POVERTY, U. S. A.

THE HISTORICAL RECORD

ADVISORY EDITOR: David J. Rothman

Professor of History, Columbia University

THE FARMER'S
STANDARD OF LIVING

ELLIS LORE KIRKPATRICK

Arno Press & The New York Times
NEW YORK   1971

Reprint Edition 1971 by Arno Press Inc.

Reprinted from a copy in
The University of Illinois Library

LC# 75—137173
ISBN 0—405—03112—2

POVERTY, U.S.A.: THE HISTORICAL RECORD
ISBN for complete set: 0-405-03090-8

Manufactured in the United States of America

THE FARMER'S STANDARD
OF LIVING

THE FARMER'S STANDARD OF LIVING

BY

Ellis Lore Kirkpatrick

ASSOCIATE AGRICULTURAL ECONOMIST, DIVISION OF FARM
POPULATION AND RURAL LIFE, UNITED STATES
DEPARTMENT OF AGRICULTURE

THE CENTURY CO.

New York & London

Printed in U. S. A.

PREFACE

This book is the outgrowth of several years' work of the author on the farmer's standard of living. It is intended for research workers, teachers and students, and for general readers, farm people especially, who are concerned about the present or future status of American agriculture. It is prepared with the hope that it may help bring to the fore the human element in programs for the improvement of rural life.

The work is based on information resulting from scientific investigations in the field of farm family living. It represents the first attempt to bring the available facts together in book form. It should be regarded as tentative rather than final in a field which shows promise of development with further progress in research in the rural social sciences—rural sociology, farm economics and home economics. It is not expected that the reader will find the analysis here presented completely satisfying in every respect; rather that he will find it suggestive of further thought or study.

Acknowledgment is due to the score or more or field workers and others who have assisted and coöperated with the writer in farm family living studies during the past eight years. Much aid and many helpful suggestions have been obtained from these workers.

I wish to take this opportunity to thank the many farm women who have contributed the information on the various phases of family living. I wish also to express my appreciation to the Bureau of Agricultural Economics, United States Department of Agriculture, for the opportunity to study the human side of farm life and for the privilege of using freely the data which have appeared from time to time in different preliminary reports and bulletins.

Finally, I wish to express my gratitude to C. J. Galpin for encouragement in the preparation of the manuscript.

E. L. KIRKPATRICK

Washington, D. C.,
May, 1928

CONTENTS

LIST OF TABLES

xi

CHARTS

THE FARMER'S STANDARD
OF LIVING

CHAPTER I

INTEREST IN FARM FAMILY LIVING

"I'VE never thought about it at all and I wouldn't try to make a guess," is the usual reply made by farmers to the question "How much money should the farmer have to provide a good living for his family annually?" Occasionally this reply is followed by some such remark as, "It depends to some extent on the number [of persons] in the family," "It might be different for different years," or, "It wouldn't be the same in some places that it would in others." Only rarely does the farmer express the idea that the ability to spend money wisely, to consume goods economically or to use time advantageously plays any part in the provision of a more satisfactory living for the farm family.

The reaction of farm women to the question of the money needed to provide a good family living is more encouraging. Charged with the responsibilities of making homes and of rearing families in the country, farm women are showing a keen interest in the different elements of farm family living. This interest is evident in their eagerness to adopt new practices in home-making, in their desire to coöperate with the home demonstration agents employed under the Smith-Lever act and in their willingness to furnish information to investigators who are collecting data on the many problems confronting American agriculture and rural life.

For example, 3000 farm women recently furnished to investigators of the United States Department of Agriculture estimates of the quantities and values of the different kinds of goods consumed annually for family living purposes. Many of these women stated that they were considering the keeping of accounts as means of knowing where the money goes and what it provides. More than a tenth offered vital comments on or asked pertinent questions concerning the different aspects of farm family living. Of more than four hundred valuable comments offered and questions asked, one hundred and fifty dealt with family living in general, seventy-five referred to household accounts and budgeting, seventy-five referred to goods and facilities contributing to development or advancement (education, recreation, etc.), thirty referred to each: food, clothing and housing, about twenty referred to each: health and the use of time, and the remainder referred to furnishings, savings and other items of less importance.

Some of the most significant comments and questions on family living in general were: "Farmers really should know what it costs them to live," "The cost of living for different families varies widely; I believe we could live on what some families waste," "How does the farmer's living in this State compare with that in other States?" "How do we farmers in this county measure up with those of other counties?" and "How can farmers of a community like this best improve their family living?"

Among the most pertinent comments and questions on household accounts and budgets were: "Farmers should keep some account of the things they sell and the things they buy for home use," "We've started to keep a record of everything we use in the house," "Where can one get a satisfactory book for keeping a record of expenditures?" and "How can one start to make a family budget?"

Comments and questions pertaining to food included: "We farmers are awfully extravagant with the things we raise," "Farm families usually have plenty to eat," "How can one tell what the things from the garden are actually worth?" and "Is it more economical to grow and can fruits and vegetables for home use than it is to buy them already canned?"

Among the most significant comments and questions on clothing were: "Farmers usually get along on as little clothing as they can; they must learn to dress better," "The children in high school get most of the clothing money," "Do many farm women find time to do sewing?" and "About what proportion of the living expenditures usually goes for clothing?"

Other pertinent comments on the different phases of family living included the following: "We keep account of what it costs to run our car," "There's really no place to buy any furniture," "We subscribe for good farm papers and magazines and I read a lot," "We can't get a doctor or a nurse out here," and "We came over here to be near a good school and a live church."

The foregoing comments and questions are indicative of the increasing interest of farm women in the various aspects of farm family living. More and more farm women are realizing that the main purpose in farming is not fulfilled until the income from farming has been exchanged for the economic goods of family living, including legitimate savings and investments. Regardless of the size of the farm income, there is a growing tendency among farm women to spend the available income more efficiently and to use goods more economically in order to get the highest possible satisfactions or values out of farming and farm life.

The producers and distributers of goods, trades people especially, are becoming vitally concerned about the different elements of the farmer's family living. Trade organizations, including advertising, sales and credit agencies, are beginning to give consideration to the farmer's family purchases. City chambers of commerce, boards of trade, Kiwanis clubs and Rotary clubs, as well as special trades groups, are developing a keen interest in the welfare of our American farm families, 6,000,000 of which are engaged in the greatest industry of the nation.

Where does the farm family trade? To what extent are its wants for standard goods and supplies met at the crossroads general store? Can the farmer's wants and needs for clothing, for house-furnishings, for books and for recreational facilities be satisfied at the village stores? Can the larger towns and the small cities, rapidly becoming more accessible to farmers, be induced to cater to the wants and needs of the farm family as the larger cities cater to the wants of different groups of city people? Cannot the farmer resort to the mail-order house in preference to hamlet, village and small city stores for many of his purchases?

And where shall the farm family purchase its services, as well as its goods of a less material nature? Are doctors, dentists, nurses, hospitals, libraries, churches, recreational opportunities and credit facilities to be centered in the larger cities, primarily? Briefly, trade organizations and professional groups are awakening to the rich possibilities of the farmer's purchasing market. Their procedure in the development of a good farmer's town must be based for the most part on the available knowledge of what the farm family spends for the different kinds of goods used annually for living purposes.

Leaders and others who are concerned with the welfare of the farmer are fast making family living the major issue in the development of American agricultural policy. This idea is not new in other industries.

It is now quite generally conceded that a good family living for industrial workers is essential to the efficient production of American goods. "Pauper or poverty level," "minimum of subsistence level" and "minimum of health and comfort level" of living have been determined and used effectively as a means of obtaining higher wages for labor. Thus, for the American industrial laborer, the way has been opened for more and better food, better housing, in fact for better conditions of living generally, and for more leisure time in which to live, to grow and to develop mentally and spiritually. Night schools and occasionally day schools for workers are now being provided by factories of certain industries.

Family living studies have been made from which family budgets have been determined for the laborers' families and professional groups of different municipalities, different cities and different geographical divisions of the country. Wholesale and retail price changes of the important articles consumed are now recorded in a number of the cities, and index numbers of prices of goods used by city families are issued monthly by the United States Bureau of Labor Statistics.

It is not too much to expect that the "good family living" idea will become basic to American agriculture. The farmer's cry of the disparity between what he gets and what he pays will go unheard by the American public until it becomes imbued with the concrete objective of an efficient family living, "a condition of living with respect to food, housing, clothes, leisure, education, insurance, amusement, religion, of which an American need not be ashamed."

Farm family living merits this increased interest and concern which it is receiving. Farming has 6,000,000 families of consumers as well as producers. And "the history of farm life shows that, in the past, farmers who have appreciated a balanced variety of the economic goods of life have left farms for cities in order to exchange their financial profits for goods not obtainable in farming communities, especially such goods as are furnished by modern institutions."

CHAPTER II

THE STANDARD OF LIVING DEFINED—INFORMATION AVAILABLE

THE growing interest in farm family living raises at once the questions of its cost and the variety, quantities and qualities of the economic goods which it contains. Those who are most concerned with the matter want to know what the farmer's living means in terms of cash outlay annually. And they want to know and need to know something of the value of the family living goods furnished by the farm without the immediate expenditure of money, but not without the expenditure of time and effort. Have we any actual knowledge as to the cost or value and the content of family living among farmers? Have we any definite information on the economic values and the relative importance of the different kinds of goods, such as food, clothing, housing and health facilities, used by typical farm families? Is there any effective measure, any common denominator of the kinds, quantities and qualities of goods, facilities and services consumed annually? Are farm families mastering the details of family living annually? Does the farm family compare rationally one set of wants with another? Can wholesome wants essential to normal, healthy growth and development be filled from the present source of goods, facilities and services accessible to the farmer?

Fortunately for those who are concerned in the matter, definite information on the different aspects of farm family living is being rapidly accumulated. During the five years just past the United States Department of Agriculture, in coöperation with a dozen state colleges and universities, has determined by the survey method the average cost or value of goods used for family living purposes by approximately 3000 farm families of moderately prosperous farming areas. Quantities of the different kinds of food, clothing, furnishings, fuel and other supplies have been ascertained for almost half of these families. Adequacy of the diet and the clothing of a part of these families is being carefully analyzed and interpreted. These studies are being superseded by a series of studies covering both farm business and family living activities in regions near the bottom of agriculture. In addition, a number of separate studies of food, clothing, housing and the use of time by both the survey and the accounting method are under way in the different colleges and universities.

Time and money are being devoted to the accumulation and interpretation of all possible information related to the various phases of farm family living. Just as attention was centered for the past quarter of a century on the study of the type or quality of living for the farmer's horses, cattle, hogs and sheep, it is now being directed to a study of the quality of living for the farm family. The many studies completed and in progress are accelerating the demand for additional information which will be accumulated and used in bringing the human side of farm life into its own; that is, in making the farm family and the farm family's living the ultimate goal in farming.

Explanation and clarification of terms used. Most of the data on family living have been obtained from studies which had as their main objective a determination of the cost of living. Many of these studies were described and are now commonly referred to as studies of the standard of living, as are practicaly all of the recent studies of farm family living. The growing popularity of the term standard of living in this respect, as well as in common parlance, calls for an explanation of what it means to those who use it. In this explanation it is worth while to note first the use of the terms standard of living and standard of life by economists, sociologists and social workers.

In the "Economics of Enterprise," Davenport defines the standard of living as "a level of consumption so fixed in habit that any falling short is felt as a privation." [1] Fetter holds that the standard of life "expresses the complex thought of that measure of necessities, comforts and luxuries considered by an individual to be indispensable for himself and his children; that measure which he will make great sacrifices to secure." [2] From the standpoint of the pressure of the wants, Ely characterizes the standard of life as "the number and character of the wants which a man considers more important than marriage and family." [3]

As defined above, the standard of living or the standard of life encompasses the idea of the intensity or pressure of wants, in varying degrees. Among the authorities who make no reference to the intensity or pressure of the wants are Nearing, who defines the standard of living as "the measure of livelihood for any given family in terms of income and expenditure"; [4] Fairchild, who regards it as "the amount of necessaries, comforts and luxuries enjoyed by the typical family" of a group of people, [5] and the writer, who holds it to mean "the economic goods contributing to the mainte-

[1] H. J. Davenport, "Economics of Enterprise," p. 3, 1918.
[2] Frank A. Fetter, "Economic Principles," p. 417, 1920.
[3] R. T. Ely, "Outlines of Economics," p. 433, 1923.
[4] Scott Nearing, "Financing the Wage Earner's Family," p. 45, 1914.
[5] Henry Pratt Fairchild, "Outline of Applied Sociology," p. 83, 1916.

nance of health, transportation, education, recreation and social relationships of the family, as well as those goods satisfying the more material needs—food, housing, fuel and clothing." [6] These authorities, it will be noted, deal with the content of living without any reference to the intensity and the fulfilment of wants as experienced by members of "the group" involved or conceived as desirable or essential by any outside interest or agency.

Other authorities have defined one or other of the two terms from the standpoint of the content of the family living regarded as necessary by some outside interest or agency. Among these authorities are Comish, who holds that "an efficient standard of life means sufficient nourishment, sleep, activity, recreation and comfort to make efficient producers and appreciative consumers"; [7] Hawthorn, who characterizes the standard of life as "a norm or measure of welfare which varies with the occupation, size of family, race and age," [8] and Chapin, who holds that "a normal standard of living is one which permits each individual of a social unit to exist as a healthy human being, morally, mentally and physically." [9]

Standard of living or standard of life? The confusion among the foregoing definitions from the standpoint of the content of the living and the intensity or pressure of the felt wants is multiplied by the interchangeable use of the two terms standard of living and standard of life. For the most part these two terms are used synonymously, and few authorities make any attempt to distinguish between them. In a study of 402 farm families of Livingston county, New

[6] U. S. Dept. Agriculture, Bul. 1466, 1926.
[7] Newell H. Comish, "The Standard of Living," p. 71, 1923.
[8] Horace B. Hawthorn, "The Sociology of Rural Life," p. 68, 1926.
[9] Robert Coit Chapin, "The Standard of Living in New York City," p. 255, 1909.

York, the writer has made a distinction between the two terms as follows: "The standard of life . . . deals with the subsistence and the satisfactions of the people with whom it is concerned. It may be regarded as a measure of life in terms of the sum total of values enjoyed by the family, as evidenced through the acquisition and expenditure of income, and through the use of time in the satisfaction of wants for things both material . . . and spiritual. . . . The standard of life includes more than does the standard of living. It comprises more than the amount of consumable goods to which the family is entitled through the expendiure of income. While the standard of living regards economic or pecuniary values as basic, the standard of life holds the realization of the highest human values attainable as the ultimate criterion of satisfaction." [10]

Level of living, plane of living, scale of living. The term standard of living is made less definite by the different usages of "level of living," "plane of living" and "scale of living." These terms are used interchangeably with standard of living by some authorities and distinguished from the standard of living by other authorities. Under the caption "standards of living," Tugwell, Munro and Stryker discuss family living as follows: "Economists . . . differ considerably as to just where the line should be drawn between the various levels [of living]; what one calls 'comfort' another calls 'minimum for health and decency.' . . . But the first requirement for an understanding of conditions is not to decide where these names belong; it is to form some idea what the levels themselves mean; what a certain income will buy." [11] These authors go on to discuss the "subsis-

[10] Cornell University Agricultural Experiment Station, "The Standard of Life in a Typical Section of Diversified Farming," Bul. 423, 1923.
[11] Tugwell, Munro and Stryker, "American Economic Life," p. 55, 1925.

tence plus level," the "comfort level," and the "comfort standard."

Andrews makes the following distinction between standard of living and plane of living: "One's expenditures organically related to each other and to the spender, and to the social group of which he is a part, constitute his standard of living. By one's standard of living one may mean only the actual commodities and services which he is able to secure, or may also include the ideal items desired but not yet secured. A distinction has sometimes been made by calling the larger complex of both desired and realized items one's standard of living and the realized items alone one's plane of living." [12]

Lescohier draws a clear-cut distinction between standard of living and scale of living. "One's standard of living is in his mind. It is the conception of the way he wishes to live. It is the embodiment of his desires. One's scale of living is the way he lives, not the way he wants to live. If one who is living in a tenement wants to own a home; if he patronizes movies when he wants to go to operas; if he walks when he craves an automobile; if he toils six days a week when he wants to spend the winter traveling in Europe, he has a standard of living far above his scale of living." [13]

In summary at this point, "standard of living" in ordinary usage necessarily conveys different ideas to different people. To many it means the economic goods meeting only the material needs of the family—that is, food, clothing and housing. To others it means primarily the satisfactions or values accruing from the acquisition and the use of goods and the use of time in the fulfilment of human wants. And to still others it means a sort of goal or ideal toward

[12] Benjamin R. Andrews, "Economics of the Household," p. 83, 1924.
[13] Don D. Lescohier, "The Labor Market," p. 95, 1919.

which to direct one's efforts at material, personal or social improvement regardless of the degree or extent of fulfilment of the felt wants or desires.

For the present purpose what specific meaning shall be given to the standard of living? What should be regarded as its scope? Should the term include in addition to economic goods the satisfactions accruing from the uses of these goods? If so, what about the satisfactions accruing from the production of goods? And what about the satisfactions accompanying certain unattained desires? And what use shall be made, then, of the term "standard of life"?

Standard of living defined. The basic step in the clarification of standard of living is a clear-cut definition of the term "family living." This term as here used refers to the *variety, quantity and quality of the goods used to meet the physical and psychic, both personal and social, needs of the different members composing the family (or group of families, on an average).* Among these goods are food, clothing, housing, furnishings, household operation, religion, government, life- and health-insurance and personal. Thus, family living includes the economic goods satisfying the more material needs as well as the economic goods contributing to the less material needs growing out of the social relationships of the family. Family living implies nothing as to the satisfactions evolving from the different uses of the available goods. It refers to the goods, facilities and services rather than to the satisfactions accruing from their use. Family living implies a content of living; goods used for living purposes.

Standard of (family) living. Any "standard" involves an established or set-up measure with reference to which something is valued or estimated. Standard of living "implies a measurement, an evaluation or a judgment" of family living according to some accepted or desired model. Any *standard of living* is a measure of the content of that living. It is the *measured or the evaluated amounts of the different kinds and qualities of economic goods involved in meeting the physical and psychic needs and wants of the different individuals composing the family.*

From the standpoint of clarity, the use of the terms "level of living," "plane of living" and "scale of living" to represent the array of goods actually used, in contradistinction to the array of goods desired or held essential for use, is regarded as questionable. The array of goods used in meeting the needs and wants of the family can be better expressed in terms of the actual or the prevailing standard of living. The array of goods desired or regarded essential to meet the needs and wants can be best expressed in terms of the desired standard of living. The different levels or planes of living can be most adequately designated or described in terms of minimum, average or maximum, or low, medium or high prevailing standards of living. Also, the qualifying phrases, minimum, average, maximum, etc., may be applied to desired standards of living as well as to prevailing standards of living.

Family life. As distinguished from family living, *family life as here used means the satisfactions or values evolving from the acquisition and the use of goods and the use of time in the fulfilment of human wants.* Family life is regarded as the objective, the end in view, the dynamic of the standard of living.

Values constituting family life—that is, values accruing from the acquisition and the use of goods and the use of time—are intangible. They vary with the temperaments, the capacities and the social relationships of individuals composing the family. No satisfactory method has been found of standardizing these values, and there is as yet no usable measure of family life. On this account the term "standard of life" is regarded as in no way synonymous or interchangeable with the term standard of living. The standard of life cannot be used as a fixed concept until the development of a scheme of measuring with scientific precision the satisfactions or values composing family life.

Cost of living a measure of standard of living. Cost of living is here accepted as the most satisfactory available measure of the standard of living. Cost of living means the expenditure annually for goods—that is, *the value (dollars' worth) of goods used annually and the distribution of this value among the principal groups of goods.* The distribution of the total value of goods is expressed relatively—that is, in the percentages or proportions that the values of the principal groups of goods are of the value of all goods used.

There are obvious objections to the use of costs or expenditures as a measure of the standard of living. Costs or market values of goods are not always typical of similar quantities and qualities of goods. The "dollars per year" for food is not an exact indication of the actual food available for nourishment of the different members of the family. Money spent for clothing may not always tell how well the different members of the family are clad. The rental cost of the house may give little or no suggestion of the comforts which the house with its surroundings provides as a home. Expenditures for goods of a cultural nature—schooling, travel, recreation and religion—may not be indicative of the knowledge and the opportunities available to those for whom the expenditures are made. The expenditure of money may not constitute a complete index of the actual content of family living generally, for inefficient and wasteful expenditure of a given amount of money by one family may buy less "values" in goods than an efficient and wise expenditure of the same amount of money by another family. In regard to farm families, a considerable portion of the goods used are furnished by the farm without the direct expenditure of money.

On the ground that it "is largely indeterminable," Zimmerman objects to the cost of living as a measure of the "living content" of farm families.[14] One of his "theoretical" objections is that living content is a matter of satisfactions and not of outlay of money and effort to secure them, and that using costs to measure living content is comparable to using farm expenditures as a measure of receipts. Another of his objections is "that money and effort outlay are measures of input, and living content is output."

Most of the objections to cost or economic value as a measure of the standard of living seem to be based on the implication that the dollars involved constitute the actual goods consumed. This is not the situation, however. The money spent for goods is merely an expression of the variety, quantities and qualities of the goods in terms of a common denominator. The goods, facilities and services used are fundamental and are so regarded by most of the authorities who accept cost as a measure of these goods. As stated by Nearing, "the basic factor in the standard of living is the 'goods' consumed. Since the more important items in a standard—food, housing and clothing—are definitely measurable in terms of the quantity of each needed to maintain a standard, any community may ascertain, by a little investigation of prices, the exact cost, in that community, of a fair standard of living." [15] Fairchild characterizes cost or outgo as the amount of money spent for the

[14] Carle C. Zimmerman, "Objectives in Rural Living Studies," "Journal of Farm Economics," Vol. 9, No. 2, p. 230, 1927.
[15] Scott Nearing, op. cit., p. 80.

actual necessities, comforts, luxuries and savings consumed by the family during a year.[16]

The objection to the cost of living as a measure of the standard of living, on the basis that expenditures are not indicative of the satisfactions or values accruing from the use of goods which they provide, is granted, for these satisfactions or values are intangible. They are as yet immeasurable in terms of money spent for goods, as well as in terms of either quantities or qualities of the different kinds of goods available for use. These values cannot be discerned from mere measurement of the goods in terms of cost, quantity or qualities. They await scientific study in the light of the modes of living and the attitudes of the different consumers of the goods.

But while other measures of the different principal kinds of goods, and of the satisfactions or values resulting from the uses of these goods, are being sought and determined, cost of living or expenditures—that is, the "dollars' worth" of goods, implying variety, amount and quality of goods— is selected as the best means available of comparing the actual standards of living of families of different years, different localities or different occupations. Similarly, this measure is probably more indicative than any other available of the desired standard of living of families of different groups, different years and different occupations. The cost or value of goods used, through the distribution of this value among the principal groups of goods, reveals the relative importance which the family assigns to various things —goods, facilities and opportunities. It discloses better than any other one measure or factor the balance of consumption from food and shelter on the one hand to formal schooling and tobacco on the other hand.

[16] Henry Pratt Fairchild, *op. cit.*, p. 92.

Farm household and farm family. The "household" as here used means all the persons sheltered in one dwelling and fed at a common table. The family includes parents and sons and daughters (blood relation or adopted) who are at home or who, while away at school or elsewhere, are supported from the family purse. The farm household accounts for relatives, hired help, boarders and others, often residing with or boarding with the family. These relatives and others are taken into account in connection with the goods provided for them from a common income. When goods are not provided for them from the common income they are not taken into account except in connection with food, fuel and other goods shared jointly.

To avoid as much as possible the variations due to differences in the make-up of households or families, studies of farm family living have been limited to families having an adult man operating the farm and an adult woman acting as home-maker. In most of these families the farm operator and the home-maker were husband and wife. In a few families, with the husband dead, an adult son, brother or nephew was regarded as the farm operator. Similarly, in a few families, with the wife dead, an adult daughter, sister or niece acted in the capacity of home-maker. In a few instances also a farm owned or rented jointly by several brothers or sisters was operated by one of the brothers while an adult sister acted as home-maker. Several households included, in addition to the immediate family, another family related by marriage.

Owing to the absence of hired helpers, boarders and occasionally relatives and others included in the household, the farm family is often smaller and of less variable make-up than the farm household. Variations in the average size of family for the different groups of farm homes studied by the United States Department of Agriculture appear slightly less significant than corresponding variations in the average size of household. On this account, as well as from a social and from an economic point of view, size of family is looked upon as being slightly more satisfactory than size of household as a basis for comparisons, and will be referred to in succeeding pages except where household is specified.

Adequacy of the family as a unit of comparison. In most standard of living studies made in the past, both households and families, when as variable in make-up as farm families, have been regarded unsatisfactory bases of comparison. The family has been pointed out by different workers as failing to take account of the fact that the number, sex and age of individuals composing the family make a difference in the needs for food, rent, clothing and other economic goods. The use of the "family" as a common basis of comparison makes no allowance for certain first costs or basic costs which are borne by all families or households regardless of the number and ages of the persons who compose them. These first costs differ for the principal groups of economic goods, as do the relative demands made against them by the third or fourth or other additional member of the family.

The widest variations due to different make-up of the family or household have been avoided in some standard of living studies by selecting the "standard" family—that is, the family consisting of husband, wife and three children, the sex and age varying somewhat with the different investigators. This plan has received less consideration than have efforts to reduce families of varying composition to a common basis of comparison. The per capita unit, the adult equivalent, the adult male equivalent, the ammain and the cost consumption unit represent some of these efforts. The per capita unit fails to take account of the variations in individual demands due to sex and age requirements. The adult equivalent unit, which counts two children as equal in their requirements to one adult, also ignores sex and accurate age requirements. Improvement in this respect has been made by considering each child over twelve years of age as an adult; yet the factor of sex is disregarded and the results are only approximate.

Adult male equivalent. The discrepancy due to both age and sex has sometimes been partially removed through use of the adult male equivalent unit, which divides the children among several arbitrary age groups and apportions the allowance for each group in accordance with age.

Among the first attempts at reducing the family to an adult male equivalent figure was that of Engel, who started with one unit for the individual at infancy and added one unit for each year of age up to and including the twentieth year for females and the twenty-fifth year for males.[17] Expenditures for all purposes were considered. This plan, of course, was purely arbitrary.

The United States Labor Commissioner, 1892, adopted the following scale of adult male equivalent units for food:[18]

	Units
Adult male	100
Adult female	90
Child of 11 to 14 years inclusive	90
Child of 7 to 10 years inclusive	75
Child of 4 to 6 years inclusive	40
Child of 3 years or under	15

[17] Ernst Engel, "Die Lebenskosten belgischer Arbeiter-Familien früher und jetzt," p. 5, 1895.

[18] United States Labor Commissioner, "Cost of Living," annual report 7, p. 859, 1892.

This scale of units was not based on scientific data as to the relative consuming power of the individual. Though purely arbitrary, the units are still used by the United States Bureau of Labor Statistics.

Another development in the way of an adult male equivalent scale for food resulted from the nutrition investigations of the Office of Experiment Stations of the United States Department of Agriculture.[19] This scale, based on the knowledge of theoretical requirements for food only, started with the requirement of an adult male person at moderate muscular work (consuming 3000 calories a day) as 100 and weighed against this the demands of individuals of both sexes and different ages. The scale of units as revised a few years later is as follows:

	Units
Average person over 12 years of age	90
Man or boy at severe muscular work	130
Man or boy at moderate muscular work	100
Man or boy at light muscular work	90
Woman or girl at severe muscular work	100
Woman or girl at moderate muscular work	80
Woman or girl at light muscular work	70
Child 10 to 12 years of age	70
Child 6 to 10 years of age	60
Child 2 to 6 years of age	50

This scale, devised for the purpose of reducing food requirements of the family to a per capita per diem basis, has been used by many investigators for families of different composition with reference to expenditures for food as well as for all purposes. Results obtained from its application to factors other than food requirements are, only roughly if at all, approximate. Though truly scientific from

19 C. F. Langworthy, "Food and Diet in the United States," Year Book, 1907, U. S. Dept. Agriculture, pp. 361-378, 1908.

the standpoint of the nutritive value of food, the scale was not developed as a means of measuring in terms of adult males even the cost of the food consumed. Since in many instances cost is not related directly to the nutritive value of food, no scale of factors may prove a satisfactory measure of both.

Ammain. The ammain scale of units developed by Sydenstricker and King for the United States Public Health Service covers all the content of family living.[20] This scale, which is an abbreviated form of "adult male maintenance," bases the total expenditure for all goods used by the separate members composing the family against the total cost of goods used by the male twenty-three to twenty-six years of age at the maximum of consumption. The relative demands rated against the money value of all economic goods consumed by the male at this age—taken as unity or 1— are varied from .22 at the first year of age up to 1.00 at the twenty-third to twenty-sixth year of age and down to .74 at the eightieth year of age for males; and from .22 at the first year of age up to .79 at the twenty-first to twenty-ninth year of age and down to .62 at the eightieth year of age for females. The ammain scale takes account of the variations in demands due to sex and age, but it makes no allowances for the different relative demands made by the third or fourth or other additional member of the family on any one of the principal groups of goods used.

Cost consumption unit. The "cost consumption unit" scales proposed by the writer in connection with the study of two groups of farm families were designated to account for this variation, in addition to all other variations, due to

[20] United States Public Health Service, Public Health Report, Vol. 35, No. 48, U. S. Treasury Dept., 1920.

different number, sex and ages of persons composing the family.[21] The requirements of the adult male are taken as a unit for a given group of needs, and the scale which is set up for each group measures the needs of individuals of different sex and age groups in terms of this unit.[22] The unit is termed a cost consumption unit. The number of units which represent the needs of a household in respect to food, clothing or other goods is called the household size index for that item, and the total expenditure for that item divided by its household size index gives the cost per cost consumption unit, the figures by means of which different households may be compared with regard to any group of goods.

The need of careful study of the relative accuracy and effectiveness of the above units as bases of comparing the standards of living among different families and different groups of families is here recognized. The cost consumption unit needs to be tested thoroughly in the analysis of a larger number of records than are now available. It is yet to be determined whether for general comparison of the standard of living of families of different groups the sum of costs per cost consumption unit—obtained by dividing the total cost of the different groups of goods per family by the household size indexes—will be much more effective than the total value of goods used per family. But until more complete data on the effectiveness of the different units of comparison for all goods and for the different groups of goods are available from the results of further study, the family is here accepted as the most usable means

[21] U. S. Dept. Agriculture, Bul. 1382, 1926

[22] The age groupings for both sons and daughters are five years or less, six to eleven years, twelve to fourteen years, fifteen to eighteen years and nineteen years or over. Points of division between the years are arbitrary and might be placed between other years.

of comparing the standards of living of different groups of people.

In connection with food, further consideration will be given to the dietary scales which have been developed for measuring the nutritive needs of the family. Similarly, further attention will be given to the per capita method of comparing the adequacy of clothing and possibly other goods not shared jointly by all members of the family.

Classification of family living goods, facilities and services. Many items enter into the idea of family living. For example, there are the major items of food, clothing and housing, each of which breaks up into a multitude of minor items. Foods include many more varieties than one ordinarily suspects. Meat, milk products, cereals, vegetables, fruits are of many different kinds, grades and conditions. Clothing has various articles of manifold makes and styles. Housing, including furnishing and equipment, has almost no end of different articles. Then there are the wider ranges of goods devoted to personal uses and to development or advancement. Thus, one sees the need for some scheme or plan of classification of the goods, facilities and services consumed annually.

In general, no thoroughly satisfactory scheme of classification of these goods, facilities and services has yet been devised. Practice is more or less uniform as regards food and clothing, although different investigators and teachers subdivide these headings differently. The items usually included under housing vary considerably, and those grouped as operation still more. Some workers make a separate division for furnishings and equipment; while others consider that the more permanent articles, such as dining-room or bedroom sets, belong under investment or housing, and the things more frequently renewed under operation. Personal goods are sometimes made to include services and facilities for the maintenance of health, as well as the various minor items, such as stationery or toilet articles, otherwise placed under operation, clothing or sundries.

The goods which are most difficult to classify and on which opinion and practice are most divided are those filling the less material or the cultural needs. Various designations have been used for this group of goods, facilities and services, perhaps the most generally adopted being "advancement." Here are usually found the goods and facilities connected with school and college attendance; general self-improvement; physical and social recreation; religious, philanthropic, civic and social organizations; attendance at lectures, concerts, games and entertainments of various kinds; and travel for pleasure or personal improvement. Savings and the facilities and services contributing to the maintenance of health should also be placed here, some workers hold; while others prefer to keep these separate.

A further difficulty comes in the case of goods that serve a mixed or indefinite purpose, especially in farm homes. The cost of the telephone, for example, should be divided between the farm business and the home; but even as used for the home it serves partly to carry on the business of the household and partly to keep up the social contacts of the family. Shall the household charges for it then be listed as operation expenses or advancement, or must one divide the cost between the two? The same applies to the radio and the automobile; the former "brings in" market reports, menus, recipes, lectures, concerts, etc.; and the latter provides for the transportation of farm supplies, groceries, clothing, the children to school, and the family to church and on pleasure trips. Should one attempt to list these goods under all of their different uses?

In case of musical instruments, a piano seems to belong with furnishings, but how about a cornet or a banjo? Some authorities tend to lump these under sundries, miscellaneous or incidentals; but the more discriminating workers are inclined to distribute them as far as possible under more definite heads, so that the unclassified goods may represent a very small proportion of the total except in the case of some emergency.

Usually, there are involved no principles so vital that the classification of the more doubtful goods in one way or another is a matter of great importance. The trouble comes from the fact that there is as yet no general agreement and consequently no assurance that the classifications used by the different authorities give generally comparable results. The one here proposed as being most satisfactory for use among farm families has been arranged from the standpoint of the practices of reliable teachers and investigators and of the logical relation of the different kinds of goods used to the standard of living. This classification makes possible comparisons of the values of goods filling specific needs or purposes, and affords through the distribution of the total cost or value of goods among the principal groups of goods a more satisfactory index than total value of goods of the standard of living. It provides for the determination of the proportion or percentage of the total value of goods devoted to advancement, a figure equally as significant as the cost or value of all goods used of the prevailing standard of living. The main groups of goods in this classification are shown in the following outline, together with the lists of goods and facilities included in the main groups.

SUGGESTED CLASSIFICATION OF FAMILY LIVING GOODS

1. Food includes meats, poultry and dairy products, syrups, honey, flour, meal, vegetables, fruit and nuts furnished by the farm valued at conservative prices, and groceries and other food products purchased at prices prevailing in the local stores.
2. Clothing includes garments and materials purchased, and sewing, dry-cleaning, pressing and shoe repairing hired or purchased.
3. Housing includes taxes, insurance, improvements, repairs and depreciation on the house during the year; 10 per cent. of the total value of house is used arbitrarily as the annual cost of rent.
4. Furnishings and portable equipment (costs include purchases and repairs). Bedding and household linens. Cleaning equipment—Brooms, brushes, carpet-sweepers, vacuum-cleaners, etc. Curtains, portieres and window shades. Floor coverings—Carpets, rugs, linoleums, etc. Furniture—Beds, including springs and mattresses, chairs, sofas, tables, etc. Gas engines (portable). Kitchen utensils, including electrical appliances for cooking purposes, canning equipment and the like. Lamps, lamp-chimneys, bulbs, etc. Laundry equipment—Washing-machines, wringers, irons, ironing-boards, etc. Musical instruments. Pictures, vases, clocks and ornaments. Screens, shades (when not included under housing). Sewing equipment—Machine, cutting-table, dress-form, etc. Stoves and heaters. Tableware—China, glass, silver, cutlery. Tools (for household use only). Trunks, suit-cases, baby carriages, etc. Wash-bowls, basins, etc.
5. Operation. Automobile costs include tax, insurance, operation, accessories, repairs and depreciation at 15 per cent. of the value of the car at beginning of year; after all costs are computed, what appears a reasonable proportion of the total, say 25, 40 or 50 per cent., is attributed to household use; the cost of the car when used for vacation trips is computed separately and placed under advancement. Fuel includes kerosene, gas and electricity for heat, light and power. Household labor (hired). Ice and water (proportion of total cost chargeable to all household uses). Insurance on furnishings and equipment. Laundry work hired done outside. Postage, stationery, express, freight and drayage. Travel by bus, trolley and train in connection with family and household business. Supplies for cleaning, laundry and miscellaneous purposes; soap, matches,

paper, tacks, etc. Telephone (proportion of total cost chargeable to all household uses, usually 50 per cent.).

6. Maintenance of health. Doctors', dentists', oculists', nurses' and hospital services. Medicines and prescriptions filled. Eyeglasses. Travel to hospitals or for special treatments.

7. Advancement. Formal education. Tuition and lessons. Schoolbooks and supplies. Lodging, board, necessary travel, and sundries at school or college. Reading matter. Books other than school-books. Papers and magazines. Music—Sheet music, music books, phonograph records, etc. Indoor games— Checkers, dominoes, cards, etc. Apparatus and supplies for amateur scientific work—Photography, radio, etc. Physical recreation and sport—Athletic supplies, attendance at ball games, etc. Church organizations, missions and welfare work. Social and educational organizations—Clubs, lodges, fraternal orders, etc. Social gatherings—Dances, parties, picnics, fairs. Concerts, lectures and amateur performances. Moving pictures. Vacation and other pleasure trips (costs include special trips by automobile or other means of travel not necessary for the business of the household, and food and lodgings specially provided for such trips).

8. Government (taxes for the maintenance of local and county government units and for schools, roads, etc., not included under advancement).

9. Personal. Services of barber, hair-dresser, etc. Candy, chewing-gum, sodas, treats. Gifts to families or friends. Jewelry (costs include repairs). Tobacco, pipes, etc. Toilet articles.

10. Life- and health-insurance.

11. Savings. Saving accounts. Investments—Real estate, government securities, bonds, etc.

12. Unclassified: Exceptional items, emergencies, etc.

While the foregoing suggestive classification may be inadequate in many respects, it is regarded as being the best suited for use among farm families. Explanation of several minor points in connection with its adaptation to different sets of statistical data on farm family living need to be made as these data are presented. Among these points are the omission of taxes and savings from the family living data.

CHAPTER III

HOW THE STANDARD OF LIVING EVOLVES

SEVERAL years ago a teacher in one of the leading state agricultural colleges was offered a position in a secondary state school at no increase in salary. He accepted the offer primarily on the assurance that living costs for his family would be noticeably lower at the secondary school, which was located in the open country about twenty miles from a county seat town of 2500 and more than two hundred miles from a city of 250,000. "Out there," he was advised, "everybody is a part of one big family. You make your own good times, and your expenses for recreation, amusements, personal improvement and even household furnishings and clothing should be light. Your house is provided and you should be able to save quite a bit of your salary without stinting yourself or your family."

Anticipating the probable needs, for the ensuing year at least, the teacher's family, in view of their moving two hundred miles from a satisfactory shopping center, decided to lay in a few additional goods for use in their new location. Among these goods were several pieces of furniture: a duofold, a leather-covered rocker, a Wilton rug and a living-room table; and new articles of clothing: coat, suit, hat and shoes for different members of the family.

A few weeks in the new location convinced the family of the folly of these purchases. Some of the goods were found to be unnecessary and others could scarcely be used

31

to advantage. The new furnishings were unsuited to the house—an old non-modern structure poorly equipped and not well arranged. The articles of clothing were superfluous. In fact, they proved to be in the realm of "conspicuous consumption," so much so that they were soon laid aside. Clothing worn in the old location proved good enough, from the standpoints of both style and quality, for the new location.

The teacher's family "made their own good times." They subscribed for additional magazines, and ordered more books and broadened the scope of their reading. They purchased a violin, but wearied in the effort to master the technique of playing it without the guidance of a teacher. They wrote for mail-order house catalogues and spent an occasional evening "window shopping" around the fireside. Several times they went on overnight hikes to the hills and mountains. Once they made their way on foot and by train to the county seat town of 2500 people, where they spent the week-end to go to a moving-picture show, to visit the library and to attend church; as they expressed it, "just to make sure we don't forget how to enjoy such things."

At the end of a year the family took stock in regard to its prevailing and its desired standard of living. They had saved money, a considerable part of their income. They had saved the new clothing. They had had comfortable quarters in which to live. They had had food in sufficient quantity and of good quality.

In taking stock the teacher and his wife counseled with each other. "It has been quite a venture," they agreed, "but we had better go some place where we can continue to raise our standard of living. This is without a doubt a cheap place to rear a family, but think of the effort we must make to keep ourselves and our children from accepting a lowered standard of living."

The above incident, indicative of the struggle usually made to maintain or to raise a given standard of living, brings to the forefront the question of its development. Out of what does the standard of living originate? How does it evolve? What directs its trend? And what factors set the actual or prevailing standards of living of different groups of people at different levels?

The origin of the standard of living is found in the "inborn tendencies of man attempting to realize themselves in ways afforded by the environment." According to Kyrk, "all activity . . . goes back to these native tendencies or dispositions to feel and to act in certain ways as the external world provides an outlet."[1] And these tendencies or dispositions to feel and act constitute the raw material from which spring the human wants for goods necessary to organic and social existence.

Human wants are either physical or social in nature. The former are, of course, basic or fundamental. Ordinarily they develop and multiply with the normal growth of the individual. A newly born baby has no social wants and only a few physical wants. "His material needs," says Zimmerman, "are quite insignificant. He consumes milk, requires a baby's crib and demands clothing for protection only.[2] Five years later his physical wants have increased. He consumes more goods in order to meet his physiological or physical needs; eats more food, requires more space than is afforded in his little crib and demands more clothing for protection. Twenty years later his physical wants have still grown, to

[1] Hazel Kyrk, "A Theory of Consumption," p. 194, 1923.
[2] Carle C. Zimmerman, "Rural Standards of Living," unpublished thesis, North Carolina State College, 1921.

somewhere near the maximum of physical consumption. He eats still more food, uses still more space and demands still more clothing for protection. His physical wants have increased more than twenty-fivefold since babyhood.

But the wants which are socially determined have increased also, at the age of five and again at the age of twenty-five. Indeed, the social wants have developed and multiplied with rapidity since babyhood. They have pressed with increasing intensity and vigor during the twenty-five years of physical growth and development. In addition to the needs for food for subsistence, for housing for shelter and for clothing for protection, the person once a baby but now a man is obsessed with a "thousand and one" social wants. He must procure other than physical satisfactions from his food, live in a costlier house, wear more fitting clothes, go many places, obtain an education, participate in recreation and so on *ad libitum*. His tastes and his wants for goods filling the social needs have far outstripped those for goods filling the physical needs.

Normally, social wants appear to "grow by what they feed on." Smart contrasts the rapidity of the growth of social wants over physical wants by the presentation of a "striking difference between animals and man. Our brothers in the field," he points out, "continue to seek the same food. . . . They try no experiments in new diets; and if food is abundant they never overeat. They wear the clothes they were born with; live in holes where their ancestors burrowed or on trees where they perched. . . . They ask no change of air, they invent no games. In short, they accept their environment and conform to it. But man never has enough . . . there is only one kind of human appetite that is at all limited, the appetite . . . for food. We, to-day, cannot . . . eat more loaf-bread or more potatoes or more

beef and mutton than our great-grandfathers did. . . .
But as to the appetite of the eye, the ear, . . . the mind,
. . . there is no satisfying it. . . . Man is a complex of
needs, desires, energies all craving for satisfaction. . . .
This satisfaction is life; and as life widens and deepens,
desires become needs, comforts become necessities, things
which before were superfluities beyond reach become luxuries to be sought after." [3]

Barring limitations set by environment, the sum total of
satisfactions for any individual or any group is concordant
with the scope or range of the felt wants. Capacity for
the formation of new wants is essential to human progress. [4]
Were the desires of human beings to cease with the provision of food, shelter and clothing—that is, were the capacity
for discovering new desires, and thereby receiving new
satisfactions, removed—lack of progress and of culture
would be evidenced. Fortunately from the standpoint of
culture, when the desires of human beings for food, shelter
and clothing are fulfilled, there comes the opportunity for
the formation of new desires, which, when met, mean new
satisfactions. When appetites for necessities are appeased,
attention may be turned to other interests, such as education, music, literature, art and recreation. Attention to
these interests incites new interests, through the attainment
and satisfaction of which comes all that is best and highest
in human life.

Normally, the growth and satisfaction of wants for individual consumption goods may be enhanced or retarded
by the prevalence of other wants growing out of the inborn
tendencies to reproduce one's kind, to acquire and own

[3] William Smart, "Second Thoughts of an Economist," p. 25, 1924.
[4] Cornell University Agricultural Experiment Station, "The Standard
of Life in a Typical Section of Diversified Farming," Bul. 423, 1923.

things for the sheer love of possession, to create or make things, to achieve, to attain distinction, to play and to feel thrills.

The use of goods by one's self may provide fewer satisfactions or values than would be forthcoming from the sacrifice of these goods for the sake of one's children. The acquisition and the ownership of goods may afford satisfaction not accruing ordinarily from the mere use of goods. The tendency to make things, to work over materials for the pleasure of seeing the visible results of craftsmanship, may give satisfactions not obtained from the consumption of goods. Satisfactions from the fulfilment of the desire to achieve may be as gratifying as satisfactions resulting from the use of goods. The attainment of distinction may influence materially the satisfactions or values to be obtained from the consumption of goods. And the liking for play, for excitement and thrills may constitute the sources of satisfactions or values not otherwise obtainable.

While the formation and the development of wants are grounded in the innate tendencies or interests of the individual, the trend of the standard of living is directed largely by the stimuli provided and the limitations imposed by society. The individual's modes of activity, his culture patterns and his choice-making with respect to goods are determined for the most part by the social group or groups of which he is a part. Thus, while inborn tendencies to act may be much the same wherever man is found, standards of living vary from family to family, from class to class, from country to country and from period to period in accordance with the degree of socialization, the freedom from custom and tradition, and the prevailing stage of the arts.

Socialization has been defined as the "income" which

the individual receives from his contacts with people, scenes and things.[5] The individual who has many contacts of a stimulating character is usually well socialized. "Human personality is developed through contacts," says Taylor. "Civilization grows out of contacts. It always follows in the path of communication and transportation. The trade routes of the world for a long time dictated the location and expansion of civilization."[6] The development of the different means of communication has been a fore-runner of both desired and prevailing or actual standards of living. Printing, photography, telegraphy, wireless and the like, improved methods of travel, increased trade facil-ities, advertising, education—all have contributed to the stimulation of wants and desires for the goods, facilities and services embodied in the standard of living.

Freedom from custom and tradition permits the "rapid diffusion of contemporary ideals" among the individuals composing any group. Only in the absence of conventional rituals and traditional codes will the wants and desires of the individual and the family find their fruition in the economic goods constituting the standard of living. The prevalence of rituals and codes makes it difficult for the individual to "break away" and experiment in the use of new goods.

About twenty years ago a member of a rural community group which was closely bound by ritual purchased an automobile. Immediately he was ostracized by the group until he agreed not to use his car within the confines of his community.

The prevailing stage of the arts exerts a modifying influ-ence upon the standard of living of different groups of

[5] Horace B. Hawthorn, "The Sociology of Rural Life," p. 56, 1926.
[6] Carl C. Taylor, "Rural Sociology," p. 131, 1926.

people. The range of choice is usually conditioned by the resources available in a given time or in a given place. The individual "cannot command for his consumption goods which are not yet produced or invented." There must be development in the production of goods before there can be noticeable expansion in the standard of living. Thus, as stated by Kyrk, "The standard of living is but a plan of life which makes the best adjustment to the situation, to the resources at hand and within control of the group in question. This adjustment is one that must be worked out by every income group." [7]

Rational desires; goods, facilities and services to be drawn upon; and buying power (in terms of time or money) constitute the materials out of which the standard of living of any group is shaped. Each group must adjust itself to the common fund of goods, facilities and services; and, with due regard to experience and knowledge, to its relative share in that fund of goods, facilities and services. In this respect the farmer is not an excepted group.

The welfare of the farmer depends upon his inclination and ability to draw effectively upon the "common" fund of goods, facilities and services available for family living purposes. The production of goods for general consumption is gaged by the fulfilment of the needs and the satisfaction of the legitimate desires of workers. Does the farmer have access to the facilities sufficient to satisfy all his legitimate or rational desires? If not, can he gain this access?

Briefly, and perhaps bluntly, can the farmer obtain the facilities needed to satisfy his felt desires and to stimulate the unrestricted growth and development of other rational wants or desires?

[7] Hazel Kyrk, *op. cit.*, p. 209.

Engel's laws of consumption. Statement has been made that rational desires, supplies of goods to be drawn upon and buying power constitute the materials out of which prevailing standards of living are shaped. The question of how these factors actually work out in a given situation must be answered. What are the needs or demands of people for family living purposes annually? What is known of the consuming habits of people? Is there any evidence or data to show what people actually do in the process of consuming food, clothing, shelter, transportation goods, educational, recreational and other goods and facilities? Fortunately some data are available.

Studies of the consuming habits of individuals and families date back to about 1800, when Sir Frederick Morton Eden made an investigation of the laboring class of England. By the use of the survey method, Eden collected data on the conditions and costs of living among a number of the poorest families that could be found. The schedule used by Eden included questions on the laborer's usual diet, the annual income and expenses per family and the prices and quantities of all goods consumed. Clergymen and their friends provided one hundred reports, of which fifty-four are published collectively in Appendix 12, Volume 3, of Eden's work, 1797, and others are incorporated with workhouse accounts in Volumes 2 and 3.

Le Play, a professor in Paris, started an investigation of the cost of living about 1830. For a quarter of a century he spent a part of his vacation studying the living conditions of workingmen's families in various countries of Europe. After locating typical families, through clergymen and teachers, Le Play made arrangements to live with each until he obtained sufficient information to prepare a family monograph. His "Les Ouvriers européens" includes ten volumes on methods of study and monographs, the last of which appeared in 1899.

In 1855 Ducpétiaux and Vischer collected approximately 1000 household accounts. Typical dependent, poor and comfortable families were represented in this study.

Ernst Engel applied the statistical method to the materials gathered by Eden, Le Play and Ducpétiaux. Through careful analysis of a number of the available schedules and monographs, along with a number of other accounts kept by workingmen's families, he calculated the distribution of the expenditures among the principal kinds of goods and constructed a table showing the percentage of expenditures for various purposes with laboring, middle-class and well-to-do families. His table may be summarized somewhat as follows:

PERCENTAGE OF EXPENDITURES FOR VARIOUS PURPOSES.

Items of Expenditure	Type of Family		
	Laboring	Middle-class	Well-to-do
Subsistence	62 ⎫	55 ⎫	50 ⎫
Clothing	16 ⎪	18 ⎪	18 ⎪
Lodging	12 ⎬ 95	12 ⎬ 90	12 ⎬ 85
Fire and lighting	5 ⎭	5 ⎭	5 ⎭
Education, public worship, etc.	2.0 ⎫	3.5 ⎫	5.5 ⎫
Legal protection	1.0 ⎪	2.0 ⎪	3.0 ⎪
Care of health	1.0 ⎬ 5	2.0 ⎬ 10	3.0 ⎬ 15
Comfort, mental and bodily recreation	1.0 ⎭	2.5 ⎭	3.5 ⎭
Total	100.0	100.0	100.0

Engel formulated several principles which have become known as Engel's laws of consumption. Stated in brief, these are:

1. As the family income increases, a smaller percentage is spent for food.
2. As the family income increases, the percentage for clothing remains approximately the same.
3. The percentage of expenditures for rent, fuel and light remains invariably the same.
4. As the income increases, the percentage of expenditures for cultural wants rises constantly.

In studies of the cost of living in workingmen's families conducted by the Massachusetts Bureau of Statistics of Labor, 1874, 1885 and 1902, and by the United States Labor Commissioner, 1892 and 1904, efforts were made to determine the annual wage necessary to support an average industrial family.

In 1904 Louise Bolard More studied the living cost of some two hundred families on the lower west side of New York city. In 1907 R. C. Chapin conducted an investigation of four hundred families in New York city. Several years later F. H. Streightoff analyzed all available data on living conditions and costs of industrial people in America, from which analysis he proposed three revisions in Engel's laws —viz., that as the income increases, (1) the percentage of expenditure for clothing decreases, (2) the percentage of expenditures for rent decreases slightly for the country at large and rapidly in New York city, and (3) the percentage of expenditures for fuel decreases.

The results of a general study of living conditions and costs among approximately 12,000 workingmen's families in ninety-two localities throughout the United States, by the United States Bureau of Labor Statistics, about 1918,

bear out Streightoff's revisions of Engel's laws, with the
exception that the percentage of the expenditure for rent
appears to decrease rapidly for the country at large. The
results of several recent studies of living conditions and
costs among more than four thousand farm families, by
the United States Bureau of Agricultural Economics, coin-
cide with Streightoff's revision, excepting the percentage
for rent in New York city, when total expenditures are
substituted for income.

Several authorities question the applicability of Engel's
laws, both in the original and the revised form, to present-
day conditions, with reference to farm families especially.
In regard to farm families, these authorities hold that the
investment in farm-land, other property, stocks, bonds and
savings cuts into the expenditures for consumption goods,
of a cultural nature especially, to the extent that the laws
are rendered invalid. In regard to all families, the authorities point out that in view of the diversification and expansion in the kinds, quantities and qualities of goods used
during the past two decades one cannot assume that the
distribution of expenditure among the principal groups
of goods has remained even approximately constant.
Present-day expenditures for food, they say, are modified
materially through a multiplicity of choices of perishable
foods resulting from new methods of packing, refrigerating,
transporting and marketing. Rent is said to have a different
meaning for both city and country than it had ten years
ago. House-furnishings of the many labor-saving types
make new and unusual demands on income. The automobile, the radio and other means of communication throw
out of balance the percentage of expenditure for the less
material goods formerly termed cultural.

But while the need for a reappraisal of the percentage

distribution of expenditures is recognized, one can safely proceed on the generalization that as the family income, and consequently as the total value of all goods, increases, a larger proportion of this total value is for purposes other than food, rent, fuel and light. On the other hand, as the income rises, the proportion going for the so-called necessities falls noticeably. Stated in another way, higher percentages of the total value of goods devoted to purposes other than the so-called necessities, to advancement purposes especially, means higher standards of living, possible of course from higher incomes.

Advancement goods are the least material in nature and cover a wider range of uses than any other one group of goods in the standard of living. As stated elsewhere, they include educational and recreational facilities, reading matter, provision for travel, participation in clubs and organizations, benevolences, religion and all other goods of a social or a spiritual nature. In the several studies among farmers, referred to above, the percentage of the total expenditure for, or value of, all goods devoted to advancement purposes increased more markedly than did the percentages of expenditures for other groups of goods filling the more material uses. This tendency of the percentage of the total expenditure for advancement to rise as the total expenditure for all purposes increases merits further consideration of the percentage of expenditures for advancement as a means of comparing the standards of living of different families or groups of families.

The acceptance of the existing laws of consumption as a basis of procedure should not restrict our consideration to the goods which are ordinarily transferred in the markets. Many forces and factors inherent in farming and farm life have not been formulated into laws or principles of consumption; in fact, not as yet summarized statistically. These must be kept in mind when one attempts to compare families of different localities, of different periods and especially of different occupations.

Comparisons of the welfare of farm families cannot be made irrationally, and inferences or conclusions as to which fares the better cannot be drawn hastily. Urban findings cannot be applied wholesale fashion to farm conditions, and vice versa. The plan or scheme of farm life differs from that of the city. The major satisfactions of farm life come from very different sources and may be much less dependent on money than those of urban life. Farmers often derive no small amount of satisfaction from an interest and a pride in pure-bred live stock which they keep, or in high-yielding strains of choice grains or fruits which they are trying to develop. Farm women frequently get real pleasure from showing and from serving to friends home-grown and home-preserved fruit and vegetable products, and the care of the garden is often a pleasure. Farm boys and girls have an opportunity for apprenticeship unequaled in any other trade or occupation. The whole scheme of farm life and farm interests must be kept in mind when inferences or conclusions are being drawn from comparisons of expenditures, on the whole or item by item, for farm and city families.

Similarly, comparisons of the welfare of individual families in any one locality, period or occupation cannot be made without reservations. Families as well as individuals vary widely in their tastes, their desires, their ambitions and their ideals. In the final consideration each family must be regarded as a dynamic process and not as a static thing. Families, as individuals, come into being, grow or develop, and decline. The scene shifts from youth and buoyancy through responsibility and amenability to serenity and composure. Family life is not always consonant with the goods, facilities and services available for consumption. The satisfactions or values accruing from the acquisition and the use of goods and the use of time in the fulfilment of human wants, as reflected in the group—family, community or nation—are the final criterion of progress.

But there are certain measurable things which have come to be regarded by the public as essential to any life "if that life is to be worth living." These things have been listed and described under a "scheme of classification." The quantities and qualities of these "essential" things vary according to individual tastes, to occupational needs and to immediate and remote environment. Through a period of years the consumption of these essential things seems to have worked out along certain general lines or principles which may be accepted as basic until other principles or laws are formulated. It is next in order to consider the extent to which the farm family gets the economic goods regarded by the public as essential to "life worth living."

CHAPTER IV

THE PREVAILING STANDARD OF LIVING OF FARM FAMILIES

UNDOUBTEDLY the best approach to an understanding of the consuming habits, aims and ideals of the farm family lies in the analysis and interpretation of the available data on the prevailing standards of living among farmers. It will be recalled that the standard of living as here used means the variety, quantity and quality of goods (measured in terms of cost or value) used during a year for family living purposes. For the present, attention will be centered on the several aspects of the total value of all goods used, including the proportion of the total value of goods furnished by the farm and the distribution of the total value of goods among the principal groups of goods. Later, consideration will be given to cost or value, variety, quantities and qualities of the principal kinds of goods, facilities and services, including foods, clothing, housing, health maintenance, advancement, personal and the like, in so far as data are available. Adequacy of some of these goods, of food and housing especially, in meeting the needs and wants of the family will be stressed.

The most complete set of data on the prevailing standard of living among farmers shows the average value of all goods used during one year, 1922-24, by 2886 families of selected localities in eleven States to be $1598 per family.[1]

[1] U. S. Dept. Agriculture, "The Farmer's Standard of Living," Bul. 1466, 1926.

Figures from which this average value of goods was obtained were collected by the survey method by the Bureau of Agricultural Economics, United States Department of Agriculture, in coöperation with a dozen or more colleges or universities. The schedule used for gathering the data provided for enumeration of the following items: Tenure; acres per farm and value of land per acre; sex, age and schooling of the members of the family and household; quantities and value of food, fuel and other materials furnished by the farm during the year just preceding the date of visit by the field worker; quantities and costs of food, fuel, furniture and furnishings, household supplies and household labor purchased during the preceding year; clothing purchased for the various members of the family; expenditures for the maintenance of health, education, reading matter, recreation, travel, religious and social contacts, and for personal and miscellaneous needs. The schedule showed also the value and the general character of the house, including its equipment and furnishings. Thus, the average value of family living among 2886 families, $1598, covers all the goods, facilities and services used during a year in so far as these could be enumerated or estimated for the households visited.

The information from which the average was obtained was usually given by the home-maker, with whom the investigator went over the goods, item by item, asking for the quantities used and the prices of each per piece, per pound, per dozen or per bushel. Prices given by the home-makers were checked with those current in the stores where the families did most of their trading and again with those reported by the Division of Crop Estimates, United States Department of Agriculture. Thus, goods were charged at about what they were worth at the farm or in the immediate locality rather than at prices prevailing in some distant city.

It is of interest to note the range of the prevailing standards of living among the 2886 families. Two per cent. of the families, 58 in number, averaging 3 persons each, used less than $600 worth of goods per year. Almost a tenth of the families, 280 in number, averaging 3.4 persons each, used $600 to $899 worth of goods. A fifth of the families, 579 in number, averaging 3.7 persons each, used goods valued at $900 to $1199. More than a fifth of the families, 679 in number, averaging 4.1 persons each, used goods valued at $1200 to $1499. Seventeen per cent. of the families, 492 in number, averaging 4.8 persons each, used goods valued at $1500 to $1799. More than a tenth of the families, 332 in number, averaging 4.8 persons each, used goods valued at $1800 to $2099. Almost 7 per cent. of the families, 196 in number, averaging 5.3 persons each, used goods amounting to $2100 to $2399 in value. More than a tenth of the families, 335 in number, averaging 5.8 persons each, used goods amounting to $2400 or more in value.

Just what can be said of levels of farming represented by the 2886 families using the $1598 worth of goods annually, in comparison with levels of farming in general? How far may these families be regarded as typical of all farm families? Roughly, what degree of profitableness of farming are involved? What types of farming and what farming regions are represented by these 2886 families?

While the 2886 families were selected at random, except colored families and a few foreign families not able to understand or speak English, the localities in which they lived were chosen on the basis of the economic level of farm business resources and returns, in so far as these could be ascertained from experiment station and extension directors, county extension agents and from local bankers, farmers or others interested in farming and farm family living. For the first concerted attempt to define the prevailing standard of living among farmers, the United States Department of Agriculture deemed it best to paint the family living picture neither too dark nor too light. Therefore, localities in which at least average farming conditions prevailed were chosen for study in so far as actual conditions could be predicted. Localities with indications of extremely high or extremely low economic levels were avoided, with the exception of one or two cases where the economic level of the locality in question seemed to be about average for an entire county.

New Hampshire, Vermont, Massachusetts, Connecticut, Kentucky, South Carolina, Alabama, Missouri, Kansas, Iowa and Ohio compose the States in which the localities containing the 2886 homes are situated. The number of localities in the different States, as well as the number of families in the different localities, varies from one locality of almost four hundred families in Ohio to at least eight localities of approximately forty families each in Alabama. Localities in New Hampshire, Vermont, Massachusetts and Connecticut, five in number, represent the types of farming most prevalent in New England dairy farming and general farming with one exception—a locality typical of a region of more intensified farming, where the production of milk, poultry, vegetables and fruits for roadside and city markets is important. Localities in Kentucky, South Carolina and Alabama, fifteen or more, represent the types of farming predominant in the South primarily. Localities in Missouri, Kansas, Iowa and Ohio are typical of the Central West, where general farming prevails with corn, small grains, hogs and cattle as the principal products marketed.

That the $1598 value of goods represents standards of living which are about typical or average is indicated by results from studies of families nearer the border line in either direction. One of these studies dealing with 402 farm families of Livingston county, New York, 1921, shows an average of $2012 worth of goods used per family.[2] There were 4 persons per family or 4.9 persons per household in the 402 Livingston county families, in comparison with 4.4 persons per family or 4.8 persons per household in the 2886 families.

Mention should be made of the prevailing price levels at the time each of the two studies, conducted similarly, were made. Although the 402 Livingston county families were visited during the fall of 1921, when prices of farm products and other commodities were slightly lower than in 1922-24, the time when the 2886 families were visited, these families may have been inclined to report the still higher prices which had prevailed during 1920. Differences in price levels would account for only a small part of the $400 difference in the prevailing standard of living for the two groups of families, however. The Livingston county families represent a locality selected as typical of one of the best farming counties in the United States, a prosperous section where diversified farming prevails.

Another set of data representing 798 farm families of Schoharie county, New York, 1924, and of selected localities of Jackson, Meigs and Vinton counties, Ohio, 1926, shows an average value of only $1023 worth of goods used per family.[3] There were 3.7 persons per family and 4.2 persons per household in the 798 families.

[2] U. S. Dept. Agriculture, "Family Living in Farm Homes," Bul. 1214, 1924.
[3] U. S. Dept. Agriculture, Preliminary Reports, 1924 and 1928.

In comparison with the $1598 value of goods used by the 2886 families, little if any allowance need be made for differences in prices, since the Schoharie county study was made in 1924 and the Ohio study in 1926, when price levels of both agricultural and non-agricultural products were about the same as in 1924, with a five-year average, 1909-14, taken as a base.

The Schoharie county locality, comprising 498 of the 798 families, is typical of the "hill farming region" of southern New York, a region where farming is held to be less prosperous than in most of the regions represented by the 2886 families. In this particular locality the land, which is hilly to mountainous, comprises a high plateau cut by large and small streams. Much of the land, formerly devoted to the growing of wheat, corn and hops, is now given to hay and forage crops, which are utilized for feeding purposes. Dairying is the main farm enterprise, with market milk as the principal source of income.

The Ohio localities, representing the other 300 of the 798 families, are typical of much of the hill land drained by the Ohio River and its tributaries. The topography grades from rolling to very steep and is often rocky. As in the southern New York region, the land is only fairly productive and is comparatively low priced.

Apparently, then, the $1598 standard of living is somewhere near typical of the prevailing standard of living among white families of moderately prosperous farming sections. At any rate, it is here assumed to be so, and this assumption is strengthened by the results of several studies of less magnitude among farmers of moderately prosperous farming regions for the period represented by the larger studies, 1922-26. One of these studies, conducted by the farm accounting method among sixty-five farm families of

North Dakota, 1923-25, shows an average value of $1508 worth of goods used for family living per year.[4] There were 5.1 persons per household in this study. Another study conducted by the household accounting method among twenty-five farm families, averaging 4.5 persons each, in Ohio, 1924-25, gives an average value of $1425 worth of goods used for family living purposes, not including rental charge for use of the farm-house.[5]

Limited data obtained by the survey method show an average value of $611 worth of goods used by 154 colored farm families for family living purposes during one year, 1919-21.[6] These 154 families comprise approximately all the colored farm families residing in several localities in Kentucky, Tennessee and Texas, which localities contained more than 800 white farm families when the study was made. The value of goods used by the white families, 861 in number, obtained at the same time and by the same method, amounted to $1436 per family.[7] The white families average 4.6 persons each in comparison with 4.8 persons in the colored families.

Thus, the figures for the 2886 farm families, averaging $1598 per family, are regarded as sufficiently typical for further analysis and comparisons both from the standpoint of the value of all goods used and of the different kinds of goods filling specific needs and purposes.

Family living furnished by the farm. In all considerations of the prevailing standard of living among farm families distinction must be made between the goods which are furnished by the farm and the goods which are pur-

[4] U. S. Dept. Agriculture, Preliminary Report, 1928.
[5] Ohio State University, "Cost of Family Living on the Farm," Preliminary Report, 1926.
[6] U. S. Dept. Agriculture, Preliminary Report, 1925.
[7] U. S. Dept. Agriculture, Preliminary Report, 1924.

chased. Usually from one third to one half of the farm
family's living represents food products, use of the house
and fuel furnished from the farm without the direct or the
immediate expenditure of money. This part of the family
living is not obtained without cost, however. It represents
labor (paid or unpaid), capital and sometimes credit, if
not a small outlay of cash for storage purposes or for
preparation for use of the goods furnished.

Value of family living goods furnished by the farm.
Over two fifths, $684 worth, of the total value of goods
used by the 2886 farm families referred to above represents food, house rent and fuel furnished by the farm.
These furnished goods include foods amounting to $441 per
family, house rent valued at $200 per family, and fuel
valued at $43 per family.

Goods furnished by the farm for family living purposes
were charged in this study at what they were regarded to
be worth for family or household uses. For the most part
the valuations for food and fuel approximate the prices
which would have been received for the products had they
been sold. Exceptions to this would include products of a
non-marketable grade or other products for which no market was available. These non-marketable products were
charged at prices ranging somewhere between what they
would have brought if sold and what they would have cost
if purchased on the local market, usually more nearly what
they would have brought if sold. Arbitrary value of the
house, on which 10 per cent. rental value was charged for
use of the house, was set as near its actual use value as
possible, on the basis of its first cost, its replacement cost
and its contribution to the sale value of the farm.

The results of several recent studies make possible limited comparisons of the distribution of the value of goods

furnished by the farm for family living purposes. Figures taken from these studies are shown in *Table 1*, along with figures for the different regions or sections represented by

TABLE 1. Average value per family and percentage distribution of the value of goods furnished by the farm for family living purposes during one year.

States	Date of study	Fami-lies studied	Size of house-hold	GOODS FURNISHED BY THE FARM FOR FAMILY LIVING			
				All goods, total value	Proportion of total value for		
					Food	Rent	Fuel
	Number	Years	Number	Persons	Dollars	Per cent.	Per cent.	Per cent.
United States [1]...	11	1922–1924	2886	4.8	684	64.5	29.2	6.3[2]
New England..	4	1922–1924	317	4.7	656	53.4	31.1	15.5[2]
South.........	3	1922–1924	1130	5.1	707	72.8	22.1	5.1
North Central..	4	1922–1924	1439	4.6	671	59.9	34.7	5.4
New York State [3]	1	1921	402	4.8	692	57.7	33.8	8.5
New York State and Ohio [4].....	2	1924–1926	798	4.2	418	62.4	20.1	17.5
South [5].........	3	1919	861	4.7	537	71.5	25.7	2.8
United States [6]...	21	1918–1922	7738	—	518	61.8	35.5	2.7

[1] "The Farmer's Standard of Living," U. S. Dept. Agriculture, Bul. 1466.

[2] Fuel includes furnished ice averaging about 20 cents per family for all families and about $1.50 per family for New England families.

[3] Adapted from "Family Living in Farm Homes," U. S. Dept. Agriculture, Bul. 1214.

[4] Adapted from Preliminary Reports, U. S. Dept. Agriculture.

[5] "Relation Between the Ability to Pay and the Standard of Living Among Farmers," U. S. Dept. Agriculture, Bul. 1382, 1926.

[6] "The Family Living from the Farm," U. S. Dept. Agriculture, Bul. 1338.

the 2886 farm families. Three sets of these figures are taken from the results of studies referred to above, Livingston county, New York, Schoharie county, New York, and localities of southeastern Ohio, and selected localities of Kentucky, Tennessee and Texas. The other set of figures represents 7738 farm families of selected localities of different types of farming in twenty-one States.[8]

There is a noticeable similarity in the percentage distribution of the value of furnished goods, except fuel, for the two sets of data representing selected localities of the United States. Food constitutes 64.5 per cent. of the total value of goods furnished in one instance and almost 62 per cent. of this total in the other instance. Accordingly, rent constitutes 29.2 per cent. of the total value of goods furnished in one instance and 35.5 per cent. of this total in the other instance. The percentage distribution figures for selected localities as shown for the two study units of the South are similar also, except for fuel. Here food comprises 72.8 per cent. of the total value of all goods furnished in one instance, and 71.5 per cent. of this total value in the other instance. Accordingly, rent comprises 22.1 per cent. of the total value of goods furnished in one instance and 25.6 per cent. of this total value in the other instance.

Roughly, the value of food constitutes from one half to three fourths of the value of all goods furnished by the farm. Use of the farm-house is from one fifth to something near two fifths of this value, and the value of fuel varies widely between a fortieth and a fifth of all goods furnished.

The total value of goods furnished by the farm, including the distribution of this value among the different groups of these goods, is unsatisfactory as well as incomplete as a basis for comparing the prevailing standards of living of farm families. Although the goods furnished by the farm constitute a substantial part of the family living, they are

[8] U. S. Dept. Agriculture, "The Family Living from the Farm," Bul. 1338, 1925.

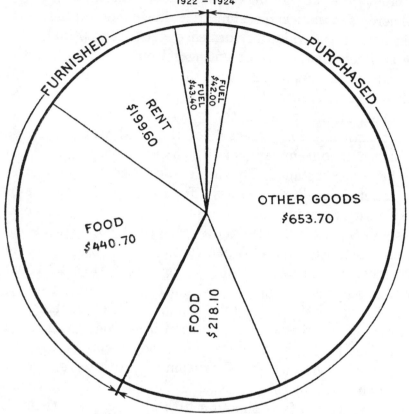

AVERAGE VALUE OF GOODS FURNISHED BY THE FARM
AND PURCHASED, FOR HOUSEHOLD USE
DURING ONE YEAR

2,886 FARM HOMES OF SELECTED LOCALITIES IN 11 STATES
1922 – 1924

FURNISHED

PURCHASED

FUEL $42.00

FUEL $43.40

RENT $199.60

OTHER GOODS
$653.70

FOOD
$440.70

FOOD
$218.10

PURCHASED $913.80
FURNISHED BY FARM $683.70
AVERAGE SIZE OF HOUSEHOLD, 4.8 PERSONS
AVERAGE SIZE OF FAMILY, 4.4 PERSONS

FIG. 1.—The value of food furnished is more than twice the value of rent and almost twice the value of both rent and fuel. The value of fuel purchased is less than one fourth of the value of all goods purchased. (*Courtesy of the United States Department of Agriculture.*)

subject to wide differences in varieties, bulk and value.
The kinds, the amount and the quality of food products
available from the farm for home use vary according to soil
types, weather conditions, and farm and family labor devoted to their production. The quantity and value of furnished fuel depends upon the supply of fuel at hand and
the labor needed in preparing it for use. The value of house
rent, although less variable from year to year than the
value of food products and fuel, does not account for the
variations due to different values of food and fuel in a
percentage distribution of the value of goods furnished by
the farm as in a percentage distribution of the value of all
family living goods used. Finally, the goods, facilities and
services provided by direct purchase constitute the major
part of farm family living and are subject to fully as
many variations as goods furnished by the farm.

Family living goods purchased. The value of family
living furnished by the farm constitutes from one third to
one half of the total value of family living, 42.8 per cent.
of the total value with the 2886 farm families and 40.8
per cent. of the total value with the 798 referred to in the
preceding pages. Thus, 57.2 per cent., $914 worth, of the
total value of goods used by the 2886 families, and 59.2
per cent., $605 worth, of the total value of goods used by
the 798 families, were provided by direct purchase. For the
eleven different States in the former of the two studies the
proportion of the total value of family living goods purchased varies from 53 per cent. in South Carolina to almost
66 per cent. in New Hampshire. For the other study the
proportion of the total value of family living goods purchased amounts to 57 per cent. in Ohio and 60 per cent. in
Schoharie county, New York. For practically all studies
of farm family living the average value of family living

goods purchased constitutes from one half to two thirds of the total value of all goods used.

As with goods furnished by the farm, the distribution of

TABLE 2.   The average value per family and the distribution of the value of goods purchased for family living purposes during one year.

Items	Selected localities of eleven States [1]		Livingston county, New York [2]		Schoharie county, New York, and Jackson, Meigs and Vinton counties, Ohio [3]	
Year of study.........	1922–1924		1921		1924–1926	
Number of families....	2886		402		798	
Persons per family.....	4.4		4.0		3.7	
Persons per household..	4.8		4.8		4.2	
Family living purchased	$914		$1320		$605	
	Dollars	Pct. of total	Dollars	Pct. of total	Dollars	Pct. of total
Food (meat, groceries, etc.).................	218	23.8	396	30.0	209	34.5
Clothing.............	235	25.7	276	20.9	156	25.8
Furnishings and equipment..............	40	4.4	43	3.3	34	5.6
Operation (fuel, supplies, etc.)..........	170	18.6	258	19.5	81	13.4
Maintenance of health.	61	6.7	83	6.3	35	5.8
Advancement goods...	105	11.5	125	9.5	53	8.8
Personal goods.......	41	4.5	48	3.6	19	3.1
Insurance, life and health.............	41	4.5	79[4]	6.0[4]	15	2.5
Unclassified..........	3	.3	12	.9	3	.5

[1] "The Farmer's Standard of Living," U. S. Dept. Agriculture, Bul. 1466.
[2] Adapted from "Family Living in Farm Homes," U. S. Dept. Agriculture, Bul. 1214.
[3] Adapted from Preliminary Reports, U. S. Dept. Agriculture.
[4] Represents an average of approximately $15 per family reported as savings.

the average value of family living goods purchased is of interest. This distribution is shown in *Table 2* for the 2886 and the 798 farm families, with a similar distribution for 402 farm families of Livingston county, New York, referred to also in preceding pages.

For the 2886 families, food (including meats, groceries and accessories) purchased comprises almost a fourth of the total value of all goods purchased. Clothing amounts to slightly more than a fourth of this total. Operation goods comprise more than a tenth of the total. Furnishings and equipment, personal goods and life- and health-insurance comprise about the same proportions, less than a twentieth of the total in each instance. The figures for the Livingston county families are similar to the figures for the 2886 families in several respects. Somewhat near the same proportions of the total are devoted to food and clothing combined, to operation goods and to the maintenance of health. The figures for the Schoharie county and the Ohio families are widely different in all respects except the proportion of the total spent for clothing.

Owing to the wide variation usually found between the proportions of family living goods furnished by the farm and purchased, the distribution of the value of goods purchased is little if any more satisfactory than the distribution of the value of goods furnished by the farm as an indication of the prevailing standard of living. The distribution of the funds available for family living purposes varies with the amount of these funds and with the variety, quantity and value of goods available from the farm without the expenditure of money. At best, the goods provided by direct purchase constitute only a part, although the major part in most instances, of the family living, and comparisons of

DISTRIBUTION OF THE AVERAGE VALUE OF GOODS AMONG
THE PRINCIPAL GROUPS OF GOODS, FURNISHED BY THE FARM
AND PURCHASED, FOR HOUSEHOLD USE, DURING ONE YEAR
2,886 FARM HOMES OF SELECTED LOCALITIES IN 11 STATES
1922 – 1924

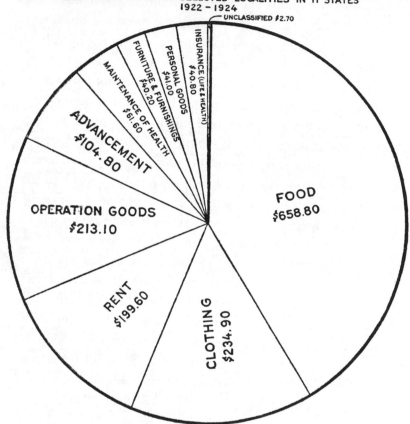

UNCLASSIFIED $2.70

INSURANCE (LIFE & HEALTH) $40.80

PERSONAL GOODS $41.00

FURNITURE & FURNISHINGS $40.20

MAINTENANCE OF HEALTH $61.60

ADVANCEMENT $104.80

OPERATION GOODS $213.10

FOOD $658.80

RENT $199.60

CLOTHING $234.90

TOTAL VALUE OF ALL GOODS USED, $1,597.50
AVERAGE SIZE OF HOUSEHOLD, 4.8 PERSONS
AVERAGE SIZE OF FAMILY, 4.4 PERSONS

FIG. 2.—The value of food is approximately two fifths, the value
of clothing, rent and operation goods approximately two fifths, and
the value of all other goods slightly less than one fifth of the value
of family living. (*Courtesy of the United States Department of
Agriculture.*)

the prevailing standards of living are most effective when made from the standpoint of all goods used.

Distribution of the average value of all goods used among the principal groups of goods. The distribution of the total value of goods among the principal groups of goods, according to uses, gives the most complete available index of the standard of living. The distribution of the average value of all goods among the principal groups of all goods used by the 2886 farm families is shown in *Table 3*. For comparative purposes these distributions are shown by farming sections, with similar distributions for two of the other groups of families considered above.

The distribution figures for the New England families are much the same as for the Livingston county, New York, families. These similarities are to be expected, owing to the somewhat similar types of farming, weather conditions and modes of living generally in western New York and New England. Also, there is a noteworthy similarity between the distribution figures for families of the South and families of the Schoharie county and the Ohio localities, with regard to the percentages of the total devoted to food, clothing and health maintenance especially. Housing constitutes a somewhat lower percentage of all family living in the Schoharie county and Ohio localities than in other localities. The percentage of the total value of all goods devoted to fuel is lowest for the Southern States. On the other hand, the percentage of the total going for food is highest for the Southern States.

Roughly speaking, in all the localities represented in *Table 3* the value of food materials constitutes about two fifths of the total value of all family living. Clothing constitutes about one seventh, rent about one tenth, and fuel less than one twelfth of all family living. The expenditures

TABLE 3. Average value per family and the distribution of the value of all goods used during one year.

Goods used	2886 farm families of selected localities in 11 states, 1922–1924[1]								402 farm families of Livingston county, New York, 1921[2]		798 farm families of Schoharie county, New York, and Jackson, Meigs and Vinton counties, Ohio, 1924–1926[3]	
	All families all States		317 families New England States		1130 families Southern States		1439 families North Central States					
	$1598		$1692		$1551		$1613		$2012		$1023	
	Dollars	Pct. of total	Dollars	Pct. of total	Dollars	Pct. of total	Dollars	Pct. of total	Dollars	Pct. of total	Dollars	Pct. of total
Total value....												
Food, including groceries......	659	41.2	707	41.8	691	44.6	623	38.6	795	39.5	470	45.9
Clothing........	235	14.7	221	13.1	242	15.6	232	14.4	276	13.7	156	15.2
Rent..........	200	12.5	204	12.0	156	10.1	233	14.4	234	11.6	84	8.2
Furniture and furnishings...	40	2.5	36	2.1	36	2.3	44	2.7	43	2.2	34	3.3
Operation goods...	213	13.3	255	15.1	194	12.5	219	13.6	317	15.8	154	15.1
(Fuel)........	(85)	(5.3)	(139)	(8.2)	(66)	(4.3)	(88)	(5.5)	(144)	(7.2)	(90)	(8.8)
Maintenance of health.......	61	3.8	61	3.6	49	3.1	72	4.5	83	4.1	35	3.4
Advancement goods..........	105	6.6	118	7.0	104	6.7	102	6.4	125	6.2	53	5.2
Personal goods.	41	2.6	51	3.0	37	2.4	42	2.6	48	2.4	19	1.9
Insurance, life and health....	41	2.6	36	2.1	39	2.5	44	2.7	79[4]	3.9[4]	15	1.5
Unclassified....	3	.2	3	.2	3	.2	2	.1	12	.6	3	.3

[1] "The Farmer's Standard of Living," U. S. Dept. Agriculture, Bul. 1466.
[2] Adapted from "Family Living in Farm Homes," U. S. Dept. Agriculture, Bul. 1214.
[3] Adapted from Preliminary Reports, U. S. Dept. Agriculture.
[4] ... amount of approximately $15 per family reported as savings.

62

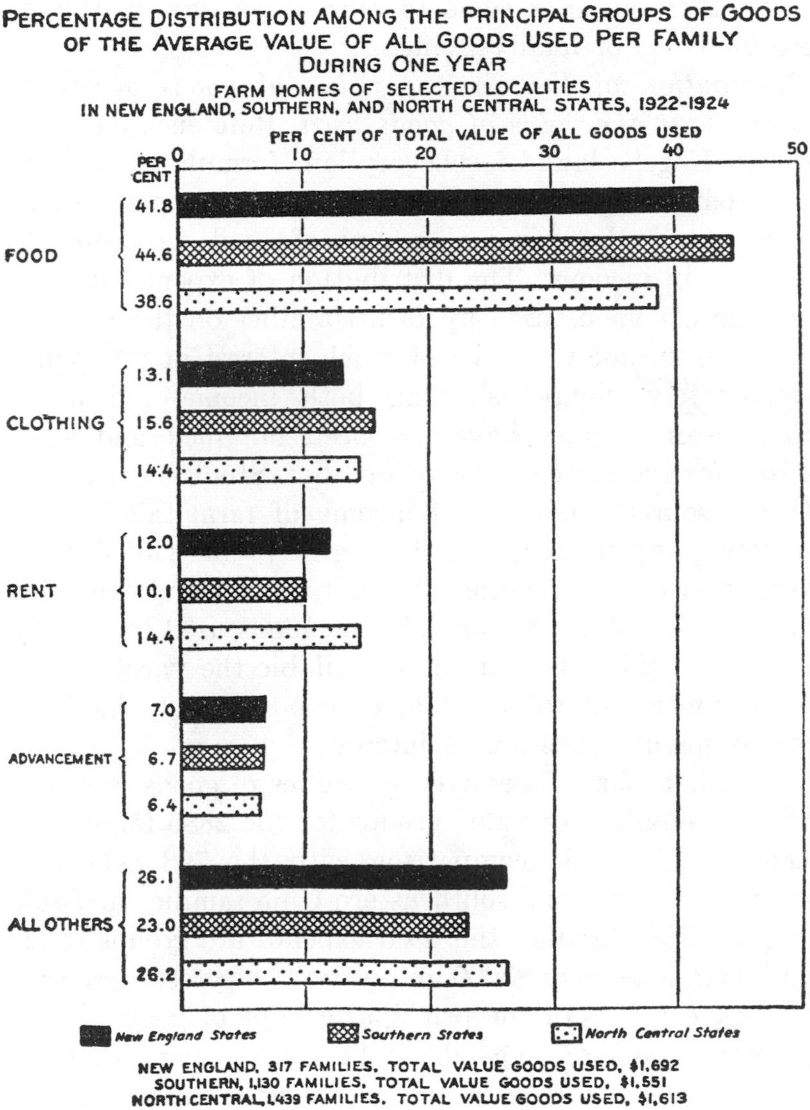
PERCENTAGE DISTRIBUTION AMONG THE PRINCIPAL GROUPS OF GOODS
OF THE AVERAGE VALUE OF ALL GOODS USED PER FAMILY
DURING ONE YEAR
FARM HOMES OF SELECTED LOCALITIES
IN NEW ENGLAND, SOUTHERN, AND NORTH CENTRAL STATES, 1922-1924
PER CENT OF TOTAL VALUE OF ALL GOODS USED
0
10
20
30
40
50
PER CENT
FOOD
41.8
44.6
38.6
CLOTHING
13.1
15.6
14.4
RENT
12.0
10.1
14.4
ADVANCEMENT
7.0
6.7
6.4
ALL OTHERS
26.1
23.0
26.2
New England States
Southern States
North Central States
NEW ENGLAND, 317 FAMILIES, TOTAL VALUE GOODS USED, $1,692
SOUTHERN, 1,130 FAMILIES, TOTAL VALUE GOODS USED, $1,551
NORTH CENTRAL, 1,439 FAMILIES, TOTAL VALUE GOODS USED, $1,613

FIG. 3.—The percentages that the values of food and clothing form of the value of all goods are highest in the Southern States. Obversely, the percentages that the value of rent and all other goods form of the value of all goods are lowest in the Southern States. (*Courtesy of the United States Department of Agriculture.*)

for all other purposes come to more than one quarter of the total value of family living.

Distribution of the average value of goods according to increase in the value of goods used. Reference has been made to Engel's laws of consumption, formulated and revised from changes in the distribution of the total expenditures among the principal groups of goods according to variations in incomes. The distribution of expenditures for (or value of) goods used by farm families on the basis of changes in income would be of much interest at this point. Unfortunately, figures showing both income and outgo among farm families have not been obtained and summarized for the same groups of families. Studies concerning both the sources and uses of income of farm families are just now being started, and these give promise of definite information on the relation of family, farm and labor income to expenditures for or value of goods used for family living. Until this information is available the variations in the distribution of total values of goods among the principal groups of goods are of interest.

The distribution of the average values of goods is shown for ten expenditure or value groups for the 2886 families of selected localities, in comparison with the 798 Schoharie county, New York, and southeastern Ohio families in *Table 4.* For the 2886 families the total expenditure groups range from less than $600 to $3000 and over. The percentages that the average values of the principal groups of goods are of the average value of all goods, and the percentages that the average values of all goods furnished by the farm and purchased are of all goods, are given for each of the ten groups.

The proportion of the total value of goods devoted to food decreases from 54.4 per cent. to 30.7 per cent. as the average total value rises from $486 to $3779 per family.

The proportion for clothing increases from 11.6 per cent. to 16.4 per cent. with the increased value of all goods used. Similarly, the proportion devoted to advancement increases from 1.9 per cent. to 13.4 per cent. The proportions for the maintenance of health and for insurance increase somewhat irregularly. The proportions for the other groups of goods remain about the same or vary without regard to the rise in the average value of all goods used.

The proportion of all family living provided by direct purchase shows a marked and quite regular increase from 44.4 per cent. to 68.3 per cent. with the rise in the average value of all goods used. Roughly, over half of the family living is furnished by the farm, without direct purchase, with families using less than $600 worth of goods, in comparison with about three tenths furnished with families using $3000 worth or more goods per year.

The distribution figures for the 798 families, with a prevailing standard of living approximately a third lower, on an average, show practically the same trends as the figures for the 2886 families. The only noticeable exception is an increase in the percentage spent for furniture and furnishings by the 798 families, goods purchased too irregularly to be of much significance with farm families.

Comparisons of the prevailing standard of living of additional groups of families—colored farm families. Reference has been made to the value of goods used during a year by 154 colored farm families. A few additional points are of interest.

About two fifths, $240 worth, of the value of all goods used, $611 worth, were furnished by the farm, and the remainder, $371 worth, were provided by purchase. The cost or value of food amounted to more than half of the family living, $327 per family. Clothing costs were 17.5 per cent.

TABLE 4. Distribution of average value of goods among principal farm and purchased, by increase in total value of goods used

Items	2886 FARM FAMILIES OF SELECTED			
				Groups of
	Below $600	$600 899	$900 1199	$1200 1499
Number of families..............	58	280	579	614
Average size of family, persons.....	3.0	3.4	3.7	4.1
Average size of household, persons..	3.3	3.6	4.0	4.5
Average value of all goods, dollars..	486	779	1055	1339
Proportion of total for food, pct....	54.4	52.1	47.6	45.3
Clothing, pct..................	11.6	11.9	12.6	13.8
Rent, pct......................	12.5	11.6	13.0	12.7
Furniture and furnishings, pct....	1.5	1.6	2.1	2.3
Operation goods, pct............	13.2	14.1	14.2	13.6
Maintenance of health, pct......	2.1	2.6	3.0	3.5
Advancement, pct..............	1.9	2.7	3.6	4.4
Personal, pct..................	2.3	2.1	2.3	2.4
Insurance, life and health, pct....	.5	1.2	1.6	1.8
Unclassified, pct...............	.0	.1	.0	.2
Total.....................	100.0	100.0	100.0	100.0
Proportion of living furnished, pct..	55.6	52.9	48.9	46.3
Proportion of living purchased, pct.	44.4	47.1	51.1	53..7
Total.....................	100.0	100.0	100.0	100.0
	798 FARM FAMILIES OF SCHOHARIE COUNTY, NEW YORK,			
Number of families..............	59	255	282	133
Average size of family, persons.....	2.4	3.0	3.8	4.7
Average size of household, persons..	2.6	3.3	4.4	5.3
Average value of all goods, dollars..	495	764	1041	1319
Proportion of total for food, pct....	57.0	50.4	47.0	42.7
Clothing, pct..................	12.0	13.7	15.4	16.7
Rent, pct......................	8.7	8.8	7.9	7.9
Furniture and furnishings, pct....	1.9	2.5	3.2	3.3
Operation goods, pct............	12.2	15.6	15.5	15.2
Maintenance of health, pct......	2.5	2.4	3.2	4.5
Advancement, pct..............	3.0	3.5	4.3	5.6
Personal, pct..................	2.5	2.0	1.8	1.6
Insurance, life and health, pct....	.2	.5	1.5	2.1
Unclassified, pct...............	.0	.6	.2	.4
Total.....................	100.0	100.0	100.0	100.0
Proportion of living furnished, pct..	48.5	45.3	41.1	38.0
Proportion of living purchased, pct.	51.5	54.7	58.9	62.0
Total.....................	100.0	100.0	100.0	100.0

[1] Adapted from Bul. 1466, U. S. Dept. Agriculture.
[3] Adapted from Preliminary Reports, U. S. Dept. Agriculture.

groups of goods and proportions of total family living furnished by
during one year.

total value of goods used

$1500 1799	$1800 2099	$2100[2] 2399	$2400 2699	$2700 2999	$3000 *and over*	*All value groups*
492	332	196	116	83	136	2886
4.8	4.8	5.3	5.4	5.7	6.2	4.4
5.1	5.3	5.9	6.0	6.5	7.0	4.8
1639	1932	2240	2529	2854	3779	1598
43.0	39.8	37.2	36.2	33.6	30.7	41.2
15.1	15.4	15.8	15.5	16.0	16.4	14.7
12.2	13.5	12.6	12.3	13.1	10.9	12.5
2.9	2.5	2.8	2.8	2.8	2.9	2.5
12.9	13.3	13.5	13.6	12.4	12.5	13.3
3.4	3.9	4.6	3.8	6.7	4.8	3.8
5.5	6.3	7.5	9.8	9.7	13.4	6.6
2.3	2.5	2.6	2.5	2.7	3.8	2.6
2.6	2.5	3.1	3.3	2.9	4.5	2.6
.1	.3	.3	.2	.1	.1	.2
100.0	100.0	100.0	100.0	100.0	100.0	100.0
44.0	42.1	39.5	38.2	38.1	31.7	42.8
56.0	57.9	60.5	61.8	61.9	68.3	57.2
100.0	100.0	100.0	100.0	100.0	100.0	100.0

AND JACKSON, MEIGS AND VINTON COUNTIES, OHIO, 1924–1926 [3]

44	15	10[2]	—	—	—	798
5.0	4.7	5.3	—	—	—	3.7
5.7	6.3	7.6	—	—	—	4.2
1605	1925	2416	—	—	—	1023
39.9	39.1	31.1	—	—	—	45.9
15.9	16.8	15.4	—	—	—	15.2
8.9	8.7	8.3	—	—	—	8.2
5.4	5.7	5.6	—	—	—	3.3
14.3	12.0	13.1	—	—	—	15.1
4.1	2.5	4.5	—	—	—	3.4
7.6	9.8	16.8	—	—	—	5.2
1.5	2.6	1.5	—	—	—	1.9
2.4	2.8	3.1	—	—	—	1.5
—	—	.6	—	—	—	.3
100.0	100.0	100.0	—	—	—	100.0
36.9	36.6	30.5	—	—	—	40.8
63.1	63.4	69.5	—	—	—	59.2
100.0	100.0	100.0	—	—	—	100.0

[2] For the 798 farm families this group is $2100 and over and contains 4 families whose total value of goods used is over $2399.

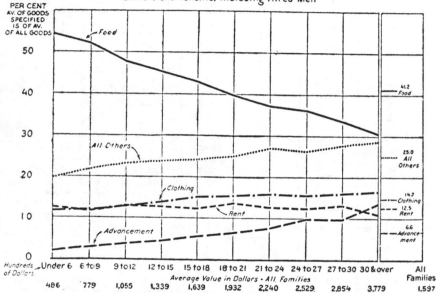

DISTRIBUTION OF THE AVERAGE VALUES OF GOODS AMONG THE PRINCIPAL GROUPS OF GOODS, BY INCREASE IN THE AVERAGE VALUE OF ALL GOODS USED, DURING ONE YEAR

2,886 FARM FAMILIES OF SELECTED LOCALITIES OF THE UNITED STATES, 1922-'24

Owners and Tenants, Including Hired Men

FIG. 4.—The percentage that the value of food forms of the value of all goods decreases from over 54 per cent. to almost 31 per cent., with an increase of approximately $3000 in the value of all goods used, on an average. Obversely, the percentages that the values of clothing, advancement and all other goods form increase, although less markedly. The percentage that the value of rent forms of the total value of all goods remains almost stationary with increased value of all goods used. (*Courtesy of the United States Department of Agriculture.*)

of the total value of all goods used, rent 6.7 per cent., furniture and furnishings .7 per cent., operation goods 9.1 per cent., maintenance of health 4.1 per cent., advancement goods 4.6 per cent., personal goods 1.5 per cent. and life- and health-insurance 2.3 per cent.

With a rise in the total value of all goods used, by $300 groups from $300 or less to $1500 or more, the percentage for food remains about the same, the percentage for clothing increases, the percentage for rent decreases slightly and the percentage for advancement goods shows a tendency to increase. The percentages for goods furnished by the farm and purchased remain about constant or vary without regard to increase in the total value of goods.

Owing to the small number of families, only 154, the figures for colored families cannot be accepted as final evidence of the prevailing standard of living among colored farm families. They are merely suggestive of conditions and trends which might be discerned through the summary and analysis of additional information representing other localities and other types of farming.

Owner, tenant, cropper and hired-man families. Fortunately, attention has usually been paid to the question of tenure in farm family living studies. The average values and the percentage distribution figures for the several tenure groups for the principal studies for which they are available are shown in *Table 5*. The first set of figures represents the 2886 farm families of selected localities in eleven States and the second and third sets represent the 861 white families and the 154 colored families of selected localities of Kentucky, Tennessee and Texas. In these sets of figures groups of goods are limited to food, clothing, house rent, operation, advancement and all other. In making comparisons of the distribution figures it is well to note

TABLE 5. Average value per family and percentage distribution of the value of goods used during one year. Farm families of selected localities of the United States, by tenure, and farm families of selected localities of Kentucky, Tennessee and Texas by color and tenure.

Color and tenure	Families	Size of family	Furnished by farm	Purchased	Total	PROPORTION OF TOTAL FOR					
						Food	Clothing	Rent	Operation	Advancement	Other
	Number	Persons	Dollars	Dollars	Dollars	Pct.	Pct.	Pct.	Pct.	Pct.	Pct.
White											
All families..........	2886[1]	4.4	684	914	1598	41.2	14.7	12.5	13.3	6.6	11.7
Owner families........	1950	4.4	728	989	1717	39.9	14.8	12.8	13.5	7.4	11.6
Tenant families.......	867	4.5	598	759	1357	44.7	14.5	11.7	13.1	4.3	11.7
Hired-men families...	69	4.4	513	725	1238	44.2	13.0	10.7	12.4	3.7	16.0
White											
All families..........	861[2]	4.6	537	899	1436	44.0	17.7	9.7	12.0	5.9	10.7
Owner families........	411	4.4	631	1004	1635	39.9	17.4	11.3	12.9	8.0	10.5
Tenant families.......	321	4.8	504	874	1378	47.8	17.9	8.0	11.6	3.7	11.0
Cropper families......	129	4.9	318	629	947	52.8	19.1	7.4	9.1	2.2	9.4
Colored											
All families..........	154[3]	4.8	240	371	611	53.5	17.5	6.7	9.1	4.6	8.6
Owner families........	35	4.8	305	378	683	52.5	17.9	8.3	8.9	7.2	5.2
Tenant families.......	47	4.9	274	399	673	54.8	18.4	5.0	8.7	4.1	9.0
Cropper families......	72	4.7	186	350	536	53.0	16.6	7.1	9.6	3.5	10.2

[1] Farm families of selected localities in eleven States, 1922–1924.
[2] Farm families of selected localities of Kentucky, Tennessee and Texas, 1919.
[3] Farm families of selected localities of Kentucky, Tennessee and Texas, 1919.

also, for each of the three sets of data, the average values of all goods used and the average size of family for the several tenure groups.

For the 2886 families, owners use more goods than do tenants or hired men, the average values of goods being $1717 for owners, $1357 for tenants and $1237 for hired men. Little, if any, allowance need be made here for difference in the size of family. Tenant families, one tenth of a person larger in size than owner families, live on approximately 20 per cent. fewer goods than do owner families. Hired-man families, the same size as owner families, consume about 28 per cent. fewer goods than do the owner families. Hired-man families, one tenth of a person smaller than tenant families, use about 9 per cent. fewer goods than do the tenant families.

Over two fifths, 42.4 per cent., of the owner's family living is furnished by the farm. A slightly higher proportion of the tenant's family living, and a slightly lower proportion of the hired-man's family living, are furnished. Thus, owner families use $989 worth of goods provided by direct purchase in comparison with $759 worth of purchased goods used by tenant families and $725 worth of purchased goods used by hired-man families.

Turning to the distribution of the value of goods among the principal groups of goods used by these 2886 farm families, owner families appear to live slightly better than do tenant or hired-man families. Less than two fifths, 39.9 per cent., of the total value of goods used was devoted to food with owners, in comparison with 44.7 per cent. of the total devoted to food with the tenants and 44.2 per cent. of the total devoted to food with the hired men. The average expenditure for clothing constitutes 14.8 per cent., 14.5 per cent. and 13.0 per cent. of the value of all goods used by each of the three tenure groups, owner, tenant and hired man. Rental values for use of the farm-house are 12.8 per cent. of the value of all goods for owners, 11.7 per cent. for tenants and 10.7 per cent. for hired men. Owner families turn a larger portion of all the money spent to advancement; that is, to formal education, recreation, church support and benevolences. For owners 7.4 per cent. of the value of all goods, in comparison with 4.3 per cent. for tenants and 3.7 for hired men, was devoted to advancement. Thus, tenants fare better in this respect than do the hired men.

Owner and tenant families appear to have about the same proportion of the total value of all goods left for other purposes, including furnishings purchased, health maintenance, life- and health-insurance and goods of a personal nature. The percentages of the total value of goods devoted to these purposes are 11.6 per cent. for owner families and 11.7 per cent. for tenant families. With hired-man families about one sixth of the total value of goods goes for these purposes.

For the 861 white farm families of Kentucky, Tennessee and Texas the average values of goods used by owners, tenants and croppers amount to $1635, $1378 and $947 respectively per family. In this instance tenant families, approximately 9 per cent. larger, consumed about 15 per cent. fewer goods than did owner families. Cropper families, about 12 per cent. larger than owner families, used about 40 per cent. fewer goods than did owner families. Owner families obtained the largest proportional part of the total value of family living goods from the farm, in this study, the proportions of the total furnished being 38.6 per cent. for owners, 36.6 per cent. for tenants and 33.6 per cent. for croppers.

As with the 2886 families, owners appear to devote a lower percentage of the total value of family living to food than do tenant and cropper families. The opposite appears to be true in connection with rent and operation goods and especially with advancement goods. Contrary to the figures for the 2886 families, percentages of the total value of family living devoted to clothing and to all other purposes are slightly lower for owner families than for tenant families.

Owing to limited numbers of families in several of the tenure groups, the figures available do not serve as final indexes of the relative prevailing standards of living of owners, tenants, croppers and hired men. Many overlappings in the so-called tenure scale have not been taken into account. It is probable that a group of tenants who are related to their landlords would have a higher prevailing standard of living than a group of typical owners. The same might be true of a group of "owner additional" farmers. Additional data are needed to ascertain the relative prevailing standards of living for different tenure groups.

Farm families with workingmen's families. While no attempt is made to compare the total values (money costs) of goods used by farm families and workingmen's families, consideration can well be given to the percentage distribution of the values of all goods used and to the change in this distribution according to variations in income, or in the total value of goods used, for each. Two sets of data resulting from studies made by the United States Department of Labor, by the survey method, one in 1902 among 11,156 families in thirty-three industrial centers and the other in 1918 among 12,096 families in ninety-two industrial centers of the United States, and a third set of data resulting from a study made by the Cornell University Agricultural Experiment Station, 1919, among ninety-two families of Groton, New York, are of interest. The percentages of the expenditure for goods devoted to the several principal groups of goods by these families are shown in *Table 6,* in comparison with similar percentages for the 2886 farm families of selected localities in eleven States.

TABLE 6.   Distribution of the average value of goods among the different groups of goods used per family during one year, farm families of selected localities in 11 States, in comparison with workingmen's families in different industrial centers of the United States.

Goods used	2886 farm families of selected localities in 11 States, 1922–1924	12,096 workingmen's families in 92 industrial centers, 1918 [1]	11,156 workingmen's families in 33 industrial centers, 1902 [2]	92 workingmen's families in Groton, New York, 1919 [3]
Total value of all goods .	$1598	$1434	$618	$1659
		Per cent. of total		
Food, including groceries	41.2	38.2	43.1	41.7
Clothing	14.7	16.6	13.0	11.3
Rent	12.5	13.4	18.1	13.1
Fuel and light	5.3	5.3 [4]	5.7	6.8
All others	26.3	26.4	20.1	27.1

[1] "Cost of Living in the United States," U. S. Dept. Labor, Bureau Labor Statistics, Monthly Labor Review, Vol. 9, No. 2.

[2] "Cost of Living and Retail Prices of Food," eighteenth annual report of the Commissioner of Labor, 1903.

[3] "The Cost of Living in a Small Factory Town," Cornell University, Bul. 431, 1924.

[4] Not including 295 families for which rent was combined with fuel and light.

About the same proportion of the total value of all goods was devoted to food, clothing, rent and fuel by the farm families and the workingmen's families studied in 1918. This proportion amounts to 73.7 per cent. of the value of all goods used by the farm families and 73.5 per cent. of the value of all goods used by the workingmen's families. Thus the proportion of the total devoted to the less material goods amounts to 26.3 per cent. and 26.4 per cent. respectively. Also, the same percentage of the total value of goods goes for fuel. The percentages of the total value of all goods going for food are not widely different for the four groups of families. The same appears to hold true with the percentages of the total value going for fuel and light. There are wider variations among the percentages going for clothing, for house rent and for all other purposes. With the wide variations in the figures for the three groups of laborers' families, it is impossible to determine whether farm families devote larger or smaller percentages of the total value of family living to food, clothing, rent, etc., than are devoted to these corresponding purposes by workingmen's families.

Some idea of the trends in the percentage distribution of expenditures among the principal groups of goods with increased expenditure or income for farm families and workingmen's families may be got from the data shown in *Table 7*. These two sets of data, representing the 2886 families and the 12,096 families referred to in preceding pages, are the most complete available.

Apparently, the downward trend in the percentage of the total value or cost of living devoted to food is most pronounced with the farm families. An upward trend of the percentage for clothing is probably most pronounced and most regular with the industrial families. There is a noticeable downward trend in the percentages for rent with the industrial families, in comparison with practically no trend in either direction with the farm families. Another simi-

TABLE 7.   Percentage distribution of average value or cost of family living goods among the important groups of goods by increase in the value of family living or income; farm families of selected localities in 11 States, in comparison with workingmen's families studied by the Department of Labor.[1]

2886 FARM FAMILIES OF SELECTED LOCALITIES IN 11 STATES, 1922–1924.

Value of living or income group	Families	Size of house-hold	VALUE OR COST OF FAMILY LIVING				
			Average value	Proportion of total for			
				Food	Clothing	Rent	All other
	Number	Persons	Dollars	Pct.	Pct.	Pct.	Pct.
Below $600..	58	3.3	486	54.4	11.6	12.5	21.5
$600– $899..	280	3.6	779	52.1	11.9	11.6	24.4
$900–$1199..	579	4.0	1055	47.6	12.6	13.0	26.8
$1200–$1499..	614	4.5	1339	45.3	13.8	12.7	28.2
$1500–$1799..	492	5.1	1639	43.0	15.1	12.2	29.7
$1800–$2099..	332	5.3	1932	39.8	15.4	13.5	31.3
$2100–$2399..	196	5.9	2240	37.2	15.8	12.6	34.4
$2400–$2699..	116	6.0	2529	36.2	15.5	12.3	36.0
$2700–$2999..	83	6.5	2854	33.6	16.0	13.1	37.3
$3000 and over	136	7.0	3779	30.7	16.4	10.9	42.0
Total......	2886	4.8	1598	41.2	14.7	12.5	31.6

12,096 WORKINGMEN'S FAMILIES OF 92 INDUSTRIAL CENTERS, 1918

Value of living or income group	Families	Size of house-hold	Average value	Food	Clothing	Rent	All other
Below $900 [2]..	332	4.3	843	44.1	13.2	14.5 [3]	28.2
$900–$1199..	2423	4.5	1076	42.4	14.5	13.9 [4]	29.1
$1200–$1499..	3959	4.7	1301	39.6	15.9	13.8 [5]	30.6
$1500–$1799..	2730	5.0	1537	37.2	16.7	13.5 [6]	32.5
$1800–$2099..	1594	5.2	1756	35.7	17.5	13.2 [7]	33.5
$2100–$2499..	705	5.7	2055	34.6	18.7	12.1 [8]	34.5
$2500 and over	353	6.4	2467	34.9	20.4	10.6 [9]	34.2
Total......	12096	4.9	1434	38.2	16.6	13.4 [10]	31.7

[1] Adapted from Bul. 1466, U. S. Dept. Agriculture.
[2] Income rather than value or cost of living groups.   Average cost of living falls outside of these groups in several instances, owing to deficit or surplus reported by a number of families.
[3] Not including one family in which rent is combined with fuel and light.
[4] Not including 44 families in which rent is combined with fuel and light.
[5] Not including 91 families in which rent is combined with fuel and light.
[6] Not including 78 families in which rent is combined with fuel and light.
[7] Not including 51 families in which rent is combined with fuel and light.
[8] Not including 21 families in which rent is combined with fuel and light.
[9] Not including 9 families in which rent is combined with fuel and light.
[10] Not including 295 families in which rent is combined with fuel and light.

larity is the upward trend in the combined percentages for all other purposes for the two groups of families. In general, the trend of the distribution of the value of goods used by the two groups of families is about the same, except the percentage for rent, which decreases rather regularly with a rise in the average cost of living per family with the 12,096 workingmen's families.

Summary. The data available show wide variations in the prevailing standards of living of different localities, different States and different regions. Families of some localities surpass families of other localities in both the values of goods and in the distribution of these values among the principal groups of goods, just as different families surpass each other in this respect. While the data show wide variations in the prevailing standards of living among each—owner, tenant, cropper and hired-man families of different regions and different States generally—owners appear to have higher prevailing standards of living than do tenants. Similarly, tenants appear to have higher prevailing standards of living than do croppers or hired men. The data available are too inadequate to show that farm families have higher actual or prevailing standards of living generally than do workingmen's families. The most complete set of data for farm families represents essentially average or above average farming and family living conditions. Another set of data, more limited in scope, represents farm families of poorer than average, yet not the poorest, of farming and farm family living conditions. The most inclusive set of data for workingmen's families represents city families probably below an average standard of living. Perchance many of these families, at the time of the study, were little if any above the poverty line. When standard of living studies among farmers include more of our poorer agricultural sections we may see in those sections a close approach to the "poverty level" in family living, especially in the expenditures for goods filling the less material needs of the different members of the family.

But it is not the purpose of the writer to draw final conclusions at this point. Consideration must first be given to the values, the varieties, the quantities and the qualities of the goods, facilities and services embodied in the prevailing standard of living, in so far as data are available.

CHAPTER V

FOOD USED BY FARM FAMILIES

"To-day, April 11," states a farm family living investigator, in notes jotted down at the close of a day's work in the field, "I arrived about 10:30 A.M. at a farm home in a region of general farming for the purpose of obtaining information on the sources and uses of farm family income. Finishing the schedule just at noon, I was invited by the home-maker, who had given the information while handling the family washing, to stay for dinner. Accepting the invitation, I waited only twenty minutes before the meal was ready.

"I was ushered from the back door through the kitchen to the dining-room, at one end of which stood a large incubator filled with hatching eggs and peeping chicks. The table, which had been pushed back to the opposite end of the room, was loaded with food: fried ham, cheese, fried potatoes, beans, rice, green onions, bread and butter, two kinds of jam or jell, apple pie, apple sauce, cake, coffee and milk. There was plenty of everything. The food was well cooked but served unattractively on a 'newspaper table-cloth.'

"During the meal some of the peeping chicks peeped so vigorously that they attracted the attention of the home-maker. Soon she was assisting one and then another out of the partially opened egg shells. Presently one of the chicks was found to have its head caught between two of the slats in the egg rack of the incubator. The home-maker called for her husband's assistance and together they labored to release the baby chick from its predicament. They returned to the table, the home-maker with drops of perspiration on her face and the husband with the remark that the chickens usually got caught in the rack just at meal-time.

"When the meal was over and payment was offered, it was accepted somewhat hesitatingly with apologies for the scanty meal which had been served. 'We have so little to cook; there's nothing in the garden this time of year, and we can't buy fresh fruits and vegetables,' said the home-maker."

The foregoing incident, which may be typical of only a relatively small percentage of all farm homes, raises several important questions in regard to the farm family's diet. In what amounts are the different kinds of food consumed? From what sources and at what costs are they provided? What is known of the adequacy of the farmer's diet? And what can be said of the adaptation of food to social uses by the farm family?

From the figures which have been presented in the preceding pages it is evident that food, in terms of value, is by far the most important item of the farm family's living. This is true of families generally, since the selection, purchase and use of food constitutes the most fundamental process of human life.

From the standpoint of the satisfactions or values which it provides, food has two chief functions, one physiological and the other social in nature. Physiologically, food serves two main purposes—namely, (1) to build up one's body to its adult size and repair wastes due to wear and tear of life, and (2) to provide energy or power for the work which the body has to do and heat to keep the body warm. Proper

physical development and good physical health are possible
only when foods are available in sufficient quantity and
variety to serve these purposes or needs. And physical
health and development are indispensable to mental health
and development. Therefore, "food is the foundation for
mental as well as bodily efficiency" of the different members
composing the family.

Socially food—the table—has always played and continues to play an important part in human life. The family
meal is a social occasion. To converse over a meal, to visit
at the table is a cherished social custom. Warren H. Wilson
holds that when religion has outgrown churches it will still
express itself in dinners, and that when art ceases to be
academic or childish it will still set a table. "A country
dinner in a remote farm-house with twenty-five . . . at
the table is a great occasion. Scientists should study the
lesson of life at a dinner party. For a country dinner party
is a social occasion." [1]

The regular family meal as well as the special dinner or
the refreshments served at any party should be and usually
is fruitful of many social satisfactions or values. Unfortunately, these social values resulting from the use of food—
values contributing much to family life—are not capable
of measurement with any scientific precision. On this
account they are given only secondary consideration, and
the discussion of food consumption by the farm family is
approached from the standpoint of the adequacy of the
farmer's diet. Preceding this discussion, it is worth while
to note again the values of foods used per year by several
groups of farm families and to consider briefly the different
kinds and amounts of foods represented by these values.

Value of food used. It will be recalled that food amounted

[1] Warren H. Wilson, "The Farmer's Church," p. 62, 1925.

to $659 per family per year with the 2886 farm families in eleven States. These families were in at least moderate circumstances. The value of food constituted approximately two fifths, 41.2 per cent., of the total value of all goods used. The values of food were $707 or 41.8 per cent. of the value of all family living in the New England States, $691 or 44.6 per cent. of the value of all family living in the Southern States and $623 or 38.6 per cent. of all family living in the North Central States. For groups of the 2886 families in different States the average value of food used ranged from $593 per family in Kentucky to $768 per family in Massachusetts. The proportion that the value of food is of the value of all goods used varied from 39.0 per cent. in New Hampshire to 47.2 per cent. in Alabama.

Slightly more than two thirds, 66.9 per cent., of the $659 worth of food used by the 2886 farm families was furnished by the farm without the direct expenditures of money. The remainder, $218 worth, was provided by purchase and included groceries, meats, vegetables and fruits, which were bought for use during the year of study. For the different States the proportion of the total value of food furnished by the farm varied from 47 per cent. in Connecticut to 76 per cent. in Alabama.

A glance at the figures in *Table 8* will show that not all farm families use food as generously as it appears to have been used by the 2886 families of at least moderate circumstances. The 861 white families of Kentucky, Tennessee and Texas referred to in the preceding chapter used $632 worth of food per year. The 798 families of Schoharie county, New York, and southeastern Ohio used only $470 worth of food during a year. Finally, the 154 colored families of Kentucky, Tennessee and Texas used only $327 worth of food during one year.

Smaller proportions of the food—that is, lower percentages of the total value—appear to be furnished by the farm with the 861 and the 798 white families and the 154 colored families than with the 2886 white families. This means the expenditure of between $200 and $250 of money or its equivalent (farm produce traded in at the store) for food purchased by the three groups of white families and approximately $150 worth for food purchased by the colored families.

For the 2886 families, owners appear to use more food (in terms of value) than do tenants or hired men. For the 861 white families of Kentucky, Tennessee and Texas, owners and tenants appear to use about the same amounts of food, approximately $650 worth, considerably more than appears to be used by the cropper families. Similarly, colored owner and tenant families appear to devote about the same amounts of money to foods purchased, while colored cropper families seem to turn considerably less money to this purpose.

Kinds and amounts of foods used by farm families. Data on amounts and costs or values of the different kinds of food used by farm families are limited to 1331 families or households of Kansas, Kentucky, Missouri and Ohio, a part of the 2886 families referred to above. The data were tabulated under the direction of the writer by the Webb Publishing Company, St. Paul, Minnesota, and summarized by Edith Hawley, food economist of the United States Bureau of Home Economics. A summary of these figures adapted from a preliminary report of the United States Department of Agriculture appears in *Table 9.*

The average value of all food used amounted to $632 for the Kansas families, $596 for the Kentucky families, $717 for the Missouri families and $570 for the Ohio families.

TABLE 8. The value of food furnished by the farm and purchased for household use during one year and the proportion of the total value furnished by the farm and purchased.[1]

Locality	Year of study	Number of families	Size of house-hold	All food		Furnished by the farm		Purchased	
				Total value	Proportion of total value of family living	Value	Proportion of total value of all food	Value	Proportion of total value of all food
				Dollars	Per cent.	Dollars	Per cent.	Dollars	Per cent.
2886 white families of selected localities in 11 States									
Owners, tenants and hired men									
All States..............	1922–1924	2886	4.8	659	41.2	441	66.9	218	33.1
New England States.....	do	317	4.7	707	41.8	350	49.5	357	50.5
Southern States.........	do	1130	5.1	691	44.6	515	74.5	176	25.5
North Central States....	do	1439	4.6	623	38.6	403	64.6	220	35.4
Owners: All States.......	do	1950	4.8	686	39.9	461	67.2	225	32.8
Tenants: All States.......	do	867	4.9	606	44.7	403	66.5	203	33.5
Hired men: All States....	do	69	4.7	547	44.2	338	61.8	209	38.2

84

861 white families of selected localities of Kentucky, Tennessee and Texas								
All families	1919	861	4.7	632	44.0	384	60.8	248	39.2
Owner families	do	411	4.6	652	39.9	428	65.6	224	34.4
Tenant families	do	321	4.9	659	47.8	387	58.7	272	41.3
Cropper families	do	129	5.0	500	52.8	236	47.2	264	52.8
798 white families of Schoharie county, New York, and Jackson, Meigs and Vinton counties, Ohio								
All families	1924–1926	798	4.2	470	45.9	261	55.5	209	44.5
154 colored families of selected localities of Kentucky, Tennessee and Texas								
All families	1919	154	5.1	327	53.5	179	54.7	148	45.3
Owner families	do	35	5.2	358	52.5	226	63.1	132	36.9
Tenant families	do	47	5.2	368	54.8	217	59.0	151	41.0
Cropper families	do	72	4.9	284	53.0	131	46.1	153	53.9

[1] Adapted from Bul. 1466 and Preliminary Reports, U. S. Dept. Agriculture.

85

TABLE 9. Average quantity and value of the various foodstuffs consumed during one year by 1331 farm families of selected localities of Kansas, Kentucky, Missouri and Ohio — 1922–1924.[1]

Kind of foodstuff	Average per family (All families)		Proportion purchased		Families using
	Pounds	Value	Pounds	Value	Number
			Per cent.	Per cent.	Number
Meat, fish, eggs—					
Beef.................	109	$21.10	52	52	1062
Mutton.............	4	0.77	24	27	76
Pork...............	374	51.03	5	7	1294
Poultry............	135	43.76	0	0	1312
Veal...............	16	2.93	29	29	166
Other meat........	1	0.15	100	100	88
Fish...............	21	4.34	90	92	1058
Eggs...............	306	45.68	0	0	1307
Milk, cream, cheese—					
Whole milk........	2370	81.16	0	0	1302
Skim milk.........	1	.09	0	0	1
Canned milk.......	—	—	100	100	2
Cheese.............	18	4.54	36	54	781
Cream.............	218	38.06	0	0	806
Fatty foods—					
Bacon, salt pork.....	137	11.26	7	24	1298
Butter.............	136	49.99	9	12	1274
Other table fats.....	2	0.69	100	100	89
Lard...............	83	7.38	15	25	1301
Other cooking fats...	—	0.08	100	100	21
Peanut butter.......	5	1.31	100	100	771
Salad oils..........	1	0.21	100	100	118
Sugar, syrups—					
Honey.............	6	1.37	47	44	414
Maple syrup.......	6	1.01	81	75	163
Molasses..........	16	1.42	99	99	470
Syrup, corn........	29	1.71	100	100	597
Sugar, granulated...	332	32.35	100	100	1320
Sugar, brown.......	23	2.10	100	100	978
Cereals—					
Bread..............	93	8.93	100	100	1005
Cornmeal..........	90	2.63	41	40	1132
Cornstarch........	4	0.43	100	100	706
Flour, white.......	806	32.10	80	80	1315
Flour, whole wheat..	22	0.85	84	75	342
Flour, other........	5	0.50	94	98	324
Macaroni, noodles...	6	1.15	100	100	1001
Rice...............	14	1.31	100	100	1131
Rolled oats........	37	3.11	100	100	958
Other cereal.......	36	3.71	95	98	1005
Other baked goods...	31	5.83	100	100	1253
Fruit—					
Fresh: Apples........	444	11.48	44	51	1268
Bananas...........	36	4.01	100	100	1193

[1] Adapted from "Average Quantity, Cost and Nutritive Value of Food Consumed by Farm Families," Preliminary Report, U. S. Dept. Agriculture.

TABLE 9 — CONTINUED

Kind of foodstuff	Average per family (All families)		Proportion purchased		Families using
	Pounds	Value	Pounds Per cent.	Value Per cent.	Number
Berries.............	58	$6.79	15	18	1076
Cherries............	52	3.05	23	23	802
Grapes.............	37	1.44	12	15	765
Lemons............	16	2.18	100	100	1219
Melons.............	168	5.05	30	45	889
Oranges, grapefruit..	52	4.52	100	100	1225
Peaches............	127	4.15	36	43	991
Pears..............	68	1.56	27	32	683
Rhubarb...........	11	0.87	5	6	641
Other fresh fruit.....	81	2.78	51	57	996
Canned..............	10	2.57	100	100	575
Dry: Prunes.........	5	1.02	100	100	675
Raisins.............	10	1.86	100	100	1066
Other dry fruit......	2	0.47	100	100	294
Vegetables—					
Fresh: Beans.........	102	4.11	2	3	1249
Beets..............	35	0.71	1	1	1121
Cabbage, cauliflower.	177	5.59	13	13	1183
Carrots............	6	0.14	6	7	295
Celery.............	18	1.43	60	65	720
Corn...............	209	5.04	1	1	1202
Cucumbers.........	118	1.90	6	6	841
Lettuce, greens......	27	3.02	8	14	1201
Onions.............	65	2.85	9	9	1282
Peas..............	40	1.69	1	1	1086
Potatoes...........	954	19.25	24	25	1318
Sweet potatoes......	90	2.43	44	44	884
Squash, pumpkin....	36	1.38	2	2	691
Tomatoes..........	281	4.58	2	2	1260
Turnips............	22	0.42	7	7	491
Other fresh vegetables	38	2.04	1	1	1147
Canned..............	25	4.58	100	100	782
Dry: Peas, beans......	56	4.09	72	65	1120
Miscellaneous—					
Chocolate, cocoa....	7	2.02	100	100	1197
Coffee.............	36	12.69	100	100	1224
Extracts............	2	1.87	100	100	1281
Gelatin.............	1	0.66	100	100	583
Olives, pickles.......	2	0.64	100	100	378
Peanuts............	4	0.77	96	98	624
Other nuts..........	12	1.17	77	92	771
Salt................	78	1.99	100	100	1298
Soda, baking powder	15	2.99	100	100	1321
Spices..............	6	1.38	100	100	1254
Tea................	4	2.35	100	100	1026
Vinegar............	43	2.60	74	77	1278
Yeast..............	1	0.46	100	100	587
Other foods.........	—	0.29	—	68	82
Total..............		615.97		33	

For all the families of these four groups it amounted to $616 per family or household and constituted 40 per cent. of the total value of all family living. About one third, 33 per cent., of the food (in terms of value) was purchased. There were 4.4 persons per household in the 1331 families. The eighty-five different kinds of foods furnished by the farm and purchased are given in terms of pounds used and cost or value per year per family. The proportions of the total amounts used, in terms of both pounds and value, and the number of families using are shown in the table.

It should be recalled that the figures are based on estimates made by the home-maker of the amount of food used in the household for the year just preceding the visit of the field worker. They may contain some appreciable errors, although every effort was made by the field workers to obtain accurate figures. Also, the estimates were usually given in volumetric terms—milk by the quart, potatoes by the bushel and apples by the box. With many of the items the units of measurement were less standardized. Onions, lettuce and the like were sometimes estimated in bunches or messes, and melons, squashes and the like were usually given in numbers. In the reduction of all these figures to pounds it is possible that in some instances the conversion factor was not correct.

Another possible source of error lies in the waste of foods due to spoilage that occurs in storage and to the throwing away of "left overs" from the table. The home-makers could not give accurate information on these points, and the errors here, to whatever extent they may be present, are doubtless on the side of larger amounts of certain foods reported for use than were actually consumed by members of the household.

The percentage of waste in food varies, of course, with

the different kinds and qualities. Usually, the poorer the grade of food the greater the percentage of waste. And it is possible that the best grades of potatoes, apples, etc., produced on the farm may have been sold, while the poorer grades were kept for home use. This would mean a larger allowance than would be made for waste ordinarily, since the figures represent the foods as provided for use. From the standpoint of the adequacy of the diet, considered in succeeding pages, allowance is made for waste in the preparation of foods for use.

Differences in the proportions of pounds and values of foods purchased, in some instances in *Table 9,* are due to differences in costs or values. Purchased foods were charged at prices which were paid for them at the grocery or market. Foods furnished by the farm were valued at prices between what would have been received for them had they been sold and what would have been paid had they been purchased, usually more nearly what would have been received had they been sold. Kinds and qualities of goods and the locality factor are involved in the prices charged for home-grown foods. For example, cottage cheese furnished by the farm was recorded at less than half as much per pound as American cheese purchased. It was regarded as being worth less as a different kind of cheese and worth less again due to its being non-salable at the local store.

Comparisons of quantities of food used by different groups of families. Data on the amounts of the different kinds of food used by 12,000 workingmen's families studied by the United States Bureau of Labor Statistics, 1918-19, show smaller amounts of practically all foodstuffs used by these families than by the 1331 farm families.[2] Of course,

---

[2] U. S. Bureau of Labor Statistics, "Cost of Living in the United States," Bul. 357, 1924.

there are exceptions in some of the different kinds of food-stuffs; the amount of beef reported used by the industrial family was two times the amount reported by the farm family, but the latter reported the use of twice as much pork, poultry, eggs and milk as did the former. The consumption of breads (expressed in terms of flours) appears to be about 25 per cent. greater for the industrial families. Table and cooking fats, including butter and lard, were used in about the same amounts by both groups of families. Twice as much sugar and syrups were used by the farm families.

Comparison of the nutriment provided by the food used is of more significance than are comparisons of the amounts of the different kinds of the foodstuffs. This comparison has been made by Hawley, against Sherman's "standard of good nutrition," which embodies 3300 calories of energy, 82 grams of protein, 0.77 gram of calcium, 1.45 grams of phosphorus and 0.0165 gram of iron.[3] These figures are shown in *Table 10*, along with similar figures for 950 farm families studied by W. C. Funk, 1912-14, on the per man per day basis.[4] Further comparisons are possible from *Table 11* on the distribution of energy among the principal food groups.

Two sets of factors or dietary scales were used in reducing the figures to the per man per day basis—that is, in allowing for differences in consumption due to differences in sex, age and activity. One of these served in the calculation of energy needs and the other in the calculation of protein and mineral needs of the family. Recent investiga-

[3] H. C. Sherman, "Chemistry of Food and Nutrition," 2d Ed., p. 383, 1918.

[4] U. S. Dept. Agriculture, "Value to Farm Families of Food, Fuel and Use of House," Bul. 410, 1916.

TABLE 10. Nutritive value of the average diet for three groups of families in terms of energy, protein, calcium, phosphorus and iron, compared with a standard of good nutrition.[1]

NUTRITIVE VALUE PER MAN PER DAY

Study	Energy		Protein		Calcium		Phosphorus		Iron	
	Calories	Pct. of standard	Grams	Pct. of standard	Grams	Pct. of standard	Grams	Pct. of standard	Grams	Pct. of standard
Standard	3300	100	82	100	0.77	100	1.45	100	0.0165	100
1331 farm families	4370	132	121	148	1.22	158	2.05	141	0.021	127
950 farm families (Funk)	4260	129	128	156	1.15	150	2.12	146	0.023	139
11,900 workmen's families........	2741	83	82	100	0.65	84	1.30	90	0.014	85

[1] Adapted from "Average Quantity, Cost and Nutritive Value of Food Consumed by Farm Families," Preliminary Report U. S. Dept. Agriculture.

TABLE 11. The distribution of energy among the various food groups in three groups of families compared with a standard of good nutrition.[1]

Study	Meat, Eggs, Cheese		Milk, Cream		Fatty Foods		Sweets		Cereals		Fruits, Vegetables	
	Cal. per man per day	Per cent. of total cal.	Cal. per man per day	Per cent. of total cal.	Cal. per man per day	Per cent. of total cal.	Cal. per man per day	Per cent. of total cal.	Cal. per man per day	Per cent. of total cal.	Cal. per man per day	Per cent. of total cal.
Standard	460	14–15	360	10–12	620	20–17	350	10–11	880	28–25	630	18–20
1331 farm families	713	16	661	15	764	18	476	11	1195	27	561	13
950 farm families (Funk)	580	14	400	9	710	17	500	12	1280	30	790	18
11,900 workingmen's families	370	14	204	7	491	18	250	9	1065	39	361	13

[1] Adapted from "Average Quantity, Cost and Nutritive Value of Food Consumed by Farm Families," Preliminary Report, U. S. Dept. Agriculture.

tions have established the fact that the growing child needs relatively more protein and minerals than the adult male.

With the adult male over sixty years of age taken as unity or 1, the relative weights attributed to other persons of different sex and age in the household are as follows:

	Age	For Energy	For protein and minerals
Adult male	18 to 60	1.2	1.1
Adult male	Over 60	1.0	1.0
Adult female	18 to 60	1.0	0.9
Adult female	Over 60	0.8	0.8
Boy	15 to 18	1.2	1.6
Girl	15 to 18	0.9	1.2
Child	11 to 14	0.9	1.2
Child	6 to 10	0.7	0.9
Child	Under 6	0.4	0.6

The adult male farmer eighteen to sixty years of age is given the maximum of consumption weights, owing to his relatively greater activity at this period of life. Also, the active adult farm woman eighteen to sixty years of age is given the consumption factors of 1.0 for energy needs and 0.9 for protein and mineral needs, instead of the factor ordinarily used for this group, 0.8.[5]

By the use of the double scale it was found that the energy need of the 1331 farm households, averaging 4.4 persons each, was equivalent to that of 4.2 adult male units, and the protein and mineral needs equivalent to that of 4.3 adult male units. All persons who lived in the home more than two weeks of the year were counted for the time they were present. That is, if a hired man lived for three months in the home, his energy requirement was consid-

[5] For the most complete and most satisfactory study of dietary scales and standards see Tech. Bul. 8, by Edith Hawley, U. S. Dept. Agriculture, 1927.

ered as 0.3, or one fourth that of an adult male. The amount of nutrients available per adult male unit was obtained by dividing the total energy yield by the factor 4.3, which expresses its protein and mineral need in terms of adult male units. Average refuse values determined by Atwater and Bryant were assumed in calculating the amount of nutrients provided from the foodstuffs available.[6]

The number of adult male units in protein and mineral needs were not determined for the 950 farm families studied by Funk and the 11,900 industrial families studied by the United States Bureau of Labor Statistics. Consequently, the figures for protein and minerals are held to be higher for these families than they would have been if the double scale had been used.

The figures in *Table 10* show that the food consumption habits of the two groups of farm families, as indicated by the amount of nutrients, are similar in most respects. Both groups appear to have used from 30 to 55 per cent. more nutrients than the "standard of good nutrition" specifies. When allowance is made for the fact that the protein and mineral values for the 950 families were calculated on a higher basis than for the 1331 families, the latter group appears to have had a much higher calcium content in their diet, due largely to the use of more milk and cream, as shown in *Table 11*.

From the standpoint of the distribution of energy among the principal food groups, *Table 11*, the 950 families used less eggs, meat and cheese and more cereals, fruits and vegetables than the 1331 families. The distribution of

---

[6] U. S. Dept. Agriculture, "The Chemical Composition of American Food Materials," Bul. 28, 1899. Reprinted 1906.

energy among the fatty foods and sweets is similar for the two groups of families.

While the food used by the two groups of farm families provided 30 per cent. more energy, 50 per cent. more protein and some more minerals than were needed, the food used by the 11,900 workingmen's families provided 17 per cent. less energy and from 10 to 16 per cent. less minerals than were needed. The protein allowance just met the "standard of good nutrition" with the workingmen's families.

Practically all the principal groups of foodstuffs figured in the differences in nutrients provided, the amount of meat, eggs and cheese in the workingman's diet being 40 per cent. below that in the farmer's diet, and the milk, cream, fruit and vegetables about 60 per cent. below. From the standpoint of the distribution of energy among the principal food groups, the proportions of the total energy yielded by milk and cream and by sweets were much lower for the workingman's family. On the other hand, the proportion of the total yielded by cereals was much higher for the workingman's family.

The comparisons here made are suggestive rather than conclusive of the range of differences which may exist between the diets of farm families and industrial families. Attention has been called already to the possible shortcomings which may be involved in the camparisons. Further studies representing other groups of families of other farming sections and other industrial situations are needed as bases for more substantial conclusions. It is possible that the figures given by farm families show considerably larger amounts of food than was actually eaten by persons of the household. On the other hand, it is possible that the very nature and variety of farm work, out of doors in all kinds of weather, calls for the consumption of more food than has been allotted in the "standard of good nutrition."

For the present, however, we may proceed on the assumption that the farmer's diet measures favorably with the workingman's diet, on an average, from the standpoint of the amount of food available. There are exceptions, of course, and these are suggested by some of the figures for some of the separate tenure groups especially, presented earlier in the chapter. In general terms, there is no "bread line" in the open country, however.

Other aspects of the use of food. But from the standpoint of the satisfactions or values accruing from the use of food, "man cannot live by bread alone," and the food problem in the farm household is not limited to the amount of food consumed. There is the question of the balance between the various kinds of food by day, by week and by season. Most farm women appreciate the difficulty, if not the impossibility, of having fresh, leafy vegetables for salads and the like during the winter months. Some farm people still attempt to span over this and possibly other dull periods in the appetite with spring tonics obtained from "patent medicine" or "quack remedy" salesmen.

Also, there is the matter of the quality of the homegrown foods used for family living purposes. Many farm families practise poor economy in using the "culls," products of small sizes and inferior grades, while saving the best for sale; sometimes to feed it to the stock later or to see it rot through failure to get it on the market. Housewives who are instructed to use the small potatoes or the apples that are "specked" from the supply in the farm cellar can scarcely be expected to get or to give a full

measure of satisfactions from preparing and serving the
family diet.

Concerning the quality of foods used on the farm, it may
be in line to mention a farmer of the writer's acquaintance
who reared his family on a "rotten apple" philosophy of
life. No matter how many grade A apples were in the
cellar, often with no market open for them, this farmer
never permitted the members of his family to eat, nor
offered the friends who came to visit them, an apple that
had not started to rot. This farmer left each of his sons
eighty acres of improved farm-land, but none of them are
farming. It is probable that the inclination always to sell
the best means poor economy for the family. "We know
the temptations, because of the scarcity of money, of saving the best products for the market," states one farmer,
"but we question whether it is any real saving in the long
run. After all, the business of life is living, and a farmer
has at hand many of the things that make life worth while
if he uses them. We believe the farm family has the right
to the first enjoyment of those good things that the farm
produces." [7]

Then there is the ever recurring problem of food preparation. One writer holds that "farm women are notably good
cooks, . . . in that they know how to cook all kinds of
food and cook them in ways that the family has learned
to like." [8] There must be learning in new ways of cooking,
however, if maximum satisfactions are to be had from the
family diet. Science is discovering and developing new tech-
niques and new methods of preparing and serving foods,
and there is as much need for the adoption of these methods
by farm families as by other families. Further, many farm

[7] M. C. Burritt, editorial, "American Agriculturist," 1925.
[8] Carl C. Taylor, "Rural Sociology," p. 111, 1926.

people, younger people especially, are learning to like foods prepared in new ways not yet learned by all farm women.

The writer referred to above might have added that farm women are good cooks in that they usually cook at the same time they are performing several other household operations; occasionally in addition to cutting the supply of wood needed to keep the meal cooking. The preparation of food for use is in reality an art when sufficient time is available, when quality foods are used and when the "artisan" obtains enough encouragement to lift her above the humdrum of everyday dull monotony.

Concerning encouragement for the "artisan," the following incident is of interest. At a rural life group meeting at one of the state colleges several years ago students and instructors were presenting problems for the consideration of the group. After some hesitation a serious-minded, farm-reared girl, a junior in home economics, stated: "My problem is just this. I learn at college how to cook and to prepare meals in new ways. For example, I learn to serve lettuce, radishes, tomatoes and the like attractively in salads. When I go home mother lets me make and serve the salads, and it would be a real treat for me if the men folks would eat them. But as soon as they get to the table they begin to make smart remarks about the salads and finally call for the lettuce, the radishes and the sliced tomatoes separately. I leave it to you if that isn't a problem."

Finally, there is the question of the surroundings and the manner in which the meal is eaten. Fresh air (free from odors of cookery, barnyard and hatchery), sunlight and comfortable table and seating arrangement may be made to add materially to the satisfactions or values obtained from meals. Sufficient time for eating, with a brief period of rest or relaxation following, may contribute much to health and to happiness of the different members of the family. Regular hours for meals and a happy atmosphere at the table may be essential to good digestion. Possibly the partaking of meals could be made the principal social hour of the family which in after-years may be recalled by men and women as the bright spots in the lives of boys and girls on the farm.

CHAPTER VI

CLOTHING WORN BY FARM FAMILIES

At a "stunt night" program of county agricultural and home demonstration agents staged in connection with a certain state conference of extension workers several years ago, the participators vied with each other to see who could characterize the farmer as the most outstanding "hick" or "rube." The actors who appeared on the stage, singly, in pairs and in groups, with trouser legs tucked in their boot tops, shingle nails for suspender buttons, alfalfa hay for chin-whiskers and the like, provoked enthusiastic applause from the audience. On being questioned by one of the audience, at the close of the performance, as to why so much energy had been spent in the attempt to picture the farmer in this fashion, one of the "actors" replied, "That's the kind of farmers I have down in my county." Questioned further as to the actual situation, this "actor" admitted that the characterizations were not applicable to more than two farm families of his acquaintance in his county.

This incident brings to the foreground the matter of clothing worn by the different members of the farm family. Fortunately, there are not many farmers who still take pride in the habit of appearing in public or elsewhere in garbs which identify them as feeders of live stock or tillers of the soil. More fortunately, there are only a few farm group leaders and farm journal publishers who fail to recognize the fact that the personal appearance need be given attention and who continue to depict farm people as being most dressed up when in their "regulars," their untidy work clothes.

Generally, farmers are realizing that it pays to keep pace with men of other affairs in the matter of dress and personal appearance. This is evidenced by the many requests for information on the different aspects of clothing for different members of the farm family received by the various state colleges and the United States Department of Agriculture, and occasionally the more substantial clothing firms and mail-order houses. These requests usually come in the form of definite questions such as, "What is a reasonable amount to pay for clothing annually?" "What percentage of one's budget usually goes for clothing?" "How is the expenditure for clothing distributed among the different types of articles of clothing?" "What types of clothing are best purchased ready-made and what types best made at home?" and "To what extent does the making of clothing at home represent a wise expenditure of money and time?"

Light is thrown on some of these and similar questions from limited data which are available. Preceding the consideration of these data attention may well be called to the principal uses and the selection of clothing.

Most authorities hold that the wearing of clothes originated primarily from a desire for adornment and secondarily from the need to shelter or protect the body and from a feeling of modesty. Although clothing may have been used first for decorative purposes, it has always provided protection from the elements, heat and cold and wind and rain; and the farmer above all workers has need for this protection. He is out in all kinds of weather. He has to wrestle with mud and snow and cold as he goes about his daily tasks and as he drives long distances by team or car.

Like food, clothing yields both physical and psychic (social and personal) satisfactions or values. Clothing needs and tastes vary widely with different families as well as with the different individuals composing the family. Some one has said that "clothing is an extension of the personality." While clothes do not "make the man," they adapt or mold his personality to mesh or "cog in" with society. Therefore, the selection, care and use of clothing must be in keeping with the needs and tastes of the individual, according to his social relations with other individuals with whom he comes in contact. This point should be kept in mind in the consideration of the number of garments purchased and average prices paid per person or per family for clothing.

Clothing costs. Clothing costs amounted to $234 per family per year for the 2886 farm families referred to in preceding chapters. This expenditure for clothing constitutes 14.7 per cent. of the total value of all goods used per family. In comparison, clothing costs amounting to $276 per family comprised 13.7 per cent. of the value of all goods used by 402 Livingston county, New York, families. Also, clothing costs averaging $156 per family constituted 15.2 per cent. of all family living with 798 farm families of Schoharie county, New York, and southeastern Ohio. Finally, the expenditures for clothing amounted to $255 or 17.5 per cent. of all family living with 861 white families and to $107 or 17.7 per cent. of all family living with 154 colored families of selected localities of Kentucky, Tennessee and Texas.

Other data representing smaller groups of farmers might be presented. For sixty-five families studied by the farm management cost accounting method in North Dakota, clothing costs averaging $173 per family comprised 11.5 per cent. of the value of all family living.[1] For twenty-five families studied similarly in Minnesota, expenditures for clothing were $141 per family, or 10.4 per cent. of the value of all goods used. Figures from other minor studies made in other periods, when reduced to the 1922-24 price levels, are quite similar.

The most complete set of figures, that for 2886 farm families, shows an expenditure of $254 for clothing for owner families, $197 for tenant families and $161 for hired-man families. The proportions that these costs are of the total value of family living are 14.8 per cent. for owners, 14.5 per cent. for tenants and 13.0 per cent. for hired men. Figures for 861 white families of Kentucky, Tennessee and Texas show an average of $255 spent for clothing by owner families, $247 by tenant families and $181 by cropper families. These expenditures are 17.4 per cent., 17.9 per cent. and 19.1 per cent. of the total values of family living. The figures for 154 colored families of the same localities show clothing costs of $122 for owner families, $124 for tenant families and $89 for cropper families, and these expenditures are 17.9 per cent., 18.4 per cent. and 16.6 per cent. of the total values of family living.

Comparison of the clothing expenditures by farm families and workingmen's families has been made by Edna L. Clarke of the United States Bureau of Home Economics.[2] Data for 1337 farm families of Kansas, Kentucky, Missouri and Ohio (the group of families referred to in the preceding chapter) and for the 12,096 families studied by

[1] U. S. Dept. Agriculture, "Annual Family Living in Farm Homes," Preliminary Report, 1928.

[2] U. S. Dept. Agriculture, "Clothing Expenditures of 86 Farm Families of Vermont," Preliminary Report, 1927.

the United States Bureau of Labor Statistics were used. The figures, classified according to the value of all family living, are shown in *Table 12*, with both clothing expenditures and costs of living of the workingmen's families adjusted to price levels of the period represented by the farm families.

TABLE 12. Average clothing expenditure per family for one year, and the proportion the clothing expenditure is of the average value of all family living, by increase in average value of all family living; 1337 farm families of selected localities of Kansas, Kentucky, Missouri and Ohio, and 12,096 industrial families of 92 industrial centers.[1]

Value of all family living	FARM FAMILIES				INDUSTRIAL FAMILIES			
	Number of families	Average value of all family living	Clothing expenditures		Number of families	Average cost of all family living	Clothing expenditures	
			Average cost per family	Proportion of average value of all family living			Average cost per family	Proportion of average cost of all family living
		Dollars	Dollars	Pct.		Dollars	Dollars	Pct.
Under $1200..	445	933	117	12.5	2755	1150	150	13.1
$1200–$1799..	513	1469	211	14.4	8283	1608	241	15.0
$1800–$2399..	245	2035	307	15.1	705	2254	381	16.9
$2400 and over	134	3113	476	15.3	353	2706	499	18.5
All groups....	1337	1559	225	14.4	12096	1574	236	15.0

[1] Adapted from "Average Clothing Expenditures of 86 Farm Families of Franklin County, Vermont," Preliminary Report, U. S. Dept. Agriculture.

Very little difference is noted in the amount spent for clothing by farm and industrial families, except in families having relatively large values of family living or incomes. The average clothing expenditure of the farm families is about $11 less than the average for the workingmen's families.

With each higher value-of-living group the proportion which clothing bears to the value of all family living increases for both farm and industrial families. As the value of all family living increases, the industrial families appear to have spent a larger proportion on clothing than did the farm families.

These figures should be of interest to rural sociologists and others who maintain that "Compared with town people, farm families spend very little for clothing." [3] While the figures are not at all final, they are suggestive of inferences that might be established by further studies among other groups of farm and city people.

Some authorities or critics hold that comparisons of expenditures for clothing as well as for other family living purposes by farmers and industrial workers are invalid, since farmers are entrepreneurs. These authorities would compare the farmer's living with that of industrial managers and business executives, who constitute a relatively small percentage of all city people. Possibly the percentage of farmers with real entrepreneurial ability is no higher than for other groups of people. At any rate, careful studies are needed to ascertain the facts in regard to this matter.

No mention has been made of size of family in connection with the above comparisons. Since clothing is so largely an individual or a personal matter, and since in the principal studies clothing costs were obtained by listing and summarizing the costs per person for the different articles of clothing, comparisons on the per person basis are possible and are regarded as more significant than compari-

[3] University of Minnesota Agricultural Experiment Station, "How Farm Family Incomes Are Spent," Bul. 234, 1927.

sons on the per family basis. The costs of clothing per person by sex and several age groups are shown for 2886 farm families of selected localities in eleven States in *Table 13*. The different age groups observed are based upon the ages at which the demands for clothing tend to change most markedly, as indicated by analyses so far made of expenditures reported per person as influenced probably by such factors as entrance to grammar school, high school or college, choice of occupation, extent of social life and preparation for marriage. The further analyses of clothing needs and costs now being made by different research workers may lead to a revision of these age groups, which as yet are quite arbitrary and somewhat tentative.

TABLE 13.   Average cost of clothing per person purchased in one year, by sex and age groups, 2886 farm families of selected localities in 11 States, 1922–24.[1]

Age group	MALE			FEMALE		
	Number	Average cost	Relative cost; average for husband, 100 Per cent	Number	Average cost	Relative cost; average for wife, 100 Per cent.
Husbands–wives...	2778	$58.80	100	2839	$59.30	100
Sons and daughters						
Over 24 years....	242	74.30	126	186	84.20	142
19–24 years.....	476	90.40	154	325	99.00	167
15–18 years.....	616	72.80	124	540	80.50	136
12–14 years.....	477	44.40	76	483	51.70	87
6–11 years.....	939	31.90	54	958	33.70	57
1– 5 years.....	729	19.10	32	698	19.00	32
Below 1 year....	106	15.10	26	108	13.50	23

[1] Adapted from Bul. 1466 U. S. Dept. Agriculture.

Sex appears to make no difference in the cost of clothing either among the heads of families or among children less than twelve years of age with farm families. Daughters of the more advanced age groups, over twenty-four years, nineteen to twenty-four years, fifteen to eighteen years and twelve to fourteen years of age, are clothed at higher average costs than are sons of corresponding age groups. The average costs of clothing for both sons and daughters of the advanced age groups, over twenty-four years, nineteen to twenty-four years and fifteen to eighteen years, are considerably above the averages for male and female heads of families. Relatively, the average costs for sons of these age groups are 1.26, 1.54 and 1.24 times as high as the average costs for male heads of families. Likewise, the average costs for daughters are 1.42, 1.67 and 1.36 times higher than the average costs for female heads of the families.

Amounts, kinds and quality of clothing. These data raise at once questions as to the number of articles, the variety or kinds and the quality of clothing used by the different farm families. They suggest also the question of adequacy of clothing worn by the farm family—that is, the warmth and comfort which it provides, and the satisfaction with which it permits the members of the family to appear in public groups or social circles.

Figures showing the average number of articles per person and the average cost per article for husbands and for sons nineteen to twenty-four years of age in 1337 farm families are given in *Table 14*. Likewise, these figures are given for wives and for daughters nineteen to twenty-four years of age for the same families in *Table 15*. The numbers of persons purchasing each article are shown also in the two tables.

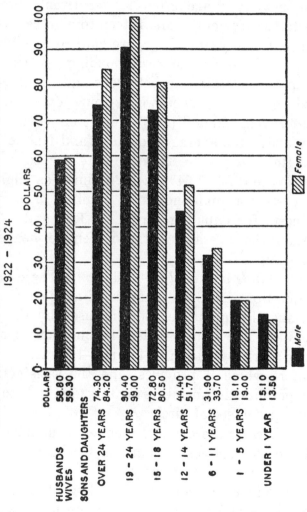

AVERAGE COST OF CLOTHING PURCHASED DURING ONE YEAR FOR PERSONS OF DIFFERENT SEX AND AGE

2,886 FARM HOMES OF SELECTED LOCALITIES IN 11 STATES
1922 – 1924

DOLLARS

	DOLLARS
HUSBANDS	58.80
WIVES	59.30
SONS AND DAUGHTERS	
OVER 24 YEARS	74.30 84.20
19 – 24 YEARS	90.40 99.00
15 – 18 YEARS	72.80 80.50
12 – 14 YEARS	44.40 51.70
6 – 11 YEARS	31.90 33.70
1 – 5 YEARS	19.10 19.00
UNDER 1 YEAR	15.10 13.50

Male   Female

Fig. 5.—Average annual costs of clothing for husbands and wives are about equal. Sons of the higher age groups are clothed at lower costs than are daughters. (*Courtesy of the United States Department of Agriculture.*)

TABLE 14. Average quantities and costs of articles of clothing purchased in one year for husbands and sons 19–24 years of age; 1337 farm families of selected localities of Kansas, Kentucky, Missouri and Ohio, 1922–23.[1]

Articles	HUSBANDS (1252)			SONS 19–24 (165)		
	Persons Purchasing	Average Number of Articles	Average Cost per Article	Persons Purchasing	Average Number of Articles	Average Cost per Article
	Number	Per person	Dollars	Number	Per person	Dollars
Headwear—						
Hats....................	824	.92	2.70	106	.99	3.39
Caps....................	409	.44	1.45	105	.87	2.31
Outer Garments—						
Sweaters................	278	.23	3.67	55	.35	4.87
Raincoats and mackinaws .	130	.10	8.88	22	.13	13.50
Overcoats...............	192	.16	18.49	42	.25	22.30
Suits....................	384	.33	28.63	116	.84	31.10
Extra trousers...........	403	.59	3.01	56	.56	3.65
Overalls.................	1020	3.24	1.85	128	2.64	1.85
Jackets, denim...........	430	.55	1.74	36	.31	1.81
Coveralls................	—	—	—	1	.01	3.50
Work shirts..............	1191	4.29	1.09	157	3.90	1.15
Dress shirts.............	704	1.03	1.99	138	2.11	2.35
Undergarments—						
Underwear: Summer......	782	1.59	1.09	128	2.22	1.10
Winter.......	681	1.15	1.98	87	1.17	1.76
Night garments..........	222	.49	.82	28	.35	1.12
Footwear—						
Socks...................	1172	8.66	.27	147	9.05	.35
Shoes...................	1181	2.07	4.38	159	2.49	4.99
Rubbers.................	273	.26	1.83	32	.25	1.88
Arctics and felts	483	.44	3.27	54	.38	3.15
Rubber boots............	439	.37	4.47	51	.34	4.16
Accessories—						
Gloves and mittens.......	892	8.24	.22	115	7.65	.27
Collars.................	392	1.14	.29	97	3.15	.33
Ties....................	401	.60	.80	100	1.82	.92
Belts...................	154	.13	.93	55	.41	.82
Suspenders..............	360	.45	.56	7	.06	.45
Garters.................	395	.62	.31	99	1.44	.34
Handkerchiefs...........	436	2.15	.15	65	2.76	.16
Miscellaneous...........	1	—	—	—	—	—
Upkeep and repair—						
Cleaning................	145	—	—	42	—	—
Pressing................	16	—	—	13	—	—
Shoe repair.............	425	—	—	63	—	—
Average cost per person for all clothing......... 56.76						89.00

[1] Adapted from "Average Quantities and Costs of Clothing Purchased by Farm Families," Preliminary Report, U. S. Dept. Agriculture.

A few explanatory notes may aid in the interpretation of the figures. The line of distinction between summer and winter underwear is not at all definite. Summer underwear was listed first on the schedules, and it is probable that some of the purchases of winter underwear were included with the summer. Underwear includes, in addition to union suits, underdrawers and undershirts for men and boys, and combinations, chemises, undershirts and drawers for women and girls. "Gloves and mittens" include cotton, leather, canvas and woolen. Most of the purchases for men and boys were cotton work gloves. "Miscellaneous" includes minor articles of clothing such as spats, shoe polish and bedroom slippers. It should be noted that the average number of articles purchased is based upon the number of all persons in the particular age group and not on the number of persons purchasing.

On an average, the farmer appears to buy a hat each year, a cap every two years, a suit of clothes every three years and an overcoat every ten years. The hats represent an expenditure of about $2.75 each, caps about $1.50, suits nearly $30 and overcoats $18.50. Other articles purchased sparingly, probably for "dress-up" wear, in part at least, include raincoats, sweaters, extra trousers and dress shirts. Articles adapted to work purposes appear to have been purchased more frequently, three pairs of overalls and four work shirts per year. Nine pairs of socks, two pairs of shoes and eight pairs of gloves per person were purchased during the year.

Because he buys them so seldom and because of the seemingly high price which he pays for them, the farmer attaches much more significance to the purchase of a suit of clothes every three years or an overcoat every ten years than to the purchase of three pairs of overalls per year

TABLE 15. Average quantities and costs of articles of clothing purchased in one year for wives and daughters 19–24 years of age; 1337 farm families of selected localities of Kansas, Kentucky, Missouri and Ohio, 1922–23.[1]

Articles	WIVES (1270)			DAUGHTERS 19–24 (117)		
	Persons Purchasing	Average Number of Articles	Average Cost per Article	Persons Purchasing	Average Number of Articles	Average Cost per Article
	Number	Per person	Dollars	Number	Per person	Dollars
Hats........................	758	.86	4.87	101	1.51	5.32
Outer Garments—						
Aprons...................	907	3.18	.65	53	1.76	.81
Dresses: House...........	1079	3.28	1.44	91	2.88	2.06
Other...........	855	1.53	9.01	98	2.26	11.35
Waists..................	359	.46	3.28	39	.67	3.01
Skirts...................	164	.16	5.14	34	.42	5.21
Suits....................	129	.10	26.86	20	.23	20.83
Sweaters.................	164	.14	5.06	38	.45	4.43
Coats...................	334	.27	23.98	69	.63	24.18
Furs....................	13	.01	14.73	3	.03	4.50
Undergarments—						
Petticoats...............	483	.69	1.40	67	1.38	1.67
Bloomers................	11	.02	.96	6	.14	.92
Corsets..................	613	.59	3.12	50	.62	2.19
Underwear: Summer......	868	2.10	.87	90	2.63	.95
Winter.......	558	.97	1.49	47	1.14	1.34
Night-dresses............	570	1.05	1.07	67	1.29	1.27
Kimonos.................	32	.03	2.44	9	.08	3.17
Bathrobes...............	14	.01	3.96	—	—	—
Footwear—						
Stockings...............	1193	5.90	.63	108	5.59	1.17
Shoes...................	1201	2.03	4.65	112	2.91	5.00
Rubbers.................	456	.44	1.14	40	.34	1.35
Arctics.................	147	.13	2.12	15	.13	3.33
Accessories—						
Gloves and mittens.......	534	.75	1.14	65	.93	1.62
Handkerchiefs...........	492	3.02	.15	58	3.36	.18
Neckwear...............	69	.08	.84	10	.28	.85
Garters.................	224	.28	.24	30	.46	.24
Ribbons.................	—	—	—	4	—	—
Miscellaneous............	14	—	—	1	—	—
Upkeep and repair—						
Cleaning................	121	—	—	19	—	—
Pressing................	29	—	—	5	—	—
Shoe repair..............	416	—	—	45	—	—
Sewing.................	138	—	—	8	—	—
Average cost per person for all clothing......... 61.81						103.36

[1] Adapted from "Average Quantities and Costs of Clothing Purchased by Farm Families," Preliminary Report, U. S. Dept. Agriculture.

involving the expenditure of more than $15 in three years or more than $55 in ten years. Questioned by family living workers as to the total expenditure for his own personal clothing during a year, the farmer usually formulates his answer in terms of a suit of clothes, an overcoat or a "dress" hat, forgetting that he has had to provide overalls, work shirts, underwear, socks, work shoes and the like for everyday uses. A good many farmers have to be reminded that the garments worn daily constitute a considerable part of their clothing, and that costs for these must be counted in the total expenditure for clothing.

Sons nineteen to twenty-four years of age appear to purchase caps, suits of clothes, overcoats, dress shirts, in fact all articles of a "dress-up" nature, more frequently than do the husbands and fathers, *Table 14*. Also, these are purchased at higher prices per article. Both of these factors contribute to the higher cost of all clothing per person for the sons nineteen to twenty-four years of age.

It is interesting to note that the farm woman (wife, *Table 15*) purchased a hat a year, a coat every four years and three "better" dresses every two years, on an average. Waists, skirts, sweaters and suits were purchased sparingly, in addition. Three house dresses and three aprons were provided during the year. As with husbands, two pairs of shoes were purchased per year, but fewer stockings (than socks for the men), six pairs per person.

Blanche E. Hyde, clothing specialist at the Colorado Agricultural College, holds that house dresses are of first importance with the farm home-maker of the Western States.[4] From the standpoint of the average number of garments provided during a year, this assumption need not

[4] Colorado Agricultural College, "Clothing as an Economic Problem," Mimeographed Report, 1927.

be questioned, perhaps, unless stockings are taken into account. But from the standpoint of the cost of the garments and the comfort or satisfaction which they provide, one may ask, "Is the provision of a house dress of any more importance to the farm woman than the provision of a 'better' dress, a hat, a coat or a pair of shoes?"

Next to house dresses Mrs. Hyde regards "an afternoon dress" for visits to town, to church and for other social occasions "a necessity for farm women." "This dress may be of wool, silk or cotton," but "different studies made seem to indicate that silk and wool are the favorite materials. The hat problem is a comparatively simple one for the farm woman. Often one hat of silk serves the purpose the year round, especially while the habit of going barehead continues in vogue."

These assumptions, some of which are doubtless true, emphasize the need for further study of the provision and uses of the different articles of clothing by farm homemakers.

Daughters nineteen to twenty-four years of age purchase the articles of a "dress-up" type more frequently and at higher costs than do the wives or mothers, according to the figures in *Table 15*. Thus the higher cost per person for daughters of this age group in comparison with the costs for wives is accounted for, in part at least.

Corresponding figures for other age groups of both sexes might be given if space were available. Relatively, the figures appear somewhat similar for the different age groups, except those groups which fall below twelve years. Also, corresponding figures might be presented for husbands, wives, sons twelve to fourteen years of age and daughters twelve to fourteen years of age for **12,096** industrial families of 92 localities.[5] These figures are not comparable in many respects, however, owing to a more detailed listing of articles for persons of the industrial families. Apparently, persons of farm families are provided with the principal articles of clothing about as frequently and at as high prices as are persons of industrial families. Additional data obtained for the same years and classified and tabulated in the same way are needed to give further light on this point.

Farm families that are considering the idea of a family budget are interested in the distribution of expenditures for clothing among the principal groups of clothing classified according to the type of article. This distribution is shown by sex and age groups for 1337 farm families, referred to above, in *Table 16*. Six classes of articles are observed: headwear, outer garments, undergarments, footwear, accessories, and upkeep and repair.

Outer garments absorb the major portion of the costs with most of the age groups of both sexes, ranging between 57 per cent. and 44 per cent. for husbands and sons and between 59 per cent. and 43 per cent. for wives and daughters. Footwear is next in importance, comprising from 36 to 21 per cent. of the total cost for husbands and sons and 35 to 20 per cent. for wives and daughters. Undergarments come next in order, with headwear, accessories, and upkeep and repair next, practically in the order named. It is interesting to note that the proportion of the total going for outer garments increases with advancing ages of both sons and daughters. Also, the proportion devoted to footwear decreases quite steadily from about 37 per cent. to 21 per cent. for sons and from 35 per cent. to 20 per cent. for

[5] U. S. Bureau of Labor Statistics, "Cost of Living in the United States," Bul. 357, 1924.

TABLE 16. Average clothing expenditure per person for one year for clothing groups, classified by sex and age; 1337 farm families of selected localities of Kansas, Kentucky, Missouri and Ohio, 1922–23.[1]

	Number of Persons	Average Expend. for all Clothing	AVERAGE EXPENDITURE FOR										
			Headwear		Outer Garments		Undergarments		Footwear		Accessories		Upkeep and Repair	
		Dollars	Dols.	Pct.	Dols.	Pct.	Dols.	Pct.	Dols.	Pct.	Dols.	Pct.	Dols.	Pct.
Husbands.........	1252	56.76	3.12	5.5	29.80	52.5	4.41	7.8	14.98	26.4	3.51	6.2	.94	1.7
Sons—														
Over 24 years...	100	73.96	4.66	6.3	42.17	57.0	4.63	6.3	15.99	21.6	5.47	7.4	1.04	1.4
19–24 years.....	165	89.00	5.37	6.0	52.13	58.6	4.89	5.5	18.67	21.0	6.08	6.8	1.86	2.1
15–18 years.....	250	71.78	3.49	4.9	41.90	58.3	4.11	5.7	16.79	23.4	4.37	6.1	1.12	1.6
12–14 years.....	176	46.18	2.02	4.4	24.26	52.5	3.04	6.6	14.26	30.9	1.85	4.0	.75	1.6
6–11 years......	344	36.03	1.82	5.0	18.01	50.0	2.84	7.9	11.55	32.1	1.24	3.4	.57	1.6
1– 5 years......	225	18.22	.98	5.4	8.09	44.4	2.08	11.4	6.48	35.6	.48	2.6	.11	.6
Wives............	1270	61.81	4.19	6.8	32.92	53.3	7.33	11.8	13.94	22.6	1.58	2.5	1.85	3.0
Daughters—														
Over 24 years...	85	88.84	7.40	8.3	52.83	59.5	7.13	8.0	18.04	20.3	1.62	1.8	1.82	2.1
19–24 years.....	117	103.36	8.03	7.8	59.36	57.4	9.71	9.4	21.97	21.2	2.67	2.6	1.62	1.6
15–18 years.....	202	82.06	5.05	6.2	44.74	54.5	7.48	9.1	20.76	25.3	2.03	2.5	2.00	2.4
12–14 years.....	195	52.23	2.95	5.6	24.54	47.0	5.47	10.5	16.30	31.2	1.84	3.5	1.13	2.2
6–11 years......	373	32.05	1.57	4.9	13.95	43.5	3.95	12.3	10.88	33.9	1.05	3.3	.66	2.1
1– 5 years......	227	17.84	.75	4.2	7.70	43.2	2.36	13.2	6.28	35.2	.45	2.5	.30	1.7
Sons and Daughters below 1 year....	24	10.61	.30	2.8	4.89	46.1	1.60	15.1	1.68	15.8	2.14	20.2	—	—

[1] Adapted from "Average Quantities and Costs of Clothing Purchased by Farm Families," Preliminary Report, U. S. Dept. Agriculture.

daughters. The range in each set of the percentages for both outer garments and footwear extends about equally far on either side of the percentages for husbands and wives. Proportions of the total expenditure going for undergarments, headwear, accessories, and upkeep and repair vary too irregularly to suggest anything very definite in the way of trends, except headwear for daughters, where the percentage increases from about 4 per cent. to 8 per cent.

Comments from farm women interviewed in connection with family living studies strengthen the suggestions in the above considerations that the clothing of children, of school age especially, presents the most important clothing problems. "Children must be suitably clothed for the school sessions and in many cases for the long drive to and from school," they say. Warm dresses, coats, caps, hosiery and stout shoes are essential.

"With the older children, particularly the girls, there is the added problem of social affairs, with requirements of special clothing." This special clothing is sometimes regarded as unnecessary and as being desired by the young people primarily to "ape" the conditions of living and ways of dressing in city communities.

Home-made and ready-made garments. The question of making garments at home versus purchasing them ready made is gaining in interest among farm women. This is doubtless due in part to coördinated efforts of home economics extension workers during the past few years to teach the art of dress fitting, millinery and the like to the farm women as a means of keeping clothing costs of the farm family at a minimum.

Only limited information is available on "sewing at home" by farm women. A recent study made by the

United States Bureau of Home Economics among approximately 2000 women in thirty-two States gives some light on this point.[6] About 700 of the 2000 women lived on farms. Certain garments for women and for girls over fourteen years of age were reported as having been made at home by the following percentages of these farm women: Aprons 89 per cent., house dresses 88 per cent., summer wash dresses 87 per cent., nightgowns 87 per cent., slips 81 per cent., bloomers 74 per cent., petticoats 66 per cent., wool dresses 64 per cent., silk dresses 61 per cent., kimonos 51 per cent., skirts 48 per cent., blouses 47 per cent., chemises 42 per cent., hats 42 per cent. and coats 28 per cent. For over 400 of the farm families with children under fifteen years of age the following percentages of the women replying to the particular question reported the making of the children's garments as follows: Night-clothes 68 per cent., drawers or bloomers 67 per cent., cotton dresses 63 per cent., slips 58 per cent., petticoats 58 per cent., wool dresses 55 per cent., coats 46 per cent., shirts 39 per cent., rompers 38 per cent., cotton suits 34 per cent., hats 28 per cent. and wool suits 27 per cent.

Of the women who reported the making of garments for women and for girls over fifteen or more years of age 9 per cent. made one to five kinds of garments, 39 per cent. made six to ten kinds of garments and 45 per cent. made eleven to fifteen kinds of garments for women and "older" girls. Of the 417 women in whose families there were children under fifteen years of age 15 per cent. reported the making of one to four kinds, 27 per cent. the making of five to eight kinds and 17 per cent. the making of nine to twelve kinds of garments for children.

[6] U. S. Dept. Agriculture, "Present Trends in Home Sewing," Misc. Pub. No. 4, 1927.

Another recent study by the survey method among 145 farm families of ten Western States shows the following percentages of the women making all or a part of the garments specified: Dresses (probably house dresses) 83 per cent., undergarments 73 per cent., aprons 25 per cent., men's shirts 16 per cent., boys' clothing 12 per cent., men's underwear 11 per cent., coats 10 per cent., hats 6 per cent.[7] In the study of eighty-six farm families of Vermont referred to previously, Miss Clarke found that aprons and cotton dresses were being made at home for women and girls of practically all age groups.

The results of a study by the survey method among approximately 10,000 farm women of thirty-three Northern and Western States, 1919, shows 92 per cent. of these women doing "home sewing." By sections, the percentages are 86 per cent. for the Eastern States, 94 per cent. for the Central States and 95 per cent. for the Western States.[8]

In the study made by the Bureau of Home Economics comparative figures are given for over 400 village homes, about 200 "smaller city" homes and 550 "larger city" homes. In general, the percentages of the farm women making house dresses, summer wash dresses, aprons, and nightgowns decreased from the farm home to the "larger city" home. This was not the case with silk dresses, chemises and kimonos, for which the percentages were about the same for the four different locations of the homes. Farm women were making more kinds of garments for women and girls than were village and city women. Also higher proportions of farm women than city women were making

[7] Colorado Agricultural College, *op. cit.*, 1927.
[8] U. S. Dept. Agriculture, "The Farm Woman's Problem," Circ. 148, 1920.

children's garments, and the farm women appeared to be making more kinds of children's garments.

The 2000 women included in the study of the present trends in home sewing, referred to above, were asked to give reasons for making garments at home. "Lower costs of home-made garments" was the more popular reason and was given by 93 per cent. of the farm women. "Better material in home-made garments" was given by 78 per cent., "home-made garments more nearly meet individual needs" by 51 per cent. and "good stores for ready-made goods inaccessible" by 14 per cent. of the farm women. "Lower costs" and "better materials for home-made garments" were given by about the same percentages of all groups of women—that is, farm, village, "smaller city" and "larger city." A higher percentage of the farm women found "good stores for ready-made goods inaccessible" and a lower percentage found that "home-made garments more nearly meet individual needs."

Chief among the reasons given by about 450 of the farm women for the purchase of ready-made garments were "better style and design" and "saving of time and energy." Each of these reasons was given by two thirds of the farm women and by somewhat near the same percentages of village and city women. "Unable to make clothes at home" was given by 30 per cent. of the farm women and by lower percentages of the other groups of women.

Of the 145 families of the Western States, 46 per cent. preferred home-made clothing. Chief among the reasons for this preference were "better fit" and "better material." Other reasons were "better construction" and "less cost." Chief among the reasons for preference of ready-made garments were "style" and "appearance."

Over 80 per cent. of the 145 women were of the opinion that it was more economical to make garments at home than to buy them ready made. Labor costs of making the different garments were not obtained, but estimates of the time used show an average of nine hours for "coats," eight hours for "good" dresses, over four hours for hats, over three hours for house dresses, almost three hours for shirts, over two hours for slips and almost two hours for underwear. The conclusion is reached in this study that if "a definite value of the time of the farm woman per hour" be taken into account, fully as good values can be obtained in ready-made garments. The study of the 2000 homes is concluded with the statement that "as long as the woman at home has no direct source of income and her chief duty is caring for the home . . . she will no doubt consider that making a part of the clothing for the family is a wise way of 'stretching' the family income." Seemingly this would apply to the farm woman. Doubtless more data are needed to establish either of these points.

It goes without question, however, that the farm woman who sees economy in the purchase of ready-to-wear garments is in need of information on how to buy garments wisely—in short, how to select becoming garments of good qualities for herself and her family. At the same time the farm woman who sees economy in the making of certain garments at home is in need of usable information on choosing materials, designs and patterns, on using and altering patterns, and on fitting and finishing the garments.

The amount of home sewing by the farm woman depends largely on the enjoyment which she gets from it. Many of the 700 farm women and about three out of four of the 145 farm women of Western States reported that they enjoyed sewing. The woman who likes to sew should be encouraged to make garments at home, provided the product turned out does not "handicap" some member of the family in "dress" or "appearance." To many women the making of clothes may give opportunity for artistic expression, as the preparation of a meal or the furnishing of a room gives to other women.

The considerations in this chapter give no indication of the adequacy of the clothing worn—that is, the warmth and comfort which it provides, or the satisfaction with which it permits the members of the farm family to appear in public groups or social circles. Furthermore, they give no suggestion as to the clothing or dress habits which may be made to contribute so much to one's personal appearance.

Evidences of care given to clothing, of cleanliness, of attention given to the complexion, hair, nails and teeth, of proper posture, of happiness and contentment are often the deciding factors of whether one is regarded by others as being well dressed. Tasteful clothing, accompanied by pleasing personal appearance and habits, is in reality a vital part of one's social life. To the observer clothing or dress is probably the foremost index of the prevailing standard of living.

If this be true, farmers cannot afford to dress less well than other people. They must continue to give increasing consideration to clothing as one of the important elements of family living. This will demand more information from research workers and other authorities on the durability, suitability, becomingness and availability of the different garments needed to provide proper physical comfort and to permit the different members of the farm family to appear in their own social groups and in society with a fair degree of mental satisfaction.

CHAPTER VII

HOME SURROUNDINGS, HOUSING AND HOUSE-HOLD FURNISHINGS

A TEACHER of horticulture in one of the state agricultural colleges tells his students about a farm woman who asked him one time to plan and plant her back yard to look so near like her front yard that the chickens could not tell in which yard to scratch. "Pretty far from housing and housing conditions," one might say; but the approach to the farm-house is certainly across either one or the other, or both, of the two yards or two parts of the lawn. In other words, farm-houses usually appear comfortable and "homey" in so far as they stand in the midst of attractive surroundings. It is now pretty generally conceded that properly placed suitable plantings and well-kept lawn and surroundings will make almost any farm home attractive. And what is the house in the way of a home if void of trees, shrubs, flowers and green grass as a setting?

There is very little information which will throw light on the question of the extent to which farm homes are properly landscaped—in fact, little to designate the proportion of farm homes with landscape plantings of any sort. There are some impressions recorded of the way farm homes appear to different persons "driving through" the country, and a few figures on several aspects of home surroundings obtained by the survey method.

"Too many houses that could be seen were pert—not

equal to the vastness," states one observer. "The barns were more in harmony with the land; big and lofty they were. Such of the houses as were large in outline were too bare and unpainted. A few were too dressy, with fretwork on porches and trimmed gables." [1]

The following statements taken from the notes of two investigators visiting the same homes, in connection with a farm organization and farm family living survey, are of interest. "No matter how small or how large the house, how old or new it appears, or how well kept the premises are, one is impressed with the presence of plantings in the dooryards. Almost every home has its rose bushes or lilacs or peonies or something of the sort," stated one of the workers. But note the statement or comment of the other worker. "Apparently, the people living in the houses have no appreciation of the beautiful. There are roses and other flowering shrubs occasionally, but nearly every home has its ducks or chickens or pigs running all over the lawn, or its unsightly machinery or pig-pens obstructing the view from and to the highway."

Going a step beyond "observations," workers obtained information on the prevalence of plantings and the care of the lawn on 402 farmsteads of Livingston county, New York, 1921.[2]

While less than a twentieth of all these homes were without shade trees of some kind, over two fifths had no shrubs of any sort and not more than one fifth showed evidences of attractive or proper arrangement of the shrubs which were present. Almost seven eighths of the homes had the front lawn mowed, and half of them had the back lawn mowed in

[1] Adapted from "Fit and Misfit Rural Homes," Emily N. Blair, "Country Gentleman," January, 1928.

[2] Cornell University Agricultural Experiment Station, *op. cit.*, 1923.

addition. A similar study including 451 families in central Iowa showed that less than a twentieth of the homes had no shade trees and approximately an eighth had no shrubbery. Differences between owner and tenant homes were not significant in either study.[3]

The few data from these studies may not be indicative of the extent generally to which farm homes are planted or farm lawns are kept in shape. More information is needed on these and other aspects of farm home surroundings.

Notwithstanding the lack of data, however, there is a pretty general agreement among landscape architects and other authorities, and among farmers who are concerned with family living, that too few farm homes are properly or effectively landscaped.

This raises the question of what is implied in proper landscaping of the farm home. No attempt will be made to give a definite answer to this question—that is, to lay down principles of landscape architecture. These can be obtained freely from the different colleges of agriculture and the United States Department of Agriculture.

The point to be made here is that in the plan of arrangement—the layout of the farmstead—the location and the surroundings of the house be given first consideration. Are not the inhabitants of the house more important than the inhabitants of the barn, although neither can well get on in farming without the other? Does the home, the house and its immediate surroundings need to be subordinate to the barns and farm service yards, in either location, state of repair or general appearance?

Farm housing. There is an abundance of information on

[3] U. S. Dept. Agriculture, "Cost of Living in Farm Homes of Iowa," Preliminary Report, 1924.

certain aspects of farm housing, especially on the extent of modern improvements and conveniences and of labor-saving devices of various kinds and types. Sources of this information include surveys made by rural health specialists, rural sociologists, farm economists and others, the United States Census figures for 1920, and the building codes worked out by housing and zoning boards or commissions of different cities.

Little of the available information pertains to the adequacy of housing for the farm family, however. With few exceptions the data stop with size of the house, by number of rooms, the extent of modern improvements, and rental charge for use of the house (as yet somewhat arbitrarily determined for farm-houses). Type of construction, proportions between the different dimensions, cubic feet of air space, square feet of floor space, provisions for light and ventilation, convenience in arrangement and style of architecture have scarcely received serious consideration in connection with farm housing.

But there are many things of interest in the data which are available, such as the value or cost of housing, the number of rooms and the extent of modern equipment per house. Preceding the consideration of some of these points of interest mention may well be made of the principal uses of housing.

Housing (shelter) has always been one of man's needs. The house has a direct bearing on the physical life of man in that it shelters him from the exigencies of the weather, from dampness from the ground and from dangers and diseases incident to mankind. Also, it protects and safeguards personal property from damage by weather and against loss and theft. The house has a vital relation to the social and personal life of the different members of the family in that it provides separateness and privacy needed for individual development, makes possible the associations of home life and gives an opportunity for expression of the esthetic.

Throughout time the house, like land, has become pretty much established as immovable property. House ownership gives access to a certain amount of land usually, and both represent fairly stable economic values which, like investments, can be drawn upon to meet different emergencies or unexpected needs.

Generally, the house is thought of as consumption capital, since it contributes directly to the comfort, rest, recreation and social values of its occupants. From the standpoint of its use as a workshop for kitchen, laundry and similar purposes, it is sometimes looked upon as production capital. And from the standpoint of its use as a creamery, hatchery or store-room, the farm-house is often regarded as production capital, so much so that farm people and others overlook its use for living purposes.

Cost or value of farm housing. Recently a 4-H club leader remarked to an investigator in rural sociology, "That's a pretty complete study you have made and I put my stamp of approval on all the figures except your charge for house rent. You have reported an average of only $135 for rent during a year, and out where I live (in a suburb of Washington, D. C.) I pay $65 a month. And what do I get? Two rooms and a kitchenette and bath."

But in the matter of house rent, why should the farm family, 100 or 1000 miles from Washington, New York or Chicago, be charged with house rents prevailing in these urban centers? Is it fair to charge to the farmer's living, in the way of rent, exorbitant sums for police protection, fire protection, public utilities and social privileges to which he has no access in the open country? On the other hand, is it fair to base the rental value of the house for living purposes on what the house "adds to the value of the land" —that is, to the selling price of the farm? Would it be more satisfactory to base the rental charge on the original cost of building the house?

These are questions so perplexing that some investigators of farm family living have regarded the matter of house rent as too complex for inclusion in their analyses. Others, attempting to strike the best possible combination of these several aspects, have included housing as one of the important elements of family living, partially to stimulate further and more detailed study of farm-house evaluation and partially to remind farmers and others that use of the house constitutes an important part of the family living furnished by the farm.

Estimates of the values of farm-houses obtained in this way range from as low as $100 or less on the one hand to $8000 or more on the other hand. In several instances the estimates obtained in the field have been checked with the assessed valuation as recorded on county tax lists. Usually the two sets of figures are not widely different.

Having determined the valuation of the farm-house, what is a fair rate of charge for use of the house for family living annually? Some workers or authorities would make an annual rental charge amounting to the cash outlay needed for repairs, taxes and insurance. Other workers, however, would include some interest charge on the investment, usually 6 per cent. per annum. Most workers making studies of farm family living have arbitrarily taken 10 per cent. of the value of the house as the annual charge for rent. This percentage is intended to cover taxes, insurance, repairs and interest on the investment.

It will be recalled that average rental value for use of

the house, obtained as described above, amounted to $200 per year for 2886 farm families of selected localities in eleven States. This value constituted 12.5 per cent. of the value of all family living. By farming sections the value of rent was $204 for the New England States, $156 for the Southern States and $233 for the North Central States. These values were 12 per cent., 10.1 per cent. and 14.4 per cent. of the value of all family living. By States, the average value of rent varied from $125 for the Alabama families to $256 for the Iowa families. Rent was 7.8 per cent. of the value of all family living in the former case and 15.3 per cent. of this value in the latter case. For the 402 Livingston county, New York, families considered in previous chapters, the value of rent, amounting to $234, was 13.8 per cent. of the family living. Likewise, for the 798 families it amounted to $156 or 15.2 per cent. of the family living and for the 861 families of Kentucky, Tennessee and Texas it amounted to $140 or 9.7 per cent. For the 154 colored families, rent was $41 or 6.7 per cent. of the family living.

Other studies show the average of estimated values of about 1000 farm-houses in Nebraska to be $1800 (1923), of about 1000 Texas farm-houses to be $1060 (1924), and of nearly 8000 farm-houses throughout the United States to be about $1840 (1918-22).[4] On the basis of 10 per cent. of estimated values, annual rental charges are $180, $106 and $184 for each of the three studies.

Comparisons of the values of house rent for the several different tenure groups are possible from *Table 5*. Of more interest, however, are comparisons of size of house, extent of modern improvements, etc., which follow later.

[4] Nebraska Experiment Station Bul. 191, "Housing Conditions Among 947 White Farm Families of Texas," Preliminary Report, U. S. Dept. Agriculture, and Bul. 1338, U. S. Dept. Agriculture.

The average value of rent for over 5000 workingmen's families living in houses in ninety-two localities in the United States was $176 for the year 1918-19, when the cost of rent was about 110 per cent. above the 1913 average, in comparison with 75 per cent. above in 1922-24.[5] Also, for the same period and in the same localities the average value of rent for over 3000 workingmen's families living in flats or apartments was $178 per family.

Size of farm-houses. Size of the house, extent of modern equipment or modern improvements and condition or state of repair were given attention in arriving at the arbitrary values from which the rental figures for the farm-houses were taken. Size of the house by number of rooms is shown in *Table 17* for the several groups of families for which data are available.

For 2886 homes in eleven States an average of 6.8 rooms per family or household, excluding bath-room, pantry, halls and closets, was reported. This average divided by the average size of household gives approximately 1.4 rooms per person. By sections of the country, the New England houses were largest, 9.6 rooms each, in comparison with 5.9 rooms each for the Southern States and 6.9 rooms each for the North Central States. The average number of rooms per house divided by the average size of household gives 2.0 rooms, 1.2 rooms and 1.5 rooms per person for the three sections. Allowance should be made in this comparison for rooms reported as not furnished for living purposes by some of the families, probably about two rooms per household for the New England families and about .5 of a room per household for the southern and the north central families, on an average.

Houses occupied by the Schoharie county, New York, and

[5] U. S. Bureau of Labor Statistics, *op. cit.*, p. 333, 1924.

TABLE 17. The average number of rooms per household and per person. Farm homes of different localities in comparison with workingmen's homes in 92 localities of the United States.[1]

Tenure group and States	Homes studied	Size of household	Rooms per household		Rooms per person	
			All rooms	Bedrooms	All rooms	Bedrooms
	Number	Persons	Number	Number	Number	Number
11 States, all families—	2886	4.8	6.8	3.3	1.4	.7
New England States (4)	317	4.7	9.6	4.5	2.0	1.0
Southern States (3)	1130	5.1	5.9	3.0	1.2	.6
North Central States (4)	1439	4.6	6.9	3.3	1.5	.7
Owners	1950	4.8	7.1	3.4	1.5	.7
Tenants	867	4.9	6.3	3.0	1.3	.6
Hired men	69	4.7	6.1	2.9	1.3	.6
Schoharie County, New York and southeastern Ohio—						
All families	798	4.2	8.8	4.0	2.1	1.0
Kentucky, Tennessee and Texas, all families—	861	4.7	5.2	—	1.1	—
Owners	411	4.6	5.8	—	1.3	—
Tenants	321	4.9	4.9	—	1.0	—
Croppers	129	5.0	4.0	—	.8	—
Kentucky, Tennessee and Texas, all families—						
Colored	154	5.1	3.2	—	.6	—
Owners	35	5.2	3.3	—	.8	—
Tenants	47	5.2	3.4	—	.6	—
Croppers	72	4.9	2.9	—	.6	—
Texas, all families—	947	4.7	5.0	—	1.1	—
Owners	485	4.6	5.6	—	1.2	—
Tenants	462	4.9	4.4	—	.9	—
Industrial families—						
Living in houses	5190	5.0	5.0	—	1.0	—
Living in flats or apartments	3370	4.7	4.5	—	1.0	—

[1] Data adapted from Bul. 1466 and Preliminary Reports, U. S. Dept. Agriculture, and from Bul. 357, U. S. Bureau of Labor Statistics.

130

the southeastern Ohio families averaged 8.8 rooms each, or 2.1 rooms per person in size, with a probable average of at least one of the 8.8 rooms not used for living purposes. The houses for 861 families of Kentucky, Tennessee and Texas were smaller, 5.2 rooms each, or 1.1 rooms per person. The 947 Texas houses had 5.0 rooms each, or 1.1 rooms per person. The houses occupied by the 154 colored families were much smaller, 3.2 rooms each, or .6 of a room per person.

For over 5000 industrial families living in houses, 1918, size of the house was 5.0 rooms, one room per person, and for over 3000 industrial families living in flats or apartments the space available was 4.7 rooms per family, or 1.0 room per person. Thus, industrial families appear to live in smaller houses than do farm families, except colored farm families.

The average number of bedrooms reported furnished for use by the 2886 farm families amounted to 3.3 per household or .7 per person. There were 4.5 bedrooms per household for the New England States, 3.0 for the Southern States and 3.3 for the North Central States. There were 4.0 bedrooms per household for the 798 Schoharie county and southeastern Ohio families.

Apparently, farm owners live in larger houses than do tenants, croppers or hired men. For the 2886 families, the number of all rooms per household was 7.1 for owners, 6.3 for tenants and 6.1 for hired men. The average number of bedrooms furnished per household was 3.4 for owners, 3.0 for tenants and 2.9 for hired men. For the 841 farm families of Kentucky, Tennessee and Texas, houses occupied by owners, tenants and croppers were 5.8 rooms, 4.9 rooms and 4.0 rooms in size. For the 947 Texas families, houses of owners averaged 5.6 rooms each and houses of tenants (including a few croppers) averaged 4.4 rooms each in size. For colored families, houses occupied by owners and tenants, 3.3 rooms and 3.4 rooms each, were larger than those occupied by croppers, 2.9 rooms each.

These comparisons do not imply that owners always live in larger houses than do tenants, croppers or hired men. There are variations among different families, different localities and different gradations of tenure. In a study of about 1000 Nebraska farm homes, 1923, Rankin found that part owners (those farming some rented land in addition to that owned) were living in slightly larger houses than were owners.[6] Share-cash tenants were living in larger houses than either share tenants or cash tenants, according to the Nebraska study. In studies of 200 homes in Blackhawk county, Iowa, 1918, and 400 homes of Cedar county, Iowa, 1923, Von Tungeln found that the homes of all tenants in each locality were only 0.2 of a room smaller than the homes of all owners.[7] More data are needed to establish the assumption that farm tenants invariably occupy smaller houses than do farm owners.

Except for the colored families, there is little or no suggestion of overcrowding among the farm families, considered above, as the term overcrowded is used in housing legislation. Usually an average of one room per person, exclusive of bath, is regarded as the minimum requirement consistent with health and decency.[8] But, when the records are sorted according to the number of sons and daughters

[6] University of Nebraska Agricultural Experiment Station, "Nebraska Farm Homes," Bul. 191, 1923.

[7] Iowa State College of Agriculture and Mechanic Arts, "The Social Aspects of Rural Life and Farm Tenantry, Cedar County, Iowa," Bul. 217, 1923.

[8] Bureau of Applied Economics, "Minimum Quantity Budget Necessary to Maintain a Worker's Family of Five in Health and Decency," Bul. 7, 1920.

(at home) per family, there are suggestions of occasional overcrowding among farm families. Families with eight or more children at home appear to be living in houses averaging not more than three fourths of a room per person.

It is probable also that there are localities where farmhouses are, on the whole, less adequate in size than those represented in the figures available for comparisons. Such localities may doubtless be found in the coastal and the mountain regions of the Southeast and in the more recently settled regions of the West. Further study is needed to ascertain the adequacy of farm-houses in different regions and different types of farming. In this study adequacy needs to be reckoned in terms other than number of rooms.

Floor area, space and the ratio of window area to floor area were noted in the study of approximately 1000 farmhouses of selected localities of Texas.[9] The 948 dwellings, which housed 4.7 persons on an average, showed 5.6 rooms, 943 square feet of floor area, 8635 cubic feet of space and 113 square feet of window area each. When the 947 records were sorted according to the number of persons per household, there was little or no indication of overcrowding, in terms of floor area, cubic space or window area according to the standards of minimum comfort accepted by housing experts generally.

As with number of rooms per house, there appears to be little if any correlation between square feet of floor area or cubic feet of space and the number of persons per family or household, according to this study.

Prevalence of modern improvements and labor-saving devices in farm-houses. It is difficult to determine the degree of "modernness" in farm-houses owing to confusion

[9] U. S. Dept. Agriculture, "Housing Conditions Among 947 White Farmers of Texas," Preliminary Report, 1926.

as to the items of equipment which should be included in a so-called modern home. Some workers place the emphasis on the plumbing facilities, including running hot and cold water for laundry, kitchen, bath-room and toilet uses. Others are more concerned about the heating facilities. Still others are inclined to stress the lighting system. All of these non-portable facilities are important enough to be considered actual parts of the house and are here regarded as the final indexes of the degree of "modernness" of the home in question. Homes with central heating and central lighting systems and with running hot and cold water, including sewage disposal, for kitchen, bath and toilet uses, are regarded as completely modern. Homes with one or other of these three facilities are regarded as partly modern and those with none of them are regarded as not modern.

A glance at *Table 18* shows less than 6 per cent. of the 2886 farm-houses in eleven States modern, over 20 per cent. partially modern and almost 75 per cent. not modern. By sections, lower percentages of the houses are modern in the Southern States, due partially to the absence of central heating plants. There is of course less need for central heating plants in the Southern than in the North Central and New England States. The low percentages of modern houses in the South is not due to the absence of central heating plants alone, however, since the percentage of homes partly modern is lowest in this section also. Houses of the South appear to be about on a par with those of the Schoharie county and the southeastern Ohio regions in degree of "modernness."

The numbers and percentages of farm-houses fitted with only one or other of the three types of modern improvements were not ascertained in *Table 18*. Data gathered and tabulated under the direction of Florence E. Ward show 32 per cent. of 10,000 farm homes of eastern, central and western United States as having running water for household uses.[10] Over half, 65 per cent., of the 10,000 homes had water in the kitchen, in many instances well or cistern

TABLE 18. Numbers and percentages of modern, partially modern and not modern houses. Farm homes of selected localities of the United States, 1922–27.[1]

| Tenure groups and States | Homes studied | EXTENT OF MODERN EQUIPMENT | | | | | |
| | | Completely modern | | Partially modern | | Not modern | |
	Number	Number	Per cent.	Number	Per cent.	Number	Per cent.
11 States, all families—	2886	164	5.7	597	20.8	2104	73.5
New England States (4)	317	28	8.8	160	50.5	129	40.7
Southern (3)	1130	19	1.7	166	14.7	945	83.6
North Central States (4)........	1439	117	8.3	271	19.1	1030	72.6
Owners.............	1950	141	7.2	481	24.7	1328	68.1
Tenants............	867	21	2.4	111	12.8	735	84.8
Hired men.........	69	2	4.2	5	10.4	41	85.4
Schoharie county, New York, and southeastern Ohio— All families.....	798	8	1.0	147	18.4	643	80.6

[1] Adapted from Bul. 1466 and from Preliminary Reports, U. S. Dept. Agriculture.

water pumped in by hand for kitchen uses. Twenty per cent. of the 10,000 homes were fitted with bath-tubs and 60 per cent. of the homes had kitchen sinks with drains. The United States Census Report, Vol. 5, 1923, specifies 10 per cent. of farm homes in the United States as having

[10] U. S. Dept. Agriculture, *op. cit.,* 1920.

water piped in the house. According to the census figures, 7 per cent. of all farm homes had gas or electric lights.

A more recent study made by the General Federation of Women's Clubs in approximately 40,000 farm homes of twenty-eight States, 1926, shows 47 per cent. of these homes having "water at the house." [11] In 7.5 per cent. of the homes the water was provided by stationary engine, in 6.9 per cent. by electric motor, in 10.5 per cent. by windmill, in 11.6 per cent. by gravity or siphon, in 10.0 per cent. by hand pump and in 0.7 per cent. by public water system. Also, results of this study show 21 per cent. of the homes with bath-tubs, 17 per cent. with flush toilets and 33.3 per cent. with stationary kitchen sinks. In addition, the results show 30 per cent. of the homes as having electric or piped gas lighting systems and 17 per cent. as having acetylene, or gasoline or kerosene mantle lights. Finally, the data show 13 per cent. of the houses fitted with central heating plants and 23 per cent. with fireplaces.

Another recent study by the questionnaire method among 6000 farm homes gives 32 per cent. with water piped in the house.[12] Of over 1000 village homes included in this study, 60 per cent. had running water in the house.

"Home conveniences" of another type have been assumed to be present in connection with houses regarded as modern; the matter of screens for doors and windows. The use of screens to keep out flies, mosquitos and the like is unquestionably one of the housing needs of farm families. Screens appear to be used quite universally on the doors and windows of farm-houses of most farming localities. The study made by the General Federation of Women's

[11] General Federation of Women's Clubs, Results of Survey, Preliminary Tables, 1926.
[12] U. S. Dept. Agriculture, "Attitudes and Problems of Farm Youth," Extension Service Circular 46, 1927.

Clubs, 1926, shows 86.5 per cent. of almost 40,000 homes screened. Of the 1000 Nebraska farm homes studied by Rankin, 1923, 95 per cent. reported screens on windows and doors. Also, one half of the back porches and one sixth of the front porches were reported screened. Von Tungeln reports 80 per cent. of 400 farm-houses studied in Cedar county, Iowa, 1923, fitted with screens. The results of a recent study of 1000 North Carolina farm homes by Taylor and Zimmerman show a different picture with regard to screening. Almost 65 per cent. of all the homes of white families and 91 per cent. of all the homes of colored families were without screens on doors and windows. It is worthy of note, however, that less than 2 per cent. of these 1000 homes had each a central heating system, a central lighting system and running hot or cold water, and none of them were completely modern.[13]

The prevalence of labor-saving devices is usually considered a gage of the standard of living because it is believed to represent the importance placed on keeping the physical labor of the home-maker at a minimum. Power washing machines, power vacuum cleaners and power sewing-machines are chief among these labor-saving devices.

Of the 10,000 families studied by Miss Ward, 1920, 22 per cent. had the use of power machinery presumably for operating the washer. Of the 40,000 families studied by the General Federation of Women's Clubs, 13 per cent. had electric-power washers, 12 per cent. had other power washers and 17.5 per cent. had hand-power washing-machines. Also, 20 per cent. had electric irons and 7 per cent. had gas irons. For cleaning, 9.0 per cent. had electric-power vacuum cleaners and 8.4 per cent. had hand-power

[13] North Carolina Tenancy Commission, "Economic and Social Conditions of North Carolina Farmers."

vacuum outfits. For sewing, only 2 per cent. had electric-power machines, but 72 per cent. had foot-power machines.

The data on modern improvements and labor-saving devices are not all-inclusive and they may not be typical of all farm homes. Further study is needed here as well in the size, type of construction and arrangement of the house before the adequacy of farm housing can be definitely determined.

Furnishings and equipment. The four walls, without or with modern improvements, do not make a home. One must go beyond the four walls, at least, to the furnishings and equipment so essential for the provision of what have been designated as the "four C's" of living quarters—"convenience, comfort, coziness and cheer." " 'I can scarcely bear to leave this room, it is so beautiful,' came from the daughter in the home as she turned, on starting up to bed, and looked back at the living-room table with its softly shaded light, its alluring piles of magazines and recent books, and the bowl of orange-red blossoms whose brilliant color was echoed by the candles on a near-by piano and in the decorative pictures above the well-filled open book shelves which formed a background for the whole. Easy chairs were placed near the table, inviting one to make himself comfortable and to select the reading material which interested him. From a large fireplace, above which was a decorative panel designed for the space, a bright fire cast its warm glow over the room. It was not a palatial home nor elegantly furnished, but looked as though each piece of furniture had been selected and placed with the idea of comfort, convenience, coziness and cheer in mind." [14]

Life on the farm might be vastly fuller, richer and more enjoyable than it is to-day if more farm-houses were fitted

[14] Adapted from "National Education Journal," January, 1927.

with furnishings that would produce the effect described above. Many farm-houses are "overstocked" with an assortment of furniture which means little in the way of comfort and convenience and nothing in the way of coziness and cheer. The sentiment attached to some articles of furnishings often tends to drive cheer out. A state home management extension worker tells of the difficulty she encounters among farm women who for some reason or other cannot be led to refinish, set aside or discard certain "out-of-harmony" pieces of furniture or equipment. In a number of homes she has solved this problem through having the family set aside one room for a sort of "sentimental" store-room, usually in the attic. Thus, the way has been cleared for a new living-room or dining-room suite, a new separate article of furniture or a more convenient and cozy arrangement of those pieces which are at hand.

There are very few figures available on the value of furnishings and equipment found within the farm home. Attempts to get inventory values of these goods in connection with family living studies have not proved very successful. The farm woman, as well as the farmer, usually "sticks" on the question of what the furnishings and equipment are worth. For 451 Iowa farm homes studied in 1923 the average value of furniture and equipment reported in the home was $704. House values reported at the same time averaged about $2600. For 861 homes of Kentucky, Tennessee and Texas, 1920, the reported values of furnishings amounted to $456 per family in houses valued at $1379 each.[15]

The purchase of furnishings and equipment annually by farm families represents a relatively small part of the value

[15] U. S. Dept. Agriculture, Preliminary Reports, 1924.

of all family living. For 2886 families considered previously, the expenditure for this purpose amounted to $40 per family and constituted 2.5 per cent. of the value of all goods provided for use during the year. For the 861 families $28.50 worth of furnishings and equipment was purchased during one year and for 798 families of Schoharie county, New York, and southeastern Ohio $34 worth was purchased.

Owners appear to have the larger expenditures for furnishings and equipment, ordinarily. Owners spent $43 per year for this purpose in comparison with $32 spent by tenants, for the 2886 families. Owners spent $33 for furnishings and equipment in comparison with $27 spent by tenants and $18 spent by croppers, for the 861 families of Kentucky, Tennessee and Texas.

Workingmen's families, 12,096 studied by the United States Bureau of Labor Statistics, 1918-19, reported an average expenditure of $73 for furniture and house-furnishings per family, when furniture prices were about the same as in 1922-24, in thirty-two cities of the United States, computed on a 1913 base.[16]

In most of the studies of farm family living the percentage that the average expenditure for furnishings and equipment is of the value of all goods used remains practically the same or varies without regard to the value of goods used. This appears to be true also with regard to the percentage that the expenditure for furnishings and equipment is of family living goods purchased. In other words, as more "dollars' worth" of goods are provided for use during the year, about the same percentage of the value of these goods is devoted to furnishings and equipment,

[16] U. S. Bureau of Labor Statistics, *op. cit.*, 1924.

on an average. This would not hold true for separate families, however, since not all families in a particular group purchase furnishing and equipment during a given year and since the different articles purchased by families purchasing vary widely in cost or value.

The average expenditure per family per year for the different articles of furnishing and equipment is probably more indicative of the prevailing standard of living than is the expenditure for all articles or items taken collectively. Expenditures for most of the items, including canning and cleaning equipment, bedding, floor coverings, musical instruments, pictures, table-ware, etc., with the number of farm families purchasing each were summarized for 1299 of the families included in the study of selected localities in eleven States. The figures appear in *Table 19*, as tabulated by the Webb Publishing Company, St. Paul, Minnesota, under the direction of the writer. The 1299 families of Kansas, Kentucky, Missouri and Ohio localities had an average expenditure of $44 for all furnishings and equipment purchased. There were 4.2 persons per family and 4.5 persons per household in these families. About one third of the families were tenants, but the average expenditure for all furniture and furnishings by the two groups was about equal.

Over 85 per cent. of the families reported the purchase of brooms during the year. Next in order are household linens purchased by about 39 per cent., canning equipment purchased by 37.5 per cent., kitchen utensils purchased by 37 per cent., bedding purchased by 35 per cent., curtains including portières purchased by 32 per cent. and table-ware purchased by 27 per cent. of the families. For the items purchased less frequently only 195 of the families

TABLE 19. Average expenditure per family, and per family purchasing, for the various articles of household furnishings and equipment purchased during one year by 1299 farm families of selected localities of Kansas, Kentucky, Missouri and Ohio, 1922–23.[1]

Kind of furnishings or equipment	Families purchasing		AVERAGE EXPENDITURE	
			Per family purchasing	Per family
	Number	Per cent.	Dollars	Dollars
Canning equipment.............	487	37.5	3.80	1.40
Cleaning equipment—				
Brooms...................	1111	85.5	2.70	2.30
Brushes..................	216	16.6	2.20	.40
Vacuum cleaners............	34	2.6	15.70	.40
Furnishings—				
Bedding..................	456	35.1	10.70	3.80
Curtains and portières.......	410	31.6	6.40	2.00
Furniture.................	195	15.0	39.90	6.00
Floor covering—				
Carpets..................	29	2.2	13.80	.30
Linoleum.................	124	9.5	16.60	1.60
Rugs.....................	199	15.3	30.90	4.70
Not specified..............	25	1.9	17.60	.30
Household linens...............	503	38.7	5.40	2.10
Lamps.......................	146	11.2	9.40	1.00
Musical instruments.............	63	4.8	65.50	3.20
Pictures and ornaments..........	53	4.1	10.10	.40
Table-ware....................	345	26.6	5.60	1.50
Window shades.................	229	17.6	4.30	.80
Kitchen utensils...............	481	37.0	4.70	1.80
Laundry equipment—				
Ironing boards..............	16	1.2	3.30	.04
Irons.....................	25	1.9	4.30	.10
Tubs.....................	16	1.2	1.30	.02
Washing-machines...........	73	5.6	36.30	2.00
Wringers..................	26	2.0	4.40	.10
Not specified..............	18	1.4	4.10	.10
Sewing equipment—				
Cutting-table...............	3	.2	17.70	.04
Dress form................	22	1.7	1.20	.02
Sewing-machine............	33	2.5	31.50	.80
Miscellaneous—				
Electric appliances...........	44	3.4	24.20	.80
Gas engines (portable).......	13	1.0	40.30	.40
Stoves....................	167	12.9	42.30	5.40
Trunks and suit-cases........	60	4.6	8.60	.40
Other (inc. refrigerator)......	45	3.5	5.80	.20

Sum of average expenditure per family 44.42

[1]From "Average Expenditures for Household Furnishings and Equipment," Preliminary Report, U. S. Dept. Agriculture.

bought articles of furniture of any sort, 63 bought musical instruments, 53 pictures and ornaments, 73 washing-machines, 34 vacuum cleaners, 44 other electrical appliances and 33 sewing-machines.

The summary and analysis of inventory lists of the different items of furniture, bedding, draperies, ornaments, cleaning and cooking equipment, and table-ware owned would be more indicative than the items purchased during a given year of the comfort and satisfaction the farm family gets from its home. Unfortunately, such lists have never been obtained in full. A few of the items sometimes regarded as falling in the "realm of luxuries" have been noted and counted by some of the rural research workers. Included among these items are pianos, phonographs and radios.

Results of the study made by the General Federation of Women's Clubs, 1926, show 37 per cent. of these homes having pianos, 35 per cent. having phonographs and 22 per cent. having radios. The percentages vary for the different regions and the different States. Results of the study by the questionnaire method among almost 6000 farm homes, 1926, shows phonographs in 44 per cent. and radios in about 23 per cent. of these homes. Other figures pertaining to the prevalence of these items of "luxury" might be presented if space were available. But after all, it is questionable whether the presence of a piano, a phono-graph or a radio in the home is any more indicative of a high standard of living than are appropriate pictures or choice books or comfortable pieces of furniture. Much depends on the uses made of the various musical instru-ments or contrivances, the different pieces of furniture and the different items of equipment.

For a maximum of satisfaction or values from furnishings and equipment in the home, the proper balance must be struck between furniture, draperies, musical instruments, pictures, books and other things of interest to the different members of the family. And this balance is usually not exactly the same for any two given families.

In summary on the housing situation, it appears that from the standpoint of open space in the out of doors— with sunlight, fresh air and quiet—and of space within the dwelling, there is little evidence of a farm housing problem. Generally, we do not have in the open country the crowding in of dwellings and business establishments until the human family is "pressed out of semblance to a human home." On the farm, people are not "squeezed between buildings, squeezed below ground, squeezed skyward, squeezed to the alley, squeezed against streets—and with every squeeze a suffocation of the home." [17]

On the basis of studies made thus far, there appears to be little need for additional space and better shelter in most of the farm homes of the country. Generally, farmhouses were built some years ago when families were larger and when the costs of building and operating houses were lower; and in many farm-houses not all the rooms available are in use. There are notable exceptions to this, however, and localities can be found where the needs for additional space and better shelter are urgent. There are localities where screens, now regarded as indispensable for comfort, cleanliness and health, are little used and where modern improvements or conveniences are scarcely known. Many farm homes are still heated by means of grates, with pine as the common fuel and with walls and ceilings often smoke laden.

In the majority of farm homes old-fashioned kerosene

[17] C. J. Galpin, "Red Cross Courier," November 15, 1927.

lamps are the only source of artificial light, and for some farm families the farm women are drawing water from open wells or dipping it from springs or creeks and carrying it up long weary steps for kitchen, laundry and other uses.

There is need of further study on the adequacy of the farm-house with respect to the purely physical needs of the family. Also, there is need for ascertainment of the extent to which the kitchen and other rooms of the house are used at times for farm business purposes, as well as need for the development of a satisfactory basis for determining the rental value of the house for family living purposes.

The universal needs in connection with farm housing generally, however, pertain to the setting, including the surroundings; the style of architecture; the arrangement; the interior finish; the facilities for conveniences and labor-saving devices; and the furnishings and equipment.

The setting and the surroundings call for the demonstration by landscape architects of the beauty and harmony that may be had through the proper use of planting materials often growing like weeds on the home farm. Style of architecture merits a coördinated effort of architects and builders to plan and construct farm-houses that fit the conditions of life on the farm. Arrangement of the farm-house deserves the serious consideration of the home management experts and others in the preparation of farm-house plans that will be most economical of the home-maker's time and energy. The facilities for conveniences and labor-saving devices demand the attention of the makers of apparatus and appliances and the developers of public utilities in the manufacture and development of goods and power which will enable the farmer to overcome certain of the handicaps inherent to farm life. Interior finish and furnishings and equipment are worthy of the coördinated efforts of interior decorators, furniture manufacturers and home-designing specialists to picture and make possible for farmers the type of home which will yield a maximum of satisfaction and values to all members of the farm family.

CHAPTER VIII

HOUSEHOLD OPERATION GOODS AND SERVICES

TWENTY years ago in a certain farming locality in one of the North Central States a casual visitor at any of the farm homes during early summer would have been favorably impressed with the large pile of clean-cut and neatly corded wood, enough to supply household needs for at least a year ahead. Ordinarily there was an additional supply of wood under cover, a part of it with a year's seasoning, for use during inclement weather. There was kindling as needed and often plenty of cobs to supplement the wood in getting a fire quickly at meal-time.

On some of these farms a supply of wood is no longer available. But equal attention is given to the purchase and storing of coal, early in the season, for winter use. Likewise, attention is given to fuel for lighting purposes and to other supplies so necessary for efficient operation of the household.

The comment of a threshing crew leader in regard to household operation in this particular locality is pertinent. "I never threshed in a neighborhood where women get meals for the crew so easily and so quickly. And such meals as they are, too! No one ever leaves the table hungry. But one thing I've noticed, the women always have everything handy; wood, cobs, kerosene for the oil stove, ice, help when they need it—they have all of them."

Operation of the household involves the use of supplies,

147

facilities and services needed in connection with the preparation of food, for heating and lighting the different rooms of the house, for the cleaning of clothing, equipment and living quarters, for communication, and for various other sundry purposes. Thus, operation goods include fuel and other supplies, transportation, power, and household labor in addition to many sundry items. As here used, they do not include unpaid labor of the home-maker or other members of the family, except as noted.

Information on the quantities, the values and the adequacy of uses of the different kinds of operation goods by farm families is exceedingly meager. The most complete set of data available pertains to the goods of this type used by the 2886 farm families of selected localities in eleven States.

It will be recalled that the average value of operation goods amounted to $213 per year for these families and that this value constituted 13.3 per cent. of the value of all goods used. By sections the value of operation goods was highest with the New England families, the averages being $255 for the New England States, $194 for the Southern States and $219 for the North Central States. Also, the proportion that the value of operation goods is of the value of all goods is highest with the New England families, the percentages being 15.1, 12.5 and 13.6 for the three sections in the order named.

The average values of operation goods were $154 or 15.1 per cent. of all family living for the 798 Schoharie county, New York, and southeastern Ohio families, $173 or 12 per cent. of all family living for the 861 Kentucky, Tennessee and Texas white families and $56 or 9.1 per cent. of all family living for the 154 colored families.

Owners, tenants and hired men of the 2886 families used

operation goods amounting to $231 per family, $177 per family and $153 per family. These amounts comprised 13.5 per cent., 13.1 per cent. and 12.4 per cent. of all family living in each instance. Owners, tenants and hired men of the 861 families used $211 worth, $159 worth and $86 worth of operation goods per family, and the values of operation goods were 12.9 per cent., 11.6 per cent. and 9.1 per cent. of the value of all family living. Owners, tenants and croppers of the 154 colored families used $61 worth, $58 worth and $52 worth of operation goods, and the values of these goods were 8.9 per cent., 8.7 per cent. and 9.6 per cent. of the values of all goods used.

Fuel. It is apparent from *Table 20,* showing the average values of the different kinds of operation goods, that the higher value of all operation goods in New England homes is due to the higher value of fuel furnished by the farm, which in turn may be due to larger amounts of fuel consumed and to higher prices per unit reported for fuel. Percentage that the value of fuel furnished by the farm is of the value of all fuel used varies from 72.3 per cent. for the New England States to 54.4 per cent. for the Southern States and to 41.1 per cent. for the North Central States.

A considerable part of the value of operation goods, averaging $154 per family for the 798 families referred to previously, is absorbed by fuel amounting to $90 per family. More than four fifths, 80.8 per cent. of the $90 value, represents fuel furnished by the farm.

Just what can be said of the kinds and amounts of fuel used by farm families? The most complete set of figures available pertain to the 1337 families of Kansas, Kentucky, Missouri and Ohio, who gave estimates of the amount of wood furnished by the farm and the amounts of wood, coal, kerosene and gasoline purchased. The average value of all fuel used by these families amounted to about $86, $31 worth of which was furnished by the farm and $55 worth of which was purchased. There was 4.2 persons per

TABLE 20.   Average value per family of the different kinds of operation goods used during one year.[1]

Operation Goods	2886 FAMILIES OF SELECTED LOCALITIES IN 11 STATES				798 families of Schoharie county, New York, and southeastern Ohio
	All families all States	317 families New England States	1130 families Southern States	1439 families North Central States	
Total................	$213.10	$255.30	$193.80	$219.00	$154.00
a. Fuel—					
Furnished by farm	43.20	100.60	36.10	36.10	72.80
Purchased.......	42.00	38.50	30.30	51.90	17.20
b. Hired help........	12.40	10.70	16.80	9.30	3.20
c. Household supplies.	8.30	11.90	7.50	8.30	10.60
d. Laundry outside...	6.50	8.80	9.50	3.70	2.00
e. Automobile........	79.70	56.90	68.70	93.30	39.00
f. Horse and buggy...	8.70	5.60	15.70	4.00	.50
g. Carfare..........	1.20	1.70	.50	1.70	1.00
h. Telephone........	4.40	9.50	2.10	5.00	5.70
i. Postage, express, freight.........	3.00	4.10	3.10	2.60	1.30
j. Insurance on furniture and equipment..........	1.20	3.60	1.10	.80	.40
k. Ice and charge for city water	2.50	3.40	2.40	2.30	.30

[1] Adapted from Bul. 1466 and from Preliminary Reports, U. S. Dept. Agriculture.

family and 4.5 persons per household in the 1337 families. There were eight cords of wood and 4.3 tons of coal reported used per family. Most of the wood, 7.3 cords, was furnished by the farm. The remainder of the wood and coal were purchased. Also, about 91 gallons of kerosene, 8.9 gallons of gasoline and 26.3 boxes of matches were purchased for household uses. Unit values or costs of the different articles used were: wood furnished $4.20 per cord, wood purchased $4.40 per cord, coal $7.70 per ton, kerosene fifteen cents per gallon, gasoline twenty cents per gallon and matches seven cents per box.

All but eighteen of the families reported the purchase of matches, almost 1300 reported the use of kerosene, 1148 the use of wood (176 purchased wood), 929 the use of coal, 315 the use of gasoline, fifty-five the use of electricity and fifty-nine the use of other fuels.

For the 176 families using furnished wood the amount furnished for use averaged 5.7 cords per family. For almost 8000 families included in farm management studies summarized by H. W. Hawthorn, 1918-22, wood furnished by the farm amounted to four cords per family, charged at $3.50 per cord. The amount furnished ranged as high as sixteen cords for families in Sumter county, Georgia, fourteen cords in Niagara county, New York, and twelve cords each in Washington county, Ohio, Hillsboro county, New Hampshire, and Orange and Windsor counties, Vermont.[1]

It would be of interest to know the percentages of the farm families using wood in the different localities which have been studied. More than half, 56 per cent. of the 40,000 farm women in homes studied by the General Federation of Women's Clubs, 1926, reported the use of wood for cooking purposes. A third of the women, 33.5 per cent., reported the use of coal, 34.5 per cent. the use of kerosene or gasoline, 3.5 per cent. the use of "piped" gas

[1] U. S. Dept. Agriculture, "The Family Living from the Farm," Bul. 1338, 1925.

and 3.6 per cent. the use of electricity in the kitchen. It is evident of course that more than one kind of fuel was used in some of the homes for cooking.

It would be of further interest if some of the data could be made to show the numbers or percentages of farm women who must be responsible for having the supply of wood available for household uses when it is needed. A farm-reared city home-maker stated to the writer some time ago that her leaving the farm was due chiefly to her having to cut the wood to "feed the kitchen stove." "And," she added, "I know other girls who left the farm for the same reason." Although no figures are available as to the number or percentage of farm women who help prepare the wood for use, those obtained by Miss Ward for 10,000 homes, 1919, show that 54 per cent. of the women in these homes carry the fuel into the house and "keep the home fires burning." These 10,000 women reported the care of 1.3 stoves per family, on an average. In addition, 79 per cent. of them were caring for kerosene lamps.

The limited data which are available show rather insignificant differences in regard to fuels used by different tenure groups, as indicated by the total cost or value of these fuels. For the 1337 families, owners, 898 in number, used $100 worth of fuel per family in comparison with $85 worth used by tenants, 439 in number including 39 hired men. The higher total value for owner families appeared to be made up of proportionately balanced higher values due to slightly larger quantities of the principal kinds of fuel used.

By way of comparison of fuel used by farm families and urban families, 8000 workingmen's families living in houses in ninety-two industrial centers of the United States spent

$78 per family per year for fuel, 1918-19.[2] At that time fuel prices were about 50 per cent. above 1913 fuel prices, whereas fuel prices in 1922-24 were around 80 per cent. higher than in 1913. The $78 figure represented 1.3 tons of anthracite coal costing about $12, 3.2 tons of bituminous coal costing $22.50, 1.1 cords of wood costing $8, 29,000 cubic feet of gas costing nearly $18, 101 kilowatt-hours of electricity costing about $8, and other fuel items costing almost $10. Quantities of the different kinds of fuel used are worthy of further comment. The industrial families reported the use of 4.5 tons of coal and 1.1 cords of wood, in comparison with 4.3 tons of coal and eight cords of wood used by the 1337 farm families. The industrial families reported the use of large amounts of gas and electricity, however, in comparison with almost none of these fuels used by the farm families. Satisfactory or complete comparisons of fuels used cannot be made unless families using similar kinds of fuel are selected or unless the adequacy of different kinds of fuels be taken into account.

The figures on fuel are not conclusive or final in any respect. They are suggestive of the need of further study in regard to the adequacy, the evaluation and the availability of the different kinds of fuel used in the farm household. To what extent is wood, formerly so plentiful on many farms, becoming exhausted? Is the production of wood for home uses a practical or an economic procedure for the typical farmer? Is coal, of the better kinds or quality especially, available to the farm family at reasonable costs? If so, is the heating equipment at the farmer's disposal adapted to its uses? What about the availability to the farmer of gas, electricity and other types of heat, now

[2] U. S. Bureau of Labor Statistics, *op. cit.*, p. 391.

regarded as indispensable by the urban dweller of America? These are questions awaiting answers which can be obtained only by means of thoroughgoing study.

Household supplies. Household supplies comprised a little more than $8 worth of the $213 worth of operation goods used by the 2886 families. Among these supplies were soaps, cleaning powders, lye, etc. Figures for the 1337 families of Kansas, Kentucky, Missouri and Ohio show fifty-three bars of laundry soap, forty-two bars of toilet soap, ten boxes of cleaning powders, five boxes of lye, 6.5 boxes of laundry starch and eight packages of bluing purchased per family. Average costs per unit of these items were six cents for laundry soap, nine cents for toilet soap, ten cents for cleaning powders, twelve cents for lye, ten cents for laundry starch and eight cents for bluing. The average expenditure for all household supplies amounted to $10 for the 1337 families. The average for owner families, $9.70 per family, was forty cents lower than the average for tenant families. Similar figures for the 12,096 workingmen's families in ninety-two industrial centers, 1919, show an expenditure of approximately $12 per family for household supplies when prices for these goods were about ten points lower than in 1922-24, with prices for 1913 as a base. Quantities of the separate kinds of goods used by the workingmen's families are not available.

Ice for conserving food. The value of ice used by 2886 farm families, primarily for conserving food during the summer, amounted to only $2.50 per family. A small portion of this, twenty cents' worth, represents ice furnished by the farm in a few of the households of the New England and North Central States.

For the 2886 families no count was made of the numbers reporting the use of ice or other means of conserving food.

The prevalence of an ice refrigerator was reported in more than 24 per cent. of the 40,000 farm homes studied by the General Federation of Women's Clubs. Iceless refrigerators were reported in 6.5 per cent., electric refrigerators in .5 per cent. and cellars or caves in 26.5 per cent. of these homes.

Hired help in the household. The study of 10,000 farm families by Miss Ward, 1919, is held to show "the passing of the 'hired girl,' once so important a factor in the economic and social life of the farm home." In this study the number of homes in which help was employed the year round was almost negligible. About 14 per cent. of the families reported the employment of hired women for short periods, probably "during the peak of heavy summer work." Figures on the cost of this employed labor are not available.

The 2886 families reported an average expenditure of $12.40 for paid household labor employed during the year. By sections the expenditure for this purpose amounted to almost $17 in the Southern States, less than $11 in the New England States and about $9 in the North Central States. The expenditure for paid labor employed amounted to only $3 per family for the 798 Schoharie county, New York, and southeastern Ohio families.

The expenditure of $4 per family by the 12,096 workingmen's families in ninety-two industrial centers, 1919, for household labor is of interest. This must be noted in connection with an additional expenditure of about $12.50 for laundry sent out, however; a much higher expenditure for this than among farm families, as will be shown later.

Paid labor represents only a part of the help which the farm home-maker has in operating the farm home, on an average. Many farm women are assisted with the housework by other women or adult girls and some are aided in the heavier tasks by the men or adult boys residing in the farm household.

The value of unpaid household labor amounted to $33 per family for 402 farm families in Livingston county, New York, 1921.[3] This unpaid labor consisted of help from men or boys on the farm at washing, churning and cleaning, and from women or girls other than the home-maker, less the time spent by the home-maker and other women or girls of the household at actual farm work, such as plowing, haying or milking. Help from women or girls at household tasks was charged at $3 a week, this being considered a fair wage in addition to board, clothing and other comforts provided for in the household budget. An average value of 25 cents an hour for time from the men was used. Labor from women and adult girls at actual farm work was valued at twenty cents an hour.

There is need of more detailed and more intensive study of the different kinds, amounts and costs of labor necessary for the efficient operation of the farm household. Questions of the economy of using labor-saving devices and of having certain kinds of work done outside the farm home will be answered most effectively by information obtained from these studies.

Laundry sent out. "I just love the odor of freshly washed clothes," remarked a visitor at a farm home as the home-maker sprinkled the crisp white garments for ironing. "And I just hate the smell of washing them," replied the home-maker as she continued with the sprinkling.

Probably not a few farm women hate the smell and the labor of washing. This may account in part for the almost universal observance of Monday forenoon as farm wash-

[3] Cornell University Agricultural Experiment Station, *op. cit.*, p. 36.

day; to get it out of the way early in the week. A rural life worker tells of keeping count of the farm homes with clothes out to dry on a Monday's drive through a Central Western State. "From 8:15 A.M. to about 2 P.M., three out of every four of more than 120 homes which I passed had the family wash out to dry."

This seems to be pretty much in keeping with the results of the study of 10,000 homes by Miss Ward, 1919, which shows that 96 per cent. of the farm women do the family washing at home. Almost as high a proportion, 94.5 per cent., of the 402 Livingston county, New York, farm women, 1921, were doing the family washing at home.

The 2886 farm families referred to above reported an average expenditure of $6.50 per year for laundry sent out. This average varied from $9.50 in the Southern States to $8.80 in the New England States and $3.70 in the North Central States. The 798 families of Schoharie county, New York, and southeastern Ohio had an average expenditure of $2 for laundry sent out.

No implication is here intended as to the numbers or percentages of farm homes in which washing should be sent out. Even if suitable service were available for sending laundry out, the question of sending it out versus doing it at home would involve the consideration of a number of factors. As with sewing, there may be farm women who get certain satisfactions from washing, especially if power equipment and modern facilities are available. Quality of the work, wear and tear on the garments and comparative costs in money, time and energy are factors to be taken into account in deciding the question.

Transportation and other communication; use of automobile. "We haven't any idea what it costs to run it," and "We keep an exact account of all the costs," are the two extremes among the first responses obtained by field workers in farm family living studies to the query on the cost of operating the automobile. One of these replies is obtained about as frequently as the other. Also, the claim that the automobile is never used for family living purposes is made about as often as is the claim that it is never used for farm business purposes. Most farm families regard the automobile as filling both family living and farm business uses, however; and, while the proportion of the total for family or household use varies from nothing to 100 per cent., the average of the precentages for this purpose usually falls between 40 per cent. and 60 per cent.

Cost of operation of the automobile for household uses amounted to almost $80 per family for the 2886 farm families in selected localities of eleven States. The average varied from about $57 in the New England States to $69 in the Southern States and to $93 in the North Central States. These costs are averages for all families in each section and therefore do not represent the actual cost of use of the car (for household purposes), since not all the families reported the use of cars. For the New England States 167 or 53 per cent. of the families reported the ownership and use of an automobile. For these 167 families the expenditures amounted to $108 per family. For the Southern States, 611 or 54 per cent. of the families reported the use of automobiles, for which families the expenditures for the car amounted to $127. For the North Central States 1126 or 78 per cent. of the families were using automobiles for household purposes. For these 1126 families the costs of the car attributable to household use averaged $119.

For the 402 families of Livingston county, New York, 1921, the cost of operating the car for household uses averaged $65 per family. Cars were owned by about 76 per cent. of the 402 families and the annual expense per car was $86. The cost of operating the car for household uses amounted to $39 per family for the 798 Schoharie county, New York, and southeastern Ohio families. Cars were used by 72 per cent. of these families and the cost per car was $54.

The average cost of operating the automobile for both family living and farm business uses amounted to $212 per family for 357 farm families of Minnesota, 1925.[4] In this study farm and family uses of the car are regarded as "inextricably combined." Cars or trucks were reported on 93 per cent. of the 357 farms. "About 75 per cent. of the machines were of the types known as economical, costing less than $800: and 25 per cent. cost $1000 or more."

Other comparisons of the numbers or percentages of farmers owning cars are possible. Sixty-two per cent. of the 10,000 families studied by Miss Ward, 1919, reported household use of the automobile. Eighty-three per cent. of 1000 farm families of Steele county, Minnesota, 1922, owned cars, and about 25 per cent. of the farm women and girls reported driving the family owned cars.[5] Almost 80 per cent. of the 40,000 families studied by the General Federation of Women's Clubs, 1926, had automobiles for family uses. Eighty-six per cent. of 6000 farm families studied by the questionnaire method, 1926, reported the ownership of cars. About 76 per cent. of more than 1000 village families, studied by the same method at the same time, owned cars.

Itemized costs of operating the automobile are available for 300 farm families of southeastern Ohio, a part of the

[4] University of Minnesota Agricultural Experiment Station, *op. cit.*
[5] "The Farmer's Wife," St. Paul, Minnesota, "The Story of 1,000 Calls on Farmers' Wives," 1922.

798 families referred to previously. The 211 cars owned were operated at an average cost of $110 per car. Almost a third of this cost, $36, was spent for gasoline and oil, $32 represented depreciation, $30 went for tires, accessories and repairs, $7 was allowed for interest on money invested in the car, $4 went for license fees and $1 covered insurance on the car. Estimates obtained attributed $58 of the $110 to household use, $47 to farm use and $5 to other use. On the per family basis these estimates attribute $41 of the $77 per family cost to household use, $33 to farm use and $3 to other use.

Expenditures on cars used by the 357 Minnesota farm families referred to above, $212 per family, were classified in four groups: the purchase of cars absorbed 4.9 per cent. of the total, repairs including tires 18 per cent., gasoline and oil 24.5 per cent. and license fees and insurance 8.5 per cent.

The 12,096 workingmen's families, 1919, reported an average cost of about $16 for operation of the automobile, including motorcycles and bicycles. Only 15 per cent. of the families had expenditures for this purpose, however; and for those families having the expenditure the average was almost $106.

The figures here presented do not represent the last word in the cost of owning and operating the automobile for family living (or farm business) purposes. They are merely suggestive of some of the things which must be ascertained through further study. They call attention to the variety of uses of the farm automobile, from taking pleasure drives and going to church on the one hand to the hauling of produce, milk, eggs and pigs to market on the other hand.

Use of horse and buggy. Use of a horse (or team) and buggy (or wagon) for family living purposes is now regarded as almost *passé* among farmers, so much so that it is usually omitted from family living studies. Also, the results of studies in which it has been included seem to contribute much to this assumption.

Field workers are inclined to overlook this item and farm people are likely to underestimate its value, however. "We have the buggy and we feed the horse with the others and it isn't worth very much," they say. In addition, driving the horse to school or to town for groceries and supplies is seldom regarded as an integral part of the family living.

The most complete figures available, those for the 2886 farm families, show an average outlay of about $9 per family for use of the horse and buggy to fill household needs. This average was less than $6 per family for the New England States, almost $16 per family for the Southern States and only $4 per family for the North Central States. Less than one sixth of the 2886 families reported the use of horse and buggy. Of the 458 families reporting expenditures for this purpose 50 were from New England States, 332 were from Southern States and 76 were from the North Central States.

A part of the cost or expenditures for use of the horse and buggy represents goods furnished by the farm. Owing to the smallness of the costs and the difficulty of apportioning them between "furnished by the farm" and "purchased," all were charged as representing purchased goods.

The figures for the 798 families of Schoharie county, New York, and southeastern Ohio show a charge of less than $1 per year for family use of horse and buggy. This average covers depreciation and repair on the buggy only, with the exception of a few instances where money was actually paid out for horse hire. Therefore, the figures do not indicate that the horse and buggy method of transportation was used less frequently by these families than by the 2886 families. They suggest the need of further study to obtain information which will show more clearly the actual cost or value of this means of transportation for family living purposes.

Other methods of transportation. In addition to costs for the operation of the automobile and charges for use of horse and buggy, both the 2886 families and the 798 families reported an average expenditure of approximately $1 per family for carfare and bus fare. Also, the 2886 families had an average expenditure of $3 and the 798 families an average expenditure of $1.30 for postage, express and freight items.

The 12,096 workingmen's families, 1919, spent over $8 per family for carfare (not including fares to work) and other travel and over $2 per family for postage.

Insurance on furnishings and equipment. The 2886 families reported an expenditure of $1.20 per family per year for insurance on furnishings and equipment. In comparison, the 798 families reported an expenditure of forty cents for this purpose. Not all farm families carried insurance on furnishings and equipment. The 12,096 workingmen's families had an expenditure of about eighty cents for insurance on personal property.

The inclusion of furnishings and equipment, house and other buildings and sometimes live stock under the same policy makes the cost of insurance for any one of these items very difficult to determine for the farm family. Experience in attempting to get at this matter would lead one to assume that the farm family is usually content with carrying some insurance on the entire holdings regardless of numbers or values of items which it covers.

Summary. Operation costs or expenditures represent one of the most important groups of goods of farm family living. Owing to the wide variety of these goods, facilities and services and the many purposes which they fill, this group of elements is likely to harbor many "leaks" or pseudo-economies in family living expenditures. Economical uses of food, clothing, housing and health facilities involve the wise expenditure of money, time and energy in preparing foods, in cleaning clothing and living quarters, in providing proper temperatures and in keeping living conditions livable. No effort is here made to evaluate the home-maker's time as operation service, since the operation of the household is not an individual "procedure." Satisfactory operation of the farm household demands the active coöperation of all members composing it. The farmer may as well contribute of his time and energy as well as he may expect the home-maker, his wife, to tend the poultry, assist with the chores and "lend a hand" in the field. The entire family may well join forces in an earnest endeavor, through proper forethought and systematization, to lift the burden of overwork and drudgery from the farm home. Only the hearty coöperation of all members of the household for the attainment of common objectives in household and farm operation will provide the maximum of satisfactions and happiness.

CHAPTER IX

HEALTH MAINTENANCE, LIFE- AND HEALTH-INSURANCE

An octogenarian living in an agricultural village in one of the North Central States relates the story of how his country doctor of a generation ago built up a substantial practice. "When this doctor came to the village he had no patronage. The farmers were patronizing doctors from other places or going without medical care and attention. Pretty soon the doctor decided he was not busy enough. He got him a spirited horse and each morning he 'set out' in the direction of some place, as hard as he could drive. Later, he would return, and afternoons 'set out' hurriedly in some other direction. Pretty soon he was regarded as a busy man. People started to patronize him. His business grew. He attended to it and finally he became one of the best country doctors in the State. He gave service to those farm people and they paid him for it."

Probably this doctor was aware of the existing health needs of the farm people among whom he located. Perchance he knew something of their ability to pay for the service which he saw them needing. At any rate, the incident is suggestive of several pertinent questions in connection with the health aspect of farm family living. For example, what is the cost of health maintenance goods, facilities and services annually? What proportion is this cost of the total value of family living? What different kinds of goods and services does it represent? What, if any, are the additional sickness costs due to time lost, and what can be said of the state of health of farm people?

It will be recalled that expenditures for the maintenance of health averaged almost $62 per family for the 2886 farm families of selected localities in eleven States, and that this expenditure was 3.8 per cent. of the value of all goods used. By sections, the average was $61 or 3.6 per cent. of all goods in the New England States, $48.50 or 3.1 per cent. of all goods in the Southern States and $72 or 4.5 per cent. of all goods in the North Central States. The 402 Livingston county, New York, families, 1921, reported an expenditure of $83 per family for health maintenance, and this expenditure constituted 4.1 per cent. of all family living. The Schoharie county, New York, and the southeastern Ohio families had health maintenance costs of $34 or 3.3 per cent. of all goods used, the 861 white families of Kentucky, Tennessee and Texas $67 or 4.7 per cent. and the 154 colored families of the same localities $25 or 4.1 per cent. of all goods used.

It is probable that not all the families in any one group had expenditures for health maintenance during the particular year of study. More than a tenth of the 2886 families, 303 in number, reported no expenditures for the maintenance of health. Of these families, 33 were in the New England States, 142 were in the Southern States and 128 were in the North Central States. Similar count of the number of families reporting expenditures for this purpose was not made for the other studies.

A study of sickness in three townships of Cortland county, New York, 1923–24, shows an average expenditure of approximately $42 per family for 142 farm families.[1] This average comprises 3.9 per cent. of the value of all family living. Thirty-one village families of the same localities had an expenditure of $68.50 for health maintenance.

For the 2886 families, owners spent $63, tenants $58 and hired men $78 per family for health maintenance. These expenditures were 3.7 per cent., 4.3 per cent. and 6.3 per cent. of all family living. Livingston county, New York, owner families spent $76 or 3.8 per cent. of the value of all goods used for health maintenance, in comparison with $102 or 4.9 per cent. of the total spent by tenant families. With the 861 white families of Kentucky, Tennessee and Texas health maintenance costs were $75 or 4.6 per cent. of the total for owners, $66.50 or 4.8 per cent. of the total for tenants and $43 or 4.5 per cent. of the total for croppers. With the 154 colored families of the same localities these costs were $16 or 2.4 per cent. of the total for owners, $29 or 4.3 per cent. for tenants and $26 or 4.9 per cent. for croppers.

In comparison with farm families the 12,096 workingmen's families, 1919, had expenditures amounting to $60 for health maintenance. These expenditures cover essentially the same kinds of facilities and services as do the expenditures for farm families.

Expenditures for the different kinds of health goods and services are specified for the 300 Jackson, Meigs and Vinton county, Ohio, families included in the 798 families referred to above. Similar figures are available for 200 farm families of Ross county, Ohio, 1927.[2] The total expenditure for

[1] Cornell University Agricultural Experiment Station, "A Survey of Sickness in Rural Areas in Cortland County, New York," Memoir 112, 1928.

[2] Ohio Agricultural Experiment Station, "The Rural Health Facilities of Ross County, Ohio," Bul. 412, 1927.

health maintenance amounted to almost $30.70 for the 300 families, of which $14.40 went for doctors' fees, medicines and appliances, $6 for hospital and nurses' fees, $6.60 for dental work, $3 for oculists' services and glasses and twenty cents for carfare to doctor or hospital. Likewise, the total expenditure amounted to $39.30 for the 200 Ross county families; $27.90 for doctors' fees, medicine and appliances, $4.20 for hospital and nurses' fees, $5.60 for dental work and $1.60 for oculists' services and glasses.

Apparently, about $20.50 of the $27.90 spent by the 200 families went for physicians' services and the remainder for "unprescribed drugs and remedies." Almost a third of the 200 families had no physicians' fees and 55 had fees less than $10 for this purpose. There were 332 physicians' visits to the 200 homes, at an average cost of over $4 per visit. On an average the 200 families were located 4.9 miles from the nearest physician. There were 1174 office calls at an average cost of a little over $1 each.

As in most other health statistics, costs for confinements are included in the figures on health maintenance expenditures. Undoubtedly, the better procedure would be to treat confinement cases separately. In a "Survey of Sickness in Rural Areas of Cortland County," referred to above, Dwight Sanderson points out that childbirth is not a condition of bad health but of normal health. " . . . We can hardly take the view that a larger number of childbirths shows a lower degree of health, for the exact opposite is nearer the physiological truth . . . for though a woman in childbirth certainly is sick, this is a sickness representing a normal function and is not due to any disease of the organism."

There were 26 births reported for the Ross county families, 22 of which were attended by physicians at an average cost of about $25. This cost covers only the physician's charge for delivery, no additional visits having been made to the home preceding or following the delivery.

Less than half of the 200 families had dental work done, only six reported expenditures for hospital services and seven employed some nursing service.

Data on approximately 800 white families and 200 negro families of Texas studied by the National Child Labor Committee, 1925, are partially comparable to the Ohio figures. The white families had an expenditure of almost $43 and the negro families had an expenditure of almost $11 for doctors' services, including prescriptions, and patent medicines during the year of study.[3]

Results of the study of 357 Minnesota farm families, referred to previously, are of interest. These results show the following distribution of an average expenditure of $87 per family for health maintenance: Medical service $47, medicine $8, dental services $15, oculists' services $3, and births, deaths and cemetery expenses $14. It appears that births accounted for about $6 of the $14 allotted to "births, deaths and cemetery expenses." There were 41 reported births, at an average cost of $57 per birth. This cost includes doctor, hospital, nurse, domestic help and layette.

About 56 per cent. of the 357 families had bills of $5 or more for medical attention, 64 per cent. had expenditures for dental services, and 22 per cent. had some expenditure for oculists' services.

An average expenditure of $60 by the 12,096 working-men's families in 92 industrial centers, 1919, for health maintenance was distributed approximately as follows: Physician, surgeon and oculist $32, medicine $10.35, nurse

[3] National Child Labor Committee, "Child Labor Among Cotton Growers of Texas," 1925.

$3, hospital $4.50, dentist $8.20, eyeglasses $1.70, other twenty-five cents. These families had an expenditure of almost $2.25 per family for burial expenses. Burial expenses, tabulated under unclassified items, for the 2886 and the 798 families, amounted to less than $3 per family in each instance.

Extent and nature of illness. It would be of interest to know something of the extent and the nature of illness prevalent among the different groups of families represented by the health maintenance figures. Limited information is available for several of the smaller groups of these families.

Among the 1609 members of the 402 Livingston county, New York, families about 11,000 working days were lost by illness, or about six days per person per year. Of these days 27.5 per cent. were lost because of minor illness, and 72.5 per cent. on account of serious illness. Minor illness signifies that which, while it prevented a person from going about his regular business, did not call for much special care from others; serious illness includes cases that required constant attention, whether from a member of the family or a special nurse and whether at home or in a hospital. The 11,000 working days lost do not include the time of a dozen or more chronically disabled persons, unable to do ordinary work on the farm or in the home.

For the 200 Ross county, Ohio, families "an illness record" by individuals for the preceding twelve months was obtained from each family. Forty-three per cent. of the persons had been ill for some period of time during the year. A larger percentage of the females were ill than of the males, but part of this difference appears to have been due to child-bearing, which after all is not a condition of ill-health but of normal health. By ten-year age groups, under ten, ten to nineteen, etc., to seventy and over, noticeable differences between the sexes do not appear until the twentieth to twenty-ninth year period. The percentage of males that were ill drops after the age of twenty, while the percentage of females that were ill increases.

The causes of illness reported for the 43 per cent. of the persons who were ill during the year were classified according to the "International List of Causes of Sickness and Death" (1920 revision). Almost a third, 32.2 per cent., of the cases fell in the epidemic-infections group, 14.1 per cent. in the respiratory group, 12.9 in the digestive group and smaller percentages in each of the six or more other groups. The eight most frequently reported specific illnesses in order of frequency, from highest down, were mumps, colds and grippe, accidents, childbirths, whooping-cough, chronic rheumatism, influenza and indigestion. Seventy-two per cent. of all the cases of illness received medical care or resource from outside the family.

Illness figures are available for the 800 white families and the 200 negro families of Texas studied by the National Child Labor Committee, 1925. More than a third, 34.3 per cent. of the persons in the white families and 42.1 per cent. of the persons in the colored families, were ill during the year. Average duration of illnesses was twenty-six days per person for white families and nineteen days per person for colored families for the year. The causes of illness given most frequently were influenza and colds, 34.2 per cent. of the total number of persons ill, dengue 20.7 per cent., and stomach and bowel complaint 9.4 per cent. Among the other causes of illness reported were childbirths, children's diseases, chills and fever, pneumonia, nervousness, accidents, operations, rheumatism and kidney trouble. Approximately half of the mothers were ill in comparison with slightly more than a third of the fathers, due partially to childbirth by the mothers, no doubt.

Also, illness data are available for the farm and village families included in the "Survey of Sickness" referred to previously. There was an average of 5.2 days' sickness per capita in the farm families in comparison with 7.4 days per capita in the village families. The average lengths of cases of sickness reported by the farm families and village families were twenty-three days and 27.6 days. The higher percentage of sickness in the village is held to be due to a higher percentage of old people in the village with a higher percentage of sickness among the older people. When sickness due to confinements is excluded, days of illness are 4.5 per capita for the farm families and 7.0 per capita for village families.

The percentage of the total number of persons ill may not be indicative of the prevailing state of health of the group in question. Allowance needs to be made for accidents and other illnesses of short duration. Limited attempts have been made to get a general picture of the farm health situation. One of these attempts, pertaining to almost 400 farm families of Texas, shows the percentages of the total number of families reporting "good health" and "poor health" in the family.[4] Percentages of the total reporting "poor health" of one or more members of the family range from 34 per cent. for owner operators down to 19 per cent. for share tenants.

These figures may be little, if any, more indicative of the prevailing state of health than are cases of illness reported, however. It is probable that some families would answer the question of "good or poor health" in terms of

[4] U. S. Dept. Agriculture, "Farm Ownership and Tenancy in the Black Prairie Belt of Texas," Bul. 1068, 1922.

the way they felt at the time it was asked. It is possible that some farm families may be like the aged lady in a certain village who, when asked how she was, remarked, "I'm enjoying poor health, now."

Further, the patronage of the "patent medicine wagon" is not a satisfactory indication of the prevailing state of health of farm people. A farm family living field worker tells of the extensive purchase of "quack" remedies by farmers at a "traveling medicine show" staged in the village around which he was working last spring. "The car pulled up and parked at a crossing on the main street. The fiddler came to the rear and struck up a catchy tune. Boys of the streets, from tots to 'teens, gathered around the wagon. Out came the conjurer, fire-eater and snake-charmer. The audience grew. Men sauntered in from all directions. Cars drove up and parked at the curbing.

"Fiddling and fire-eating were over and the wonderful Indian Arrowroot was introduced; a relief for every ailment, internal and external, from headache down to corns and bunions. It was demonstrated; applied to paining corns through heavy work shoe leather, and 'patients' vouched for the relief which it gave. The sale started. Three one dollar bottles for the price of two were offered. As the self-named professor of medicine 'yodeled on,' at least twenty transactions were effected. The price was cut, two bottles for the cost of one, and at least another score of people made purchases.

"On my rounds the following week I got reports from the farm women of expenditures for Indian Arrowroot. On query as to whether it was satisfactory I got most frequently the reply that it had not been used. In several instances further information was offered to the effect that the medicine would be on hand when needed, that it was bought at a bargain price, that it had looked good and that others were buying it."

In an article on the country doctor in "Rural America" for June, 1926, Walter Burr holds that the patronage of quacks, fads and isms is playing out. "Simple rules of living, with simple wholesome advice and remedies are taking their place." It will be recalled, however, that 200 Ross county, Ohio, families spent over $7 annually for unprescribed drugs and remedies. In the study of 1000 farm families of North Carolina, by the Tenancy Commission, about 1923, more than 60 per cent. of the total number reported the use of patent medicines. The percentages varied with the different tenure groups, the highest being 96 per cent. for colored tenants. The average expenditure annually for patent medicines ranged from about $3 per family for white owners to more than $5 per family for colored tenants.

The extent to which patronage of quacks and the like is playing out may be suggestive of general improvement in the health of the farm family. It will not serve as a satisfactory or a complete index of the physical health status of the different members composing the family. This must be sought in the current death-rates and morbidity (defect and illness) rates of farm people, in comparison with people of other occupations or professions and other locations.

Rural and urban death-rates. Many articles have been written and much discussion has centered on the question of rural and urban death-rates. Most writers now hold that the rural rate is decreasing less rapidly than the urban; and this is indicated by the data showing the death-rates from all causes and from certain types of disease in the registration area of the country from 1900 to 1924. As compiled by the United States Census Bureau, the figures show a decline in the urban death-rate, from 17.7 per 1000 population for the period 1900–1904 to 13.0 per 1000 population for the period 1920–24; a decline of 4.7 per 1000 population in two decades. The rural death-rate decreased from 14.2 per 1000 to 11.2 per 1000 for the same period; a decline of 3.0 per 1000 population. Thus, the urban death-rate appears to have declined 1.7 per 1000 more rapidly than the rural death-rate during the two decades. The registration area comprised about 40 per cent. of our total population in 1900 and nearly 90 per cent. in 1924. Attention must be called to the joker in the figures, however; "rural" includes everything under 10,000 population—farms, villages, towns and small cities—in these figures. Death-rates for villages are doubtless higher than for farms generally owing to higher percentages of adult population in the villages. Until mortality statistics are recorded and summarized by place of residence or by occupation or profession, however, the matter of the farm, village and town death-rates will continue to be an unanswered question.

The situation is about the same in regard to morbidity statistics. Study of the defects found in drafted men shows a "defect-rate" of 528 per 1000 rural registrants (drafted men) in comparison with 609 per 1000 urban registrants.[5] A summary statement holds that urban registrants exceed in defects due to inferior stock and poor environmental conditions, while rural registrants exceed in accidental injuries and in hereditary and congenital defects due to inbreeding. Since "rural" in this study includes villages, towns and cities with populations up to 25,000, the figures give no indication of the defect-rate among registrants from farm homes.

Physical examination of over 500,000 "rural" and "city" school children shows that noticeably higher percentages

[5] U. S. War Department, "Defects Found in Drafted Men," 1920.

of the rural children have defective teeth, tonsils, adenoids, eyes, nutrition, glands, ears, breathing, spine, blood, lungs, heart and mind than have city children.[6] The terms rural and city are not defined in this study. Examination of over 500,000 school children in New York State, 1922–23, shows 37.4 per cent. of the rural school children in normal health in comparison with 45 per cent. of the "large village" children and 38 per cent. of city children. In this study "rural" appears to have included villages with population up to 4500. On this account these figures contribute no definite information on either the defect- or illness-rate among farm people.

Probably the most exacting study of the rural-urban defect and illness rates is that based on "observations" made by the Students' Health Service of the University of Minnesota, 1924-25.[7] Health histories or records obtained from almost 3500 male university students were classified according to place of residence, as rural, village, town, small city and city. Apparently rural corresponded closely to farm, since village next above rural includes places of 50 to 1000 population. In regard to the defect-rate this study concludes that students reared on farms show fewer physical defects than those from villages, about the same number as those from small cities and more than those from towns (1000 to 5000 population) or large cities. Students from villages had more defects and students from large cities (more than 50,000 population) had fewer defects than students from other residence groups. From the standpoint of illness, students from the farm had had more

[6] American Medical Association, "Health Essentials for Rural Schools," 1921.

[7] "Journal of the American Medical Association," 1924, and "Journal of Industrial Hygiene," 1925.

diseases than students from large cities but fewer than students from each of the other three places of residence. Students from villages had had more cases of disease and students from large cities fewer cases of disease than students of any other group. Higher percentages of the farm-reared students had had pleurisy, pneumonia, rheumatism, smallpox and tuberculosis, according to the histories, in comparison with village, town and city students. Lower percentages had had chickenpox, diphtheria, tonsillitis, typhoid fever and whooping-cough.

According to the "Farmer's Wife" for October, 1927, records kept at "baby conferences" in Illinois show an average of 2.1 significant defects per child for over 3000 farm children, in comparison with an average of 1.6 significant defects for over 2000 city children. Also, in dental inspections or examinations of about 10,000 farm school children by the Illinois State Board of Health, at least 80 per cent. were found to have one or more defective teeth.

The preceding figures on mortality and morbidity rates point to the need of well-planned, discriminating study of the prevailing health status of farm people. Birth-rates, death-rates from different causes, illness, accident and defect-rates must be ascertained for farm people—those who reside on farms and make their living from tilling the land—in comparison with those who make their living at other specific occupations. The first step in the ascertainment of these rates is the getting of vital statistics on farm population regularly. Farm population and village population must cease to be merged as rural population and the lines of distinction between village and town and town and city must be clearly drawn. Vital statistics must then be recorded in such a way that the age composition of the farm, the village, and the city groups correspond.

Health- and life-insurance. The matter of health- and life-insurance is an important consideration in connection with health maintenance of the farm family. This type of insurance, life-insurance especially, is regarded by some farm family living investigators as "savings" and by others as a form of investment. Whether paid to an insurance company or merely held as a reserve fund to meet health contingencies and to provide burial expenses in case of death, the putting aside of a certain definite sum monthly, quarterly or yearly may well be regarded as one of the principal elements of farm family living.

The 2886 farm families in eleven States had an expenditure of nearly $41 per family for health- and life-insurance, life-insurance premiums primarily. Families of the North Central States spent most for this purpose, about $44, in comparison with almost $39 spent by families of the Southern States and $36 spent by families of the New England States. Approximately 55 per cent. of all these families reported no expenditure for insurance. Of the 1305 families reporting expenditures for this purpose 145 were New England families, 465 were southern families and 695 were north central families. The 798 farm families of Schoharie county, New York, and southeastern Ohio spent $15 per year for insurance premiums, the 402 Livingston county, New York, families spent $42, the 861 white families of Kentucky, Tennessee and Texas spent $39, and the 154 colored families, of the same localities as the 861 white families, spent $14 per year for this purpose. The 357 Minnesota families referred to above had an expenditure of $38 for insurance premiums.

Owners spent $45 for insurance, among the 2886 families, in comparison with $33 each spent by tenants and hired men. Livingston county, New York, owners and tenants

spent $41 and $46 respectively for this purpose. For the
Kentucky, Tennessee and Texas study white owners, tenants and croppers spent $45, $37 and $12 per family, and
colored owners, tenants and croppers spent $12, $15 and
$14 per family for health- and life-insurance.

In comparison with farm families the 12,096 workingmen's families in ninety-two industrial centers, 1919, had
an expenditure of $39 for life-insurance and almost $3.50
for health- and accident-insurance. Over 86 per cent. of
these families carried life-insurance and almost 20 per cent.
carried health- and accident-insurance.

The average expenditure for health- and life-insurance
premiums cannot be regarded as indicating the potential
needs of any single family. The health needs are likely to
be pretty much a matter of chance, from nothing for those
families with no accidents or sickness to exorbitant sums
for those who experience prolonged serious illness. Life-
insurance premiums may well be regarded as filling investment needs in that they provide a means of meeting burial
costs and that they represent an accumulation of funds
from certain amounts set aside at regular intervals.

Further, the average expenditures for health maintenance
cannot be looked upon as covering the needs of many families. Several farm families, in the different groups considered, reported expenditures ranging between $1000 and
$2500 for operations, hospital fees and the like. Serious
illness of any duration means usually an item of "heavy
cost" to the farm family.

The data presented warrant no final conclusion as to the
prevailing status or level of health of either farm or city
people. They show somewhat near the same expenditures
for health maintenance by farm families and workingmen's
families. They suggest that the general health level of the

open country is not much above that of the city. Undoubtedly, there are farming regions where the health status is not equal to that in the larger cities of these same regions.

The country possesses an abundance of fresh air and sunshine, two basic essentials for good health, and opportunity for out-of-door life, an important aid to good health. On the other hand, the country appears to favor the "feeling" of poor health. The story is told of a certain student in class who, when asked to give reasons why married men live longer, replied, "They don't, it just seems longer." While farm people may not be less "physically fit" than people of other occupations and locations, they may feel much less "fit" owing to the inclination to think more of sickness or ailments.

Whatever the prevailing status of health, however, there is little doubt regarding the inadequacy of health maintenance facilities and the lack of enforcement of health regulations among farm people. Modern hospitals and clinics and competent doctors, nurses and specialists are farther from the farmer's reach than from the city man's reach. The health of the farm family is less adequately safeguarded by organizations and by the enforcement of health laws than is the health of the urban family. Public health supervision is within the reach of less than 20 per cent. of our farm families. The maintenance of health, although it represents usually less than one twentieth of the value of all goods used, stands as a direct challenge to all who are concerned with the welfare of the farm family. Well-planned, technical research in the field of health, and in foods, clothing and housing as related to health, of the different members of the family, is paramount in the development of a farm health program.

CHAPTER X

ADVANCEMENT AND PERSONAL GOODS, FACILITIES AND SERVICES

RECENTLY a family living field worker on returning to his headquarters at the close of a day's work made the following report to the investigator in charge of his unit of study: "I want to take you out over the hill and down the slope toward the valley to visit what I call an ideal farm home. There are two daughters and a son still at home. The son, a senior in high school, plans to go to college, one of the daughters has just entered college and the other, with three years of college work to her credit, is teaching near home in order to help the brother and sister get started in college. The three older brothers and sisters, two of whom live on farms, are college graduates. When you 'size up' the farm on which they were reared you wonder how they did it. It's about average in size and layout but kept up well, judging from appearances. The family has paid for the farm, improved the house and had a reasonably good living as they have gone along. There are evidences of good reading matter, classical and general music and wholesome recreation of different types within the home. Both the parents and the young folks support and encourage good schools, participate in church and other local organizational activities, and all enjoy occasional trips to points of interest within driving distance. The parents say they have always regarded the wise expenditures of money for non-material

180

goods a gilt-edge investment, and I can readily believe them."

Here we have pictured on the screen primarily the goods, facilities and services which have to do with "advancement" of the family. These goods are less material in nature and cover a wider range of uses than any other one group of family living goods. They include educational and recreational facilities, reading matter, provision for travel, participation in clubs and organizations, benevolences, religion and other interests of a social or a spiritual nature. Values obtained from the use of these goods are commonly accepted as significant of the degree of refinement or culture of the family or of a group of families.

For the 2886 farm families referred to in connection with other groups of goods, the average value of goods for advancement purposes amounted to $105 per family and constituted 6.6 per cent. of the value of all family living. The average was slightly more for the New England families, $118 or 7.0 per cent. of the total, in comparison with $104 or 6.7 per cent. of the total for the southern families, and $102 or 6.4 per cent. of the total for the north central families. Only 16 of the 2886 families reported no expenditures for advancement goods. Expenditures for advancement goods amounted to only $53 per family, 5.2 per cent. of all family living, for the 798 Schoharie county, New York, and southeastern Ohio families. For the 402 Livingston county, New York, families they averaged $125 per family or 6.2 per cent. of all goods used, for the 861 white families of Kentucky, Tennessee and Texas $84 per family or 5.9 per cent. of all goods used and for the 154 colored families of the same localities $28 per family or 4.6 per cent. of all goods used.

Owners among the 2886 families spent $128, 7.4 per cent.

of the value of all goods, for advancement, in comparison with $58, 4.3 per cent., spent by tenant families, and $46, 3.7 per cent., spent by hired-man families. Owners of the 841 white families of Kentucky, Tennessee and Texas spent $130, 8.0 per cent. of the total, for advancement goods, while tenants spent $51, 3.7 per cent. of the total, and croppers spent $21, 2.2 per cent. of the total, for the same purpose. Owners of the 154 colored families spent $49 or 7.2 per cent. of the value of all goods, tenants $28 or 4.1 per cent. of the value of all goods and croppers $19 or 3.5 per cent. of all goods for advancement purposes. Comparable data on the average expenditure for all advancement goods are not available for other groups of farm families nor for workingmen's families. Comparison of the average expenditures for certain kinds of advancement goods are possible for several of the groups of families considered above. The average expenditures for the principal kinds of all the advancement goods used by the 2886 families of selected localities in eleven States and the 798 families of Schoharie county, New York, and southeastern Ohio appear in *Table 21*.

Formal education. With the larger group of these families, as a whole and by sections, expenditures for formal education constitute the largest item of advancement costs, $37.90 per family for all families. The southern families spent most for this purpose, $46 per family, in comparison with $42.60 spent by the New England families and $30.50 spent by the north central families. The 798 families spent only a third as much as was spent by the 2886 families for formal education, or $12.80 per family. It should be recalled that the expenditure for formal education for these groups of families includes money spent for lessons, school-books and supplies in the elementary schools, and

tuition, books, board and lodging and miscellaneous purposes at high schools or colleges. School taxes are not
included.

TABLE 21.   Average value per family of the different kinds of advancement goods used during one year, 1922–26.[1]

| Advancement Goods | 2886 FAMILIES OF SELECTED LOCALITIES IN 11 STATES | | | | 798 families of Schoharie county, New York, and south-eastern Ohio |
	All families all States	317 families New England States	1130 families Southern States	1439 families North Central States	
Total	$104.80	$117.90	$104.30	$102.30	$53.10
a. Formal schooling...	37.90	42.60	46.00	30.50	12.80
b. Reading matter....	11.20	11.70	8.20	13.40	8.10
c. Organization dues..	3.90	6.00	1.90	5.10	2.00
d. Church, Sun. school and missions.....	28.20	26.60	29.10	27.90	12.90
e. Red Cross and other welfare..........	1.10	1.70	1.10	1.00	.30
f. Recreation........	22.50	29.30	18.00	24.40	17.00

[1] Adapted from Bul. 1466 and from Preliminary Reports, U. S. Dept. Agriculture.

Figures showing expenditure for formal education by
tenure are not available. As nearly as can be ascertained
the 12,096 workingmen's families spent approximately $8
per family for the goods, facilities and services included
under formal education for the farm families. The higher
expenditures for the different groups of farm families are
doubtless due in part to boarding and lodging costs and
possibly to tuition fees for boys or girls attending school
away from home.

The figures on expenditure are in no way representative of the extent or kinds of formal education attained by the different members of the families to which they refer. They are merely averages of the costs incurred in connection with attendance at grade school, high school or college. These costs may range from nothing for families with no children to hundreds of dollars where several sons or daughters attending college are supported from the family purse. Further, they give no indication of the adequacy or the efficiency of the educational institutions available to the farm family. These are considered briefly in a succeeding chapter. Indexes of the extent and kinds of formal education—that is, of the educational status of farm people—must be sought in the percentages of the school population attending school and in grades of schooling attained by different members of the family.

Estimates prepared by the United States Bureau of Education, 1926, show 65 per cent. of the white farm population and 53 per cent. of the colored farm population ten to twenty years of age in school.[1] By sections of the country, the percentages for white population are average for the North Central and Southern States, two points below average for the Northeastern States and three points above average for the Western States. Also, by sections, the percentages of colored population of the ages ten to twenty years in school are average for the Southern States, two points above average for the Northeastern States, two points below average for the Western States and four points above average for the North Central States. In these figures it is assumed that the per cent. of farm population in school is the same as the per cent. of rural population in school, rural including places of less than 2500 inhabitants.

[1] U. S. Dept. Interior, Rural School Leaflet 20, 1926.

An actual study of the school situation in Currituck county, a rural county in North Carolina, 1921, shows 74 per cent. of the school population, as determined by the school census, enrolled in school.[2] Another study of a strictly rural township (with no towns or villages) in Adams county, Pennsylvania, 1920, shows 86 per cent. of the census-enumerated school population in school.[3] The higher percentages of the total in school in the minor studies are doubtless due largely to the inclusion of children below ten years of age in the population. It is possible also that the per cent. of village population ten to twenty years of age in school is lower than the per cent. of farm population of the same age in school. More information on the percentages of farm, village, town and city population of similar ages in school would throw further light on the educational status of farm people.

Grades attained in school by sons and daughters still in school are incomplete indications of the educational status of the farm family, unless the grades attained are based against individual ages of those who are attending school. Few figures arranged on this basis are available. For the Livingston county, New York, study, 1921, there were 165 families with sons and daughters over seventeen years of age. In 14 per cent. of the 165 families none of the sons and daughters eighteen years of age and over had completed the eighth grade in school. In 32 per cent. at least one son or daughter had completed the eighth but had not reached the twelfth grade; in 30 per cent. at least one had finished but had not gone beyond high school; in 17 per cent. at least one had had one to two years in college; and

[2] U. S. Dept. Interior, "Suggestions for the Reorganization of Schools in Currituck County, North Carolina," Bul. 24, 1921.

[3] U. S. Dept. Interior, "Feasibility of Consolidating Schools of Mount Joy Township, Adams County, Pennsylvania," Bul. 20, 1920.

in 7 per cent. at least one had had more than two years in college. There were ninety-two of the 165 families with sons and daughters over twenty-two years of age. The percentages of these in which at least one son or daughter had had less than eight grades, eight or more and less than twelve grades, twelve grades only, one to two years in college and more than two years in college were 18 per cent., 27 per cent., 26 per cent., 17 per cent. and 12 per cent.

For 1145 farm families of Nebraska, 1923, 3.6 per cent. of the 525 sons and daughters more than nineteen years of age were college graduates.[4] More than a fourth of the owner's sons and daughters and one fifth of the tenants' sons and daughters sixteen or more years of age were high-school graduates. More than two fifths of the owners' sons and daughters and almost one third of the tenants' sons and daughters fourteen or more years of age had completed at least ten grades of high-school work. In a study of 400 farm families of Cedar county, Iowa, 1923, of 325 sons and daughters regarded as "beyond school age," 51 per cent. quit school in the grades, 41 per cent. quit in the high school and 8 per cent. quit in college.[5]

Schooling attained by the parents, also, is indicative of the educational status of the farm family. For the 2886 families in selected localities in eleven States the grade attained in school was reported for about 2350 of the operators and 2450 of the home-makers. For 12 per cent. of the operators four grades or less of schooling was reported, for 60 per cent. five to eight grades, for 22 per cent. nine to twelve grades and for 6 per cent. more than twelve grades.

[4] University of Nebraska Agricultural Experiment Station, "The Nebraska Farm Family," Bul. 185, 1923.
[5] Iowa State College of Agriculture and Mechanic Arts, "The Social Aspects of Rural Life and Farm Tenantry," Bul. 217, 1923.

The corresponding figures for the 2450 home-makers were 8 per cent., 55 per cent., 31 per cent. and 6 per cent. Four grades of schooling or less were reported for 34 per cent. of the operators in the 841 families of Kentucky, Tennessee and Texas; five to eight grades for 48 per cent., nine to twelve grades for 14 per cent. and more than twelve grades for 4 per cent. Here the corresponding figures for home-makers were 19 per cent., 55 per cent., 21 per cent. and 19 per cent. Four grades or less were given for 16 per cent. of the operators in 498 Schoharie county, New York, families; four to eight grades for 73 per cent., nine to twelve grades for 10 per cent. and more than twelve grades for only 1 per cent. Similar figures for the home-makers were 13 per cent., 72 per cent., 13 per cent. and 2 per cent. Almost a fifth of the operators in the 400 Cedar county, Iowa, families referred to previously quit school in the grades, 23 per cent. quit in the high school and 4 per cent. quit in college. Here 62 per cent. of the home-makers quit school in the grades, 33 per cent. quit in the high school and 5 per cent. quit in college. It is noteworthy that in all of the figures the home-makers appear to have attained more formal schooling than the operators.

As with expenditures for formal schooling, the grades attained are not regarded as representing in full the educational status of farm people. Continuing education and the influence of institutions and agencies other than the school are significant factors. The influence of study and reading at home and of participation in neighborhood and community activities must not be overlooked.

Reading matter. The average cost of reading matter, including newspapers, farm journals, general magazines and books not for school purposes, amounted to $11.20 per family among the 2886 farm families in eleven States. Of the 199 families who reported no expenditure for reading matter, nineteen were in the New England States, 155 in the Southern States, and 25 in the North Central States. Expenditures for reading matter were $8.10 per family for the Schoharie county, New York, and southeastern Ohio families. As nearly as can be determined from the figures available the 12,096 workingmen's families appear to have spent only $2.75 per family for reading matter—that is, for magazines and books. This figure may not cover newspapers and the like which may have been classed with "miscellaneous" goods.

The average number of the different types of periodicals taken during a year have been obtained in several studies. For about 450 Iowa farm families, 1924, owners were taking 1.5 local papers, 1.1 daily papers, 2.5 farm journals and 1.8 general magazines. Tenants were taking 1.2 local papers, 1.0 daily paper, 2.2 farm journals and 1.3 general magazines.[6] For the 402 Livingston county, New York, families reading matter of different types averaged about the same for owners and tenants; .8 local paper, 1.0 daily paper, 2.4 farm journals and 2.1 general magazines per family.[7] The study of over 1200 farm homes and almost 200 village homes of Nebraska shows about the same numbers of periodicals taken by farm and village families: one daily, almost three weekly and three monthly periodicals, on an average.[8] Farm journals were taken twice as frequently as other trade journals by village families.

Estimates of the number of books in the home library have been obtained and summarized in several studies. The

[6] U. S. Dept. Agriculture, "Cost of Living in Farm Homes of Iowa," Preliminary Report, 1924.

[7] Cornell University Agricultural Experiment Station. *op. cit.*

[8] University of Nebraska Agricultural Experiment Station, "Reading Matter in Nebraska Farm Homes," Bul. 180, 1922.

numbers of volumes reported average seventy per family for the Livingston county, New York, families and sixty-three per family for owners and forty per family for tenants of the 451 Iowa families.

There are those who hold that the periodicals and the number of books owned are little, if any, more indicative than the costs which they represent of the satisfactions or values which they provide, unless one knows the extent to which they are read by different members of the family. Appreciating the significance of this point, the workers in charge of a recent study by the questionnaire method, among almost 8000 farm and village boys and girls of the ages ten to twenty years primarily, asked each to name from the periodicals taken by the family those in which he or she read. The periodicals named were classified in five groups: newspapers, farm journals, general magazines, boys' or girls' magazines and other magazines.

For the farm boys 76 per cent. of the total reported reading in newspapers, 68 per cent. reported reading in farm journals, 36 per cent. reported reading in general magazines, 15 per cent. reported reading in boys' magazines and 11 per cent. reported reading in other magazines. Corresponding figures for the village boys were 82 per cent., 42 per cent., 49 per cent., 24 per cent. and 16 per cent. Only 3 per cent. of the farm boys and 2 per cent. of the village boys reported no reading in any periodicals. For the farm girls, 80 per cent. reported reading in newspapers, 64 per cent. reported reading in farm journals, 68 per cent. reported reading in general magazines, 12 per cent. reported reading in girls' magazines and 16 per cent. reported reading in other magazines. The corresponding figures for village girls were 78 per cent., 28 per cent., 77 per cent., 13 per cent. and 17 per cent. Two per cent. of the farm girls and 1 per cent. of the village girls reported no reading in periodicals.[9]

Also, these boys and girls were asked to name the books which they had read during the year just preceding the study. The books named were classified under fiction, books for youth, nature, history and biography, classics and poetry, and all others. Fifty-five per cent. of the farm boys and 59 per cent. of the village boys and 73 per cent. each of the farm and village girls reported the reading of one or more books of fiction. Forty-one per cent. of the farm boys and 54 per cent. of the village boys, and 51 per cent. each of the farm and village girls reported the reading of one or more books for youth. Less than 11 per cent. each of farm and village boys and girls reported the reading of books of the other classifications. Sixteen per cent. of the farm boys and 8 per cent. of the village boys, and 4 per cent. of the farm girls and 3 per cent. of the village girls, reported the reading of no books.

The amount of reading may be little if any more indicative than expenditure for reading materials of the satisfactions or values accruing from the use of these advancement goods. Recently Will Rogers told of seeing Charles Lindbergh show "splendid judgment" by picking up a book and laying it down without reading it. It is probable that for many people less random reading with more time to think or cogitate about the things read would be fully as productive of satisfactions or values.

Organization dues. Expenditures for social and educational organization dues, including fees for clubs, lodges and the like but not for religious organizations, averaged $3.90 per family for the 2886 families in eleven States and

[9] U. S. Dept. Agriculture, "Attitudes and Problems of Farm Youth," Extension Service Circular 46, 1927.

$2 per family for the 798 families in Schoharie county, New York, and southeastern Ohio. These expenditures appear to be much lower for the southern families than for the other two groups of the 2886 families.

The 12,096 workingmen's families appear to have had an expenditure of $3.50 per family for about the same organization or club dues that are included under this group of expenditures for the farm families. This figure may include some of the church "society" dues classified under contributions to church for the farm families.

These figures give no indication of the numbers of memberships involved or the time spent in fostering the different organizations. The present tendency to promote organizations among farm people raises the question of the amount of time as well as the money which may be wisely spent for this purpose.

Church, Sunday school and missions. The contribution to church, including Sunday school and missionary offerings, appears to be one of the large items of advancement expenditures. This amounted to over $28 per family for the 2886 families, with little variation for the three separate groups of States. Approximately a fifth of the 2886 families, 603 in number, reported no expenditure for church work in any form. Of the 2283 families reporting expenditures for this purpose, 239 were in the New England group, 966 in the southern group and 1078 in the north central group. Thus, for the families reporting, the average expenditures per family for church purposes are approximately $35, $34 and $37 for the three groups of States in the order named.

The 798 families had an average expenditure of $12.90 per family for church purposes. The number of families in this group having no church expenditures is not available.

The 402 Livingston county, New York, families spent $40 per family for church support. Owner families spent $45 each in comparison with $28 spent by tenant families.

The 12,096 workingmen's families had an expenditure of $10.15 for church support, probably not including some church club dues which may have been grouped with "lodges, clubs, societies, etc." About 72 per cent. of these families reported expenditures for church, and the average for those who had expenditures for this purpose was slightly more than $14 per family.

Closely allied with the church contributions is the expenditure of $1.10 per family for Red Cross and other welfare, by the 2886 farm families. Apparently the workingmen's families spent $1.35 for these and other benevolences in 1919.

It would be interesting to know something of the church affiliations and attendance of the groups of families represented by the expenditures, but information of this type is lacking. Results of a recent study among approximately 500 farm families of Oklahoma show 81 per cent. of the home-makers and 61 per cent. of the operators as having "claimed church membership." [10] Slightly more than half of the women attended church "reasonably regularly." Over 50 per cent. of the women attended church in a near-by town, 30 per cent. attended in the open country and less than 20 per cent. attended no church at all. Approximately 50 per cent. of the women attended Sunday school. Over 30 per cent. of the women reported some attendance at church organization (club or society) meetings. Children in 70 per cent. of about 400 of the families made "at least occasional contacts from attendance at Sunday school."

[10] Oklahoma Agricultural and Mechanic Arts College, "Church Activities of Farm Women and Their Families," Experiment Station Bul. 169, 1927.

It is probable that attendance at the different kinds of church services are fully as indicative as financial support of church activities of the values to be obtained from this group of advancement goods. This will remain an unanswered question until more complete data have been gathered on church attendance by the different members of the farm family and until methods of measuring the satisfactions or values from "church giving" and "church going" have been developed, however.

Recreation. Another large item of expenditure under advancement is for recreation, $22.50 per family for the 2886 families in eleven States and $17 per family for the 798 of Schoharie county, New York, and southeastern Ohio. For the 2886 families the expenditure for this item varies considerably for the three sections. Families of the New England group spent $29.30 for this purpose in comparison with $18 spent by families of the southeastern group and $24.40 spent by families of the north central group.

The 12,096 workingmen's families appear to have spent $21 per family for recreation. Almost $8 of this went for movies, $7.50 for vacations, $2 for travel and less than $1 each for excursions, concerts and the like and "other" amusements.

It will be recalled that recreation goods and facilities include concerts, lectures, theaters, movies, games, photography, radio and the like, athletic goods and vacation or pleasure trips by auto or other means of travel. The average expenditures for these goods may be less fruitful of social or spiritual satisfactions than are the uses of the goods, including participation in the activities which they represent. Information on some of the different kinds of recreational activities was obtained from the 8000 farm and village boys and girls referred to under reading material.

Answers from these boys and girls to the question, "What is there to do when you have time free from work?" ranged from "odd jobs" through the various kinds of work and types of recreation, including fancy work and dancing, to "enjoy myself." The great variety of answers made an arbitrary classification rather difficult, owing to some duplications of home work, school work, club work and summer camp activities. Answers to the two phases of this question, "when school is in session" and "during vacation," are shown in *Table 22*, classified on the basis of social activities, recreational activities, sports, work and study. Things reported to do are checked against "things done"; that is, activities actually participated in, as stated in answer to the question, "What do you (with other boys and girls of about the same age) do together?"

With things reported to do, different kinds of work appear to cut into recreation more during vacation than when school is in session. Village boys and girls seem to have or to see more opportunities for recreation than do farm boys and girls, in both instances. Some allowances must be made for differences due to arbitrary classification of the things reported to do.

From the standpoint of activities participated in with other boys and girls, village boys and girls appear to excel in the classified activities, except socials (including parties and picnics) and club work (including summer camps) for girls. In most instances, group activities—that is, activities participated in jointly—appear to be less universal than things reported to do individually or without regard to group participation.

In addition to things reported to do and activities par-

Table 22.   Things reported to do, when school is in session and during vacation, and group activities participated in; 7880 farm and village boys and girls.[1]

Items classified	PERSONS REPORTING ON DIFFERENT ITEMS							
	Living on farm				Living in village			
	Male		Female		Male		Female	
	Number	Pct. of total	Number	Pct. of total	Number	Pct. of total	Number	Pct. of total
When school is in session (total reporting)	3024	—	2825	—	314	—	998	—
Nothing	65	2.1	31	1.1	7	2.2	16	1.6
Socials, parties, picnics	137	4.5	366	13.0	12	3.8	159	15.9
Recreational, reading, movies	1129	37.3	1633	57.8	140	44.6	620	62.1
Sports, games, hikes, etc	1039	34.4	564	20.0	108	34.4	217	21.7
Work (helping parents)	1025	33.9	1176	41.6	109	34.7	359	36.0
Study, project, club work, etc.	489	16.2	545	19.3	54	17.2	208	20.8
All others	38	1.3	39	1.4	7	2.2	14	1.4
During vacation (total reporting)	2801	—	2589	—	272	—	895	—
Nothing	30	1.1	12	.5	3	1.1	14	1.6
Socials, parties, picnics	186	6.6	692	26.7	16	5.9	284	31.7
Recreational, reading, movies	528	18.8	1020	39.4	68	25.0	425	47.5
Sports, games, hikes	829	29.6	624	24.1	85	31.2	279	31.2
Work (helping parents)	1517	54.2	1291	49.9	175	64.3	425	47.5
Study, project, club work, etc.	186	6.6	369	14.2	19	7.0	115	12.8
All other	73	2.6	150	5.8	9	3.3	82	9.2
Group activities actually participated in (total reporting)	2987	—	2683	—	300	—	925	—
Nothing	111	3.7	151	5.6	11	3.7	50	5.4
Socials, parties, picnics	657	22.0	1382	51.5	52	17.3	451	48.8
Recreational, play, movies	677	22.7	939	35.0	103	34.3	458	49.5
Sports, games, hikes, etc	1187	39.7	898	33.5	189	63.0	426	46.0
Work and school	299	10.0	298	11.1	57	19.0	144	15.6
Club work, project, summer camp	231	7.7	442	16.5	20	6.7	90	9.7
All other	47	1.6	36	1.3	3	1.0	16	1.7

[1] From Extension Service Circular 46, U. S. Dept. Agriculture.

ticipated in, the boys and girls were asked to report the number of visits to town and city for pleasure or business during the year just preceding the date of filling the questionnaire. Practically a third of the farm boys and girls reported less than forty trips to town during the year, presumably trips made in addition to those in connection with school work. About a fifth made 160 or more trips to the city, as did about a fifth of the village boys and girls. Almost half of the village boys and girls reported less than forty trips to town or city during the year. The figures seem to indicate that both farm and village boys and girls get to town or city one to three times during the week on an average.

Also, the boys and girls reported the numbers of parties, picnics and fairs and festivals attended during the year. Roughly, about 60 per cent. of each of the four groups of boys and girls reported attendance at one to six parties and about 80 per cent. of each reported attendance at picnics and at fairs and festivals. Farm and village boys seem to attend about the same number of parties during the year. Similarly, farm girls and village girls each attend about the same number of parties on an average. Both farm and village girls appear to have more parties and to attend more picnics than farm and village boys. Attendance at fairs and festivals appeared to be about the same for farm and village boys and girls.

The figures on "activities participated in" as well as on number of trips to town or city and attendance at parties, picnics and the like are in close accord with the results of a survey study among over 400 farm and village boys and girls of four trade communities of Missouri, 1927.[11] In

[11] University of Missouri Agricultural Experiment Station, "Community Relations of Young People," Research Bul. 110, 1927.

this study attendance at parties, picnics, shows, movies, concerts and lectures; playing games and musical instruments; taking hikes and auto rides, and visiting in other communities and in cities stand near the top of the list of things reported as being done "now"; that is, at the time of the study.

Answers to questions on what the Missouri boys and girls would do if they "had a chance" or what they would like to learn to do were classified under recreational, educational, social, economic and religious. "Recreational" stood highest in the list of classified "activity wishes," with the other classes or types coming next in the order named above. The greatest percentage of recreational "wishes" was expressed by farm boys and the greatest percentage of educational "wishes" was expressed by farm girls. Girls expressed higher percentages of social, economic and religious wishes than boys, and boys expressed a higher percentage of recreational wishes than girls, with little difference for farm and village boys and girls in either case.

This study records the evidence of conflict between age and youth—that is, between the "old" and the "new." In the main, adults appeared to express the most friendly attitude toward the church and the least friendly attitude toward recreation and play for young people. Adversely, the young people expressed the least appreciation for the church and the greatest appreciation for recreation. Further studies are needed to show the detrimental effects of the age and youth conflict on the attainment of satisfactions or values from recreational and other advancement goods. A maximum of satisfactions from goods and facilities available will not be possible until age and youth appreciate and respect each other's "tastes" and capacities for enjoyment.

Summary. The foregoing considerations of advancement goods and facilities represent the attempt to treat as a unit the interests or factors pertaining primarily to the social or spiritual development of the different members of the farm family. It deals with the costs or expenditures of these goods and facilities at the market; that is, at the source where they become available to individual farm families. It ignores the costs expended in the form of public taxes for the provision of goods, not because these are insignificant or unimportant but because they can be handled elsewhere with less confusion to the reader.

Information on both advancement expenditures and activities is somewhat meager, and comparisons are limited owing to dissimilar classifications used by different workers of the items included in the advancement or development group. In view of the wide variety and many uses of the items which compose it, this group of goods and activities is worthy of all possible study which can be directed toward it in the future. Although they comprise only a minor part of the cost of all goods, advancement goods and facilities when used efficiently enhance the satisfactions or values obtained from the more material goods.

Personal goods. Closely akin to advancement goods are goods for personal uses. These goods, which are partly social in nature, include services of the barber and hair dresser, toilet articles, gifts, jewelry, "treats," candy, chewing-gum, sodas, tobacco, pipes, etc.

The average expenditure for goods for personal uses amounted to $41 or 2.6 per cent. of the value of all family living for the 2886 farm families in eleven States. By sections there was considerable variation in the expenditures for this purpose: $50 per family for the New England States, $42 per family for the Southern States and $37 per family for the North Central States. Only 134 of the 2886 families reported no expenditures for personal goods.

The expenditures for personal goods were $48 per family for the 402 Livingston county, New York, families, $19 for the Schoharie county, New York, and southeastern Ohio families, $17 for the 861 white families of Kentucky, Tennessee and Texas and $9 for the 154 colored families of the same localities as the white families.

Owner families spent $45 per family for personal goods, for the 2886 families, in comparison with $33 per family each spent by tenant families and hired-man families. For the 861 white families, expenditures per family for personal goods averaged $17 for owners, $18 for tenants and $12 for croppers. For the 154 colored families, owners appear to have spent less for personal goods than did tenants or croppers. Here the figures were $7 for owners, $12 for tenants and $8 for croppers. Expenditures for personal goods, as a single group, are not available for the 12,096 workingmen's families. Expenditures for some of the separate items are available, however, and these are noted in so far as they are comparable with similar items of expenditure for the farm families.

The average expenditures for the several kinds of personal goods used by the 2886 families in eleven States and by 300 families in southeastern Ohio, a part of the 798 families considered under other groups of goods, appear in *Table 23.*

Gifts comprise the largest part, over one third, of the average expenditure for personal goods among the 2886 families. Expenditures for tobacco, pipes, etc., come next in order with almost $12 per family. Expenditures for this purpose comprise almost half of the costs of personal goods for the 300 Ohio families. Expenditures for toilet articles, barber's fees and the like are somewhat near the same for the two groups of families. Considerable variation exists between the expenditures for the separate kinds of personal goods used by different groups of the 2886 families.

For the 12,096 workingmen's families the costs of toilet articles, barber's fees, etc., amounted to $14 per family. Costs for tobacco were about $16.50 per family.

TABLE 23.   Average value per family of the different kinds of personal goods used during one year, 1922–26.

Personal Goods	2886 FAMILIES OF SELECTED LOCALITIES IN 11 STATES				300 families south-eastern Ohio
	All families all States	317 families New England States	1130 families Southern States	1439 families North Central States	
Total..................	$41.00	$50.90	$37.40	$41.80	$29.20
a. Gifts..............	14.50	19.70	9.40	17.30	3.40
b. Jewelry...........	1.20	3.30	1.30	.80	1.30
c. Toilet articles, etc...	9.40	9.20	8.00	10.70	7.10
d. Candy, sodas, etc...	4.30	5.40	4.10	4.30	3.70
e. Tobacco, pipes, etc..	11.60	13.30	14.60	8.70	13.70

Goods for personal uses, although of less magnitude than most of the other principal groups of goods, are worthy of more consideration than is usually given to them in farm family living studies. These goods, which may properly be regarded as an adjunct to clothing and dress on the one hand and to advancement goods on the other hand, have been ignored in most studies, on the assumption that they represent minor costs which cannot be accounted for. The omission of these, as well as other of the so-called "less important" items, tends to minimize the total cost or value of farm family living.

Summary of costs and uses of goods, facilities and services. Attention has been given in the several preceding chapters to goods, facilities and services constituting the prevailing standard of living among farm families. Available data have been drawn upon in so far as these data were considered applicable to the principal kinds of goods and comparable in connection with different groups of families. Purposely the costs of the goods, facilities and services in the form of publicly administered funds—that is, taxes for roads, maintenance of health, formal schooling and local government—were ignored in this consideration. Tax needs or demands, the so-called tax burdens, are discussed in a succeeding chapter in connection with the sources of goods, facilities and services for the farm family.

CHAPTER XI

FACTORS WHICH CONDITION THE STANDARD OF LIVING

On the basis of the foregoing picturization of goods, facilities and services used by farm families, it is next in order to consider the factors which establish or condition the prevailing standard of living among farmers. With farm people as well as with industrial people the prevailing standard of living has become pretty generally conceived of as being determined by income. Many advocates of better living for farm families hold that if the farmer's income could be increased his prevailing standard of living would rise accordingly. It is doubtless true that increased incomes are reflected in higher prevailing standards of living. This does not mean, however, that increased incomes produce higher standards of living. They may, and they do in many cases, make possible higher prevailing standards of living through the attainment of higher desired standards of living. Briefly, the question with which we are concerned is whether the prevailing standard of living is determined by income or whether the desired standard of living is the dynamic factor which results in more income. Are family living goods, facilities and services desired before the satisfactions or values to be had from them are experienced or anticipated? Generally, are the aims or objectives or ideals of life injected in an abstract manner into the situation with or following the receipt

of income? Rather, is the perception of the needs and the
satisfactions or values growing out of past experience,
associations and relationships not the incentive for increasing the income? Specifically, does one purchase clothing
primarily to dispose of income or to fulfil the physical and
the social needs or desires? Has the automobile, which is
now a part of the prevailing standard of living of most
farm families, been adopted on account of increased income
or has its purchase, whether or not the farm family could
afford it, not been an effective stimulus to income?

The data which are available cannot be made to show
the extent to which the prevailing standard of living is
conditioned by income or the extent to which the desired
standard of living dynamically influences income. They can
be made to throw some light on the different aspects of the
question, however. For convenience in the consideration of
relationships to the prevailing standard of living the data
are grouped on the basis of three sets of factors: (1) those
regarded as influencing the demands or desires of the family
for goods, facilities and services; (2) those involving the
use of time as an aspect of the standard of living, and (3)
those indicative of the family's ability to provide the economic goods of family living. For further convenience the
principal groups of goods, facilities and services are limited
in the consideration or analysis to food, clothing, rent,
advancement and all others. This less detailed classification
will suffice, since the value of all goods and the values of
the principal groups of the more material goods are retained
and since the expenditures for advancement, covering a
wider range of uses than any other group of goods, are
fairly indicative of the cultural development of the family.
The standard of living, then, is measured as in preceding
chapters in terms of the value of goods and in the distribu-

tion of this value among the principal groups of goods, except for the less detailed classification.

Factors regarded as influencing the demands or desires of the family. The factors regarded as influencing the demands or desires of the family are treated in two groups, (a) those indicative of biological growth and development and (b) those pertaining to the cultural advancement of the family.

Factors indicative of biological growth and development of the family. Obviously, the number of persons and the different ages of persons composing the family have direct bearings upon the prevailing standard of living; that is, upon the varieties, amounts and qualities, and consequently upon the value of goods, facilities and services used for living purposes annually. The significance of the number of persons and ages of persons ordinarily is minimized or lost in family living data either from selecting the "standard family" for study or from picturing the average or "cross-section" family as a static unit and not as a process. Every family represents a biological process; a change at practically every period of its life span. Regardless of whether there are children in the family, advancing ages of the wife and husband are indicative of change or process.

Ages of home-maker and operator. The ages of the wife and husband, the home-maker and the operator, are looked upon as having a direct relation to the standard of living of the farm family. The extent of this relation is difficult to determine in view of many counteracting influences, such as providing for children of different ages and supporting other dependents, in some instances.

Results of the study of 2886 farm families of selected localities in eleven States show a fairly close relation be-

tween age of the home-maker and the prevailing standard
of living, *Table 24.* When the families were sorted by the
age of the home-maker into five-year groups extending from
twenty-four years or less up to sixty-five years and over,
the lowest average value of family living goods occurs in
the lowest-age group of home-makers, $1116 per family.
The highest average value of goods used occurs in the forty
to forty-four years of age group of home-makers, $1834
per family, and the next to the lowest average value occurs
in the highest-age group of home-makers, $1285 per family.

The average value of all goods is distributed somewhat
as might be expected among the principal groups of goods.
Except for clothing and advancement, the percentages that
the average values of the principal kinds of goods are of
the value of all goods used remain practically constant or
vary only slightly with advanced age of the home-maker.
The percentage for clothing tends to increase slightly up
to forty-five to forty-nine years of age and again to decrease slightly with the higher-age groups. Similarly the
percentage for advancement goods shows a more pronounced although a less regular trend throughout the different age groups. The higher percentages for clothing and
advancement goods are due in part to the demands of
daughters and sons who are near the maximum of consumption of these goods at this particular period of family
development.

It should be noted that the average size of a family increases from 3.1 persons for the lowest-age group of home-
makers up to 5.3 persons for the forty to forty-four year age
group. From 5.3 persons the average size of family decreases to 2.8 persons for the highest-age group of home-
makers.

Proper allowance should be made in the foregoing fig-

TABLE 24. Relation of age of the home-maker to the value per family of goods used during one year and to distribution of this value among principal groups of goods. Farm families of selected localities in 11 States, 1922–24.[1]

Age of home-maker	Families reporting	Size of family	All goods used	Food		Clothing		Rent		Advancement		All other	
	Number	Persons	Dollars	Dollars	Per cent[2]	Dollars	Per cent[2]	Dollars	Per cent[2]	Dollars	Per cent[2]	Dollars	Per cent[2]
All years	2807	4.4	1601	660	41.2	236	14.8	202	12.6	104	6.5	399	24.9
24 or less	177	3.1	1116	481	43.1	155	13.9	151	13.5	37	3.4	292	26.1
25–29	303	4.2	1322	581	44.0	176	13.3	167	12.6	47	3.6	351	26.5
30–34	402	4.6	1531	658	42.9	211	13.8	187	12.2	64	4.2	411	26.9
35–39	393	5.0	1661	703	42.3	250	15.0	195	11.8	92	5.6	421	25.3
40–44	385	5.3	1834	743	40.5	291	15.9	224	12.2	142	7.7	434	23.7
45–49	365	4.9	1795	709	39.5	294	16.4	210	11.7	157	8.8	425	23.6
50–54	305	4.3	1743	695	39.9	263	15.1	216	12.4	149	8.5	420	24.1
55–59	212	3.8	1671	674	40.3	236	14.1	237	14.2	130	7.8	394	23.6
60–64	143	3.3	1559	617	39.6	218	14.0	221	14.1	106	6.8	397	25.5
65 and over	122	2.8	1285	510	39.7	142	11.0	228	17.8	77	6.4	328	25.1

[1] Adapted from Bul. 1466, U. S. Dept. Agriculture.
[2] Per cent. of total value of all goods used.

ures for families supporting no children. For 249 of the families with no children there appeared to be no difference in the prevailing standard of living of the 119 families with home-makers less than fifty years of age and the 130 with home-makers fifty years of age or more. The 249 families included several with home-makers who were mothers, sisters or daughters of farm operators.

The results of tabulation by ages of the farm operators showed a less significant relation between ages of the operator and size of family, and also between ages of the operator and the prevailing standard of living, than was shown for the home-makers. This is doubtless true generally, since the number of children per family and the ages of these children are usually coördinate with the child-bearing ages of the home-makers.

Number of children per family. Probably the largest part of the rise and decline in the prevailing standard of living of the 2886 families, grouped according to age of the home-maker, is due to variation in the number of children per family. It has been noted that the average size of a family increased from 3.1 persons to 5.3 persons and declined to 2.8 persons with advanced ages of the home-makers by five-year periods from twenty-four or less up to sixty-five years or more.

An indication of the relation of the number of children per family appears in the summary of 1662 records for families with only the immediate members supported from the family purse included, *Table 25*. Since all households having hired helpers, boarders, relatives or others housed or fed at the family table during all or part of the year of study were excluded, these families could be classified readily on the basis of the number of persons supported during the year of study.

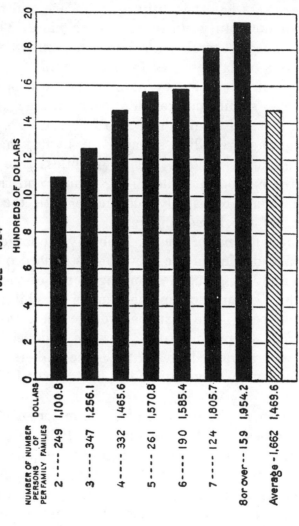

AVERAGE VALUE OF ALL GOODS FURNISHED BY THE FARM AND PURCHASED FOR HOUSEHOLD USE DURING ONE YEAR, BY FAMILIES OF DIFFERENT SIZES

1,662 FARM HOMES OF SELECTED LOCALITIES IN 11 STATES

1922 - 1924

HUNDREDS OF DOLLARS

NUMBER OF PERSONS PER FAMILY	NUMBER OF FAMILIES	DOLLARS
2	249	1,100.8
3	347	1,256.1
4	332	1,465.6
5	261	1,570.8
6	190	1,585.4
7	124	1,805.7
8 or over	159	1,954.2
Average -1,662		1,469.6

Fig. 6.—The average value of all goods used increases at the rate of approximately $140 per additional son or daughter supported per family. Allowance needs to be made for certain irregularities, especially for the six-person or the four-children-per-family group. (*Courtesy of the United States Department of Agriculture.*)

The average value of all goods used by the 1662 families was $1470. This was somewhat lower than the average value of goods used by all families of the study, $1598. The distributions of these values among the different groups of goods were not widely different, however. The percentage of the value of all goods devoted to rent was the same in both instances. The percentages for food and clothing were slightly higher with the 1662 families, whereas the percentages for advancement goods and all other goods were slightly higher with all families.

The proportion of goods furnished by the farm was higher with the 1662 families, 44.1 per cent., in comparison with the 42.8 per cent. furnished by the farm for all families. This higher percentage for the 1662 families may have been due to relatively heavier demands by the families with children for the more essential goods of family living, as food, housing and fuel, the bulk of which are furnished by the farm.

Proceeding to the relation between the number of children supported and the prevailing standard of living, the value of all family living increased from approximately $1100 for families with no children to over $1950 for families with six or more children. Were this increase distributed regularly it would mean an extra cost of slightly more than $140 per child, regardless of age or sex. There are noticeable changes in the distribution of the value of all family living among the different groups of goods with increased numbers of children per family. The proportion that the value of food is of the value of all goods used increases from 39.6 per cent. for families of no children to 47.5 per cent. for families of six or more children. This increase in the percentage for food would be interpreted ordinarily as indicating a lowering in the standard of living.

TABLE 25. Average number of rooms per house, average value of principal groups of goods for families with different numbers of selected localities of 11 States, 1922–24.[1]

Number and ages of children per family	Families studied	Rooms per house	AVERAGE VALUE OF		
			All goods used	Food	
	Number	Persons	Dollars	Dollars	Per cent.[2]
All families...............	1662	6.4	1470	622	42.4
No children...............	249	6.5	1101	436	39.6
1 child...................	347	6.4	1256	499	39.7
0– 5 years............	113	6.1	1108	454	41.0
6–11 years............	64	6.3	1307	506	38.7
12–18 years............	80	6.3	1330	543	40.8
19 or more years........	90	6.9	1340	511	38.2
2 children................	332	6.3	1466	594	40.5
0– 5 years............	90	5.5	1109	525	47.3
6–11 years............	80	6.8	1465	593	40.5
12–18 years............	88	6.5	1596	614	38.5
19 or more years........	74	6.7	1745	655	37.6
3 children................	261	6.5	1571	670	42.6
0–11 years............	127	6.1	1399	618	44.2
12 or more years........	134	6.8	1734	718	41.4
4 children................	190	6.3	1585	721	45.5
0–11 years............	105	6.0	1412	672	47.6
12 or more years........	85	6.6	1800	783	43.5
5 children................	124	6.7	1806	777	43.0
0–11 years............	67	6.8	1576	742	47.1
12 or more years........	57	6.5	2076	818	39.4
6 or more children.........	159	6.6	1954	928	47.5
0–11 years............	85	6.3	1729	876	50.6
12 or more years........	74	6.9	2213	988	44.6

[1] Adapted from Bul. 1466, U. S. Dept. Agriculture.

At the same time the increased value of all goods used indicates a rather gradual raising of the standard of living. The combination of both suggests that, although the total expenditure is greater as the number of children increases,

goods used during one year and distribution of this value among the
of children supported, grouped according to age; 1662 farm families

AVERAGE VALUE OF							
Clothing		Rent		Advancement		All others	
Dollars	Per cent.[2]	Dollars	Per cent.[2]	Dollars	Per cent.[2]	Dollars	Per cent.[2]
221	15.0	184	12.5	90	6.1	353	24.0
122	11.1	195	17.7	58	5.2	290	26.4
166	13.2	194	15.5	67	5.3	330	26.3
139	12.6	164	14.8	46	4.2	305	27.4
175	13.4	193	14.8	61	4.6	372	28.5
194	14.6	186	14.0	88	6.6	319	24.0
169	12.6	242	18.1	78	5.8	340	25.3
215	14.7	184	12.6	97	6.6	376	25.6
137	12.4	124	11.2	35	3.1	288	26.0
204	13.9	207	14.1	63	4.3	398	27.2
257	16.1	206	12.9	120	7.5	399	25.0
273	15.7	206	11.8	181	10.3	430	24.6
254	16.2	187	11.9	98	6.3	362	23.0
207	14.8	162	11.6	56	4.0	356	25.4
299	17.3	211	12.2	139	8.0	367	21.1
255	16.0	164	10.3	92	5.8	353	22.4
211	15.0	151	10.7	48	3.4	330	23.3
308	17.1	180	10.0	145	8.0	384	21.4
300	16.6	172	9.5	147	8.1	410	22.8
235	14.9	160	10.0	73	4.7	366	23.3
376	18.1	187	9.0	233	11.2	462	22.3
349	17.9	170	8.7	120	6.1	387	19.8
276	16.0	148	8.6	72	4.2	357	20.6
433	19.6	195	8.8	174	7.9	423	19.1

[2] Per cent. of total value of all goods used.

it is not sufficiently great to provide as high a standard of
living for the large families as for the small families.

The proportion that the cost of clothing is of the value
of all goods used increases from 11.1 per cent. to 17.9

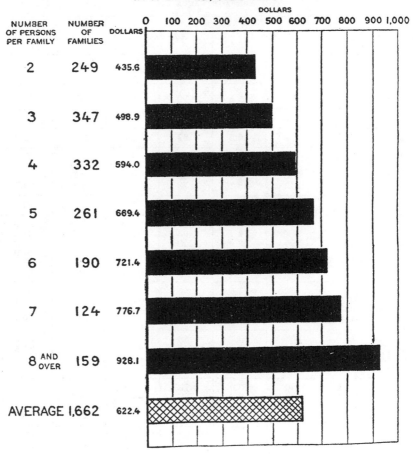

AVERAGE VALUE OF FOOD FURNISHED BY THE FARM
AND PURCHASED FOR HOUSEHOLD USE
DURING ONE YEAR BY FAMILIES OF DIFFERENT SIZES
1,662 FARM HOMES OF SELECTED LOCALITIES
IN 11 STATES, 1922-1924

NUMBER OF PERSONS PER FAMILY	NUMBER OF FAMILIES	DOLLARS
2	249	435.6
3	347	498.9
4	332	594.0
5	261	669.4
6	190	721.4
7	124	776.7
8 AND OVER	159	928.1
AVERAGE	1,662	622.4

FIG. 7.—The average value of food increases at the rate of approximately $80 per additional son or daughter supported per family. Thus, more than half of the increase in the value of all goods used, with increased numbers of children per family, is absorbed in the value of food. (*Courtesy of the United States Department of Agriculture.*)

per cent. The percentages for clothing and food move in the same direction. Apparently clothing used approaches the minimum for all groups represented and so cuts into the expenditures for less essential goods, as does food, with the large families.

The average rental value for use of the house remains practically constant or decreases slightly with increased numbers of children per family. It is of interest also that the average number of rooms per house stays about the same regardless of the number of children per family. The tendency of rent to remain constant while the value of all goods rises with increased numbers of children per family means a decrease in the proportion that rent is of the value of all family living.

Ages of children. The degree of relationship between ages of children and the prevailing standard of living cannot be determined exactly owing to wide variations between the ages of children in families with more than one child. An indication of the existence of some relationship between these two factors occurs in figures for the 1662 families considered above, however.

The 1662 families were classified roughly according to age periods or family living cycles. Age periods for 347 families supporting one child and 332 families supporting two children were taken arbitrarily as 0 to five years, six to eleven years, twelve to eighteen years, and nineteen or more years. Age periods for families of three, four, five and six or more children were placed arbitrarily at 0 to eleven years and twelve or more years. The larger span of years in each of these latter cases was necessary to accommodate families supporting the larger number of children with correspondingly wider ranges of ages, and then not all families could be classified definitely into any one group. A few were placed in those groups within which the average of the ages of all the children fell.

The average value of family living increases noticeably with increased age of children per family. For families supporting one child this increase is less regular than for families supporting two children. For families supporting more children, about the same rate of variation occurs between the average values of goods used in each instance. Relatively these averages for the higher-age groups are between 123 and 131, with the averages for the lower-age groups taken as 100 in each case.

There is evidence of a slight tendency for the percentage of the total value of family living devoted to food to decrease with advancing age groups. On the other hand, the percentages of the total value of goods devoted to clothing and to advancement tend to increase with increased ages of the children. The percentages of the total going for rent and for all other goods tend to vary without regard to ages of the children.

The decrease in the percentage for food and the increases in the percentages for clothing and advancement are indicative of a higher standard of living among the families supporting older children. This, of course, may be due to greater ability to provide by virtue of the contribution of more workers and longer periods of farming.

Summary. Generally an increase in the number of children per family appears to be accompanied by a decline in the prevailing standard of living. On the other hand, an advance in the ages of persons composing the family suggests a rise in the prevailing standard of living until the period of maximum family consumption is reached, somewhere between ages forty to forty-nine years for the home-maker, following which the reverse appears to be true. This rise in the prevailing standard of living undoubtedly accompanies or follows a rise in the desired standard of living due to increased needs or demands growing out of multiplied associations and experiences. It is made possible through an enhanced ability to provide due to increased earning capacities or to the accumulation of funds, with advancing ages of the different members composing the family.

The above considerations bring to the foreground the questions of the ages at which the farmer can afford to marry and the number of children constituting the most desirable size of farm family. Some economists would gage the prevailing standard of living by the things one "insists upon having before undertaking the responsibility of a family." If one insists on having little in the way of house, education, travel and amusement, his prevailing standard of living will be low; if many of these items, it will be high.

There are no data available, and probably none will soon be available, on the extent to which prospective farmers postpone marriage in lieu of a high prevailing standard of living. It is possible that those who are planning to farm look upon the "responsibility of a family" as an asset rather than as a liability. At any rate, science awaits the ascertainment of facts in regard to this matter.

The question of the most desirable or the proper number of children per farm family recently has been stated clearly, although somewhat abruptly, by a rural sociologist, who holds that "perhaps the time has now arrived to teach the farmer, or for the farmer to teach himself, to produce only two children per family where now he is producing four or more." [1] The "quality and opportunity factor" rather than mass production is suggested as a possible solution of the present problem of farm surpluses. Children are held to be the largest farm surplus. Two children per family, it is held, would practically provide the farm free from indebtedness through inheritance, and thus make available for living expenses "at least a major part of the interest which fixed capital earns." Increasing the opportunities of individuals within a given population is regarded as a more rapid means to progress than increasing the number of individuals within the population. Two children per family would not maintain a farm population, however. Doubtless three or more are needed.

It is recognized, of course, that in any given group not all families will have the same number of children. There will be those with none or few and those with many children. The essential point, however, is that the welfare of the children is worthy of more concern than the number of the children born or to be born to the farm family.

Factors pertaining to cultural advancement of the family. Among the factors pertaining to cultural advancement are formal schooling of the different members of the family, other educational and social agencies and organizations, and proximity to church, schools and trading or service centers. Increased amounts of or more favorable situations in regard to these factors are looked upon as stimulating the desires for higher standards of living and therefore as making demands for more kinds, larger amounts and better qualities, and consequently increased values of family living goods, facilities and services.

Formal schooling of operator and home-maker. As with

[1] George H. Von Tungeln, "The Solution—Two Children," "Farm Journal," June, 1927.

ages, the relation of formal schooling to the standard of living is difficult to ascertain in view of the cross-relationships of the many factors involved and especially to the counter-influences of the different amounts of formal schooling obtained by the different persons composing the family.

An attempt was made to account for the counter-influences of the different amounts of schooling of operator and home-maker for the 2886 families in eleven States. Those for which the grades of formal schooling were reported, 2316 in number, were grouped according to grade of schooling of the operator in conjunction with that of the home-maker, and vice versa, as follows:

Both operator and home-maker, eighth grade or less.
Both operator and home-maker, ninth to twelfth grades.
Both operator and home-maker, more than twelve grades.
Operator, eighth grade or less; home-maker, ninth to twelfth grades.
Home-maker, eighth grade or less; operator, ninth to twelfth grades.
Operator, eighth grade or less; home-maker, more than twelve grades.
Home-maker, eighth grade or less; operator, more than twelve grades.
Operator, ninth to twelfth grades; home-maker, more than twelve grades.
Home-maker, ninth to twelfth grades; operator, more than twelve grades.

There appears to be a fairly close relationship between the combined grades of schooling and the prevailing standard of living, especially with the families reporting the same grades for both the operator and home-maker, *Table 26*. The average value of all goods used by families in which both the operator and the home-maker had obtained more than twelve grades of schooling is almost $550 above the average for families in which both the operator and home-maker had obtained not more than eight grades of schooling. The average value of all goods used by the families in which the operator had received from nine to twelve grades of schooling is approximately half-way between these two averages. The percentage that the average value of food is of the total value of all goods used shows a marked decrease with advanced grades or years of schooling. The percentages that the values of clothing and rent are of the total decrease slightly and irregularly. The percentages that the value of advancement goods and all other goods are of the value of all goods used increase regularly, the former significantly and the latter slightly.

Beside substantiating the relationship suggested above, the remaining figures in *Table 26* suggest a heavier bearing of the schooling of the home-maker than of the operator on the prevailing standard of living. In all three instances of alternate cross-classifications the groups of families in which the schooling of the home-makers exceeds that of the operators show somewhat higher average values of all goods used. Because of the small number of families, this indication of a higher prevailing standard of living among families in which the home-makers excel in grades of schooling could not be traced effectively through the distribution of the value of goods among the principal groups of goods.

To pursue further the indication of a probable closer relationship of the schooling of the home-maker than of the operator to the value of goods used, the 2886 families were grouped according to the grade of schooling reported for the home-maker regardless of the grade reported for the operator. The ten groups starting with the fourth grade extended through the twelfth grade to more than twelve

TABLE 26. Relation of combined grades of formal schooling of operator and home-maker to value per family of goods used during one year and to the distribution of this value among the principal groups of goods. Farm families of selected localities in 11 States, 1922-24.[1]

Schooling of operator and home-maker combined	Families reporting (Number)	Size of family (Persons)	All goods used (Dollars)	AVERAGE VALUE OF									
				Food		Clothing		Rent		Advancement		All others	
				Dollars	Per cent.[2]	Dollars	Per cent.[2]	Dollars	Per cent.[2]	Dollars	Per cent.[2]	Dollars	Per cent.[2]
All grades..........	2316	4.4	1600	658	41.1	233	14.6	202	12.7	108	6.7	399	24.9
Both, 8th, or less..........	1303	4.6	1484	645	43.5	218	14.7	188	12.7	86	5.8	347	23.3
Both, 9th–12th..........	317	4.1	1755	692	39.4	251	14.3	217	12.3	123	7.0	472	27.0
Both, more than 12th..........	50	3.9	2032	681	33.5	290	14.3	248	12.2	211	10.4	602	29.6
Operator, 8th or less; home-maker, 9th–12th..........	327	4.1	1647	653	39.6	242	14.7	218	13.3	109	6.6	425	25.8
Home-maker, 8th or less; operator, 9th–12th..........	143	4.2	1636	674	41.2	231	14.1	199	12.2	122	7.5	410	25.0
Operator, 8th or less; home-maker, more than 12th....	46	3.9	1935	687	35.6	275	14.2	270	13.9	167	8.6	536	27.7
Home-maker, 8th or less; operator, more than 12th....	26	4.0	1835	654	35.6	233	12.7	286	15.6	158	8.6	504	27.5
Operator, 9th–12th; home-maker, more than 12th....	39	4.1	2072	682	32.9	313	15.1	212	10.2	272	13.2	593	28.6
Home-maker, 9th–12th; operator, more than 12th....	65	4.1	1904	678	35.6	278	14.6	235	12.3	191	10.1	522	27.4

[1] Adapted from Bul. 1466, U. S. Dept. Agriculture.
[2] Per cent. of total value of all goods used.

grades. Again, the families were grouped according to the grade of schooling reported for the operator regardless of the grade reported for the home-maker.

From this analysis it appears that schooling of the home-maker is more closely related to the prevailing standard of living—in terms of both values of all goods used and the distribution of this value among the principal groups of goods—than is schooling of the operator. The increase in the average value of all family living by similar groups was more pronounced with the families classified by schooling of the home-maker. Also, the decrease in the percentage that the average value of food formed of the average value of all goods, and the increase in the percentages that the values of advancement goods and all other goods formed of the average value of all goods, were more marked with families classified in this way. At the same time, reductions in the average size of family with higher grades of schooling were about the same in both cases, from 4.9 persons to four persons per family.

Further studies are needed to establish the exact relation of formal schooling of the home-maker and the operator to the farmer's standard of living. Counter-influences of the different amounts of schooling of the operator upon farm business resources and consequently on the ability to provide must be accounted for. Many data have been tabulated to prove that education pays the farmer; that is, enables him to make a larger farm or labor income. Results of these tabulations show that advanced formal schooling is usually accompanied by higher returns from farming, on an average. The extent to which education pays the farmer over or above pay for the farmer's education is yet to be determined. The higher schooling of the farmers whom "education paid" may have been due to the fact that parents of these farmers were financially able to school their sons and to give them assistance in starting at farming.

Limited studies suggest a relationship between formal schooling of the children and the standard of living of the farm family. The degree of this relationship and the extent to which of the two factors may be regarded as casual are yet unknown. Also, the influence of "continuing education," reading at home and of social participation in community organizations, agencies and activities on the inclination to increase formal schooling, as well as on the prevailing standard of living, must yet be ascertained.

Proximity to social institutions and agencies. Proximity or nearness to social institutions and agencies, including trading center, school and church, through the facilitation of multiplied contacts, should have a direct bearing on the prevailing standard of living. Ordinarily one would expect nearness to trading center, high school, church and other institutions to be reflected in higher expenditures for family living purposes, except costs for transportation to and from these institutions.

With regard to each of the three institutions or agencies named above records for the 2886 families were sorted, on the basis of miles distant, into ten groups, starting with less than 0.5 mile and continuing with one mile each to 8.5 miles or over. There was no apparent indication of relationship between nearness to the local trading center, the high school or the church and the prevailing standard of living. Also, there was no suggestion of relationship between the distance from local trading center, church or high school and the number of persons per family. It is probable that existing relationships may have been obscured by the many other factors involved.

Figures from a rural school survey of New York State show that in general the nearer the child is to high school the more likely he is to attend school.[2] Figures from different farm management studies indicate that farmers who live near markets have higher labor incomes than those living farther away. If this be true generally, the higher incomes of the farm families living near markets may mean higher prevailing standards of living, provided these markets are as efficient in the sale of family living goods as in the purchase of farm produce.

With the present facilities for transportation and other means of communication, miles are not a satisfactory index of nearness to local or other institutions. Use of the automobile on hard-surfaced roads in many instances is constantly rendering miles a less complete measure of distance. The telephone and the radio are gradually breaking down the barriers to communication and increasing the social contacts of the farm family. The distances from trading center, high school, church and other institutions, as well as other aspects of isolation for the farm family, are worthy of further study, especially if more satisfactory indexes of isolation than miles can be found.

The use of time in relation to the standard of living. "Do you know any farm people who rest?" and "I have a regular rest period" are the two extremes in the replies of farm women to the family living field worker's question, "How much time do you spend resting or relaxing daily?" Occasionally a farm woman reports, "We take a little rest each day and we find it an economical use of time in the long run."

What if any bearing has time spent at rest or at work

[2] G. A. Works, "Economic Aspects of Rural Education, Farm Income and Farm Life," 1927.

daily to the standard of living? What can be said of the leisure time and hours of work of different members of the farm family? How does the work day of farm people compare with the work day of people in other trades or professions?

The hours of leisure activities and adversely the hours of labor per day are regarded by some authorities as a better measure of the farmer's standard of living than the money value of goods used. Under ordinary circumstances the farm family is able to provide many of the essential goods of family living and to control many of its living conditions through a well-regulated use of time. The value of family living furnished by the farm may depend largely upon the hours of labor spent by different members of the family on the farm garden, orchard and lawn. The final decision of whether the farm home is to have running water in the kitchen may involve a valuation of the home-maker's time, as well as the money necessary to provide the machinery to force the water to the kitchen.

The satisfactions or values to be had from family living goods depends upon the leisure time available for their use. Access to more goods, facilities and services may contribute little or nothing to the satisfaction or happiness of the different members of the family if there is not sufficient free time in which to make full use of them.

Length of work day. The average length of work day (excluding Sunday) was found to be 11.4 hours for home-makers and 11.3 hours for operators during the year for the 2886 farm families in selected localities in eleven States. This average was determined in each case from estimates of the time reported for beginning and completing the day's work in summer and in winter. The hours from which the average was obtained start with housework or choring in the morning and end with the completion of household tasks, chores or other work in the evening. Time spent at meals and in reading or other rest during the day was excluded before the average was taken in each instance.

The 11.4 hour work day for home-makers of this group was practically the same as for 10,000 farm women studied by Miss Ward of the United States Department of Agriculture in 1919. The 11.3 hour work day for the operators of the group was considerably more than the averages for small groups of farmers in ten or more States—which ranged from 6.2 hours in Texas to 9.9 hours in Wisconsin.[3] These averages, which were obtained by the farm-accounting method, are not strictly comparable, since they represent a summary of the time spent at different tasks, and some of the less important items may not have been recorded. They do not cover non-physical duties incident to the management of the farm, including the supervision of work done by others than the operator.

The 11.3 hour day for operators indicates longer hours of labor on the farm than in the city. The difference is not so great as it appears to be, however, if the proper amount of time is allowed for the city man to get to and from his work. Also farm work offers change and variety, while city work is pretty much the same during the year. It is probable that farm women put in longer days at housework than do city women, but there are no data available for exact comparisons in regard to the matter.

A study was made of the relation of the length of work day of the home-maker to the prevailing standard of living for the 2886 families. The records were sorted into nine groups, starting with 15.5 hours or more per day and

[3] U. S. Dept. Agriculture, "Working Day of Farmers a High Average," Year Book, pp. 785-86, 1926.

dropping by one hour steps to 8.4 hours or less per day. The average value of all family living goods increased only slightly with a decrease in the length of work day from 15.5 hours or more to 8.4 hours or less per day. This increase was most pronounced in the average values of advancement goods and all other goods. Indication of a more significant relationship was evident in the percentage that the average value of advancement goods formed of the average values of all goods used. Also, the average size of family decreased from 5.1 persons to 3.8 persons, with a reduction in the hours of work per day from 15.5 and over to 8.4 and less. This is indicative of a higher standard of living among the families in which the home-maker works less hours per day, to the extent that the slightly larger amounts of goods available were shared by fewer persons per family on an average.

A similar classification of the records from the standpoint of the operator showed practically no relation between the length of work day and the prevailing standard of living. The average number of persons per family remained almost constant or varied without regard to the average number of hours of work per day of the operator.

Hours of rest per day. For all families for which data were available, an average of 2.7 hours per day, excluding Sunday, for the home-makers and 2.6 hours per day, excluding Sunday, for the operators was spent in resting. This time included minutes or hours spent in rest or relaxation (including reading) during the afternoon, in addition to any time spent in rest or recreation (including reading) between the completion of the day's work and the time of retiring. For the home-maker, both sewing and mending are considered work and are included in the actual work day.

Both home-makers and operators of the Southern States spent more time resting than did those of the New England and the North Central States. The 10,000 home-makers studied by the United States Department of Agriculture, 1919, reported an average of approximately two hours' rest per day.

To ascertain the relation of hours of rest for the home-maker to the prevailing standard of living the records were sorted on the basis of thirty-minute rest periods into ten groups beginning with 0.25 hour and extending up to 4.25 hours or more. The average value of all goods remained almost constant or varied without regard to increase in the time spent per day resting. An irregular increase in the percentage that the value of advancement goods is of the value of all goods suggested a slight relation between the time spent resting and the prevailing standard of living. The average number of persons per family decreased from 5.2 to 4 persons, with an increase in the hours of rest from 0.25 hour to 4.25 and more hours per day. This is suggestive of a higher prevailing standard of living among the families in which time is found for more rest, to the extent that the practically constant amounts of goods were used by less persons per family and thus more goods per person were available in the smaller families.

Time spent in resting by the farm operator appeared to be less closely related to the size of family than did time spent resting by the home-maker.

Vacation from work. Vacation from home or farm work, meaning periods of rest or relaxation of at least a day's duration off the farm, were reported for the majority of the 2886 farm families. Partially, these periods of vacation covered motor or other trips to cities, or to mountain or other summer or winter resorts. Often they were limited to one or two days' camping trips to near-by woods or lakes. Sometimes they meant attendance at county or state fairs, and occasionally they were visits to relatives or friends living in distant localities. They averaged 3.5 days per year for the home-makers and 2.8 days per year for the operators for whom the figures were given. About three fourths of those for whom estimates were obtained had no vacation; and the average for those who had time off the farm was thirteen days for each home-maker and operator. For 1250 of the 10,000 home-makers, referred to above, having vacations the average time off amounted to 11.5 days per year.

To study the relation of days' vacation for the home-maker to the prevailing standard of living the schedules were sorted on the basis of "days away" into six groups: None, one to four, five to nine, ten to fourteen, fifteen to twenty-nine and thirty or more. The average value of all goods rose slightly, although not regularly, as the days of vacation increased from none to thirty and over. At the same time the percentage for advancement goods increased roughly from 6.4 to 11.9 per cent.

There was a decrease in the number of persons per family with increased periods of vacation, indicating the use of more goods per individual among the families taking longer vacations.

Summary. The limited data available suggest only an insignificant relationship between the use of time and the prevailing standard of living of the farm family. Seemingly increased cost or values of family living goods are not accompanied by a corresponding increase in free time for the fullest use of these goods. If this be true, the farm family can well afford to give attention to the time aspect as well as the money aspect of the standard of living.

Whether the farmer has only long days of constant toil, whether the home-maker has a certain amount of time for leisure activities and whether the farm boy or girl has an occasional half-holiday are phases of the standard of living which must be faced squarely if the maximum of satisfactions are to be obtained from the goods, facilities and services available.

Economic ability to provide in relation to the standard of living. The relation between economic ability to provide and the standard of living among farmers is difficult to determine owing to the lack of a suitable index or measure of this ability. In the search for an index for this purpose one naturally turns first to farm income. This is not a satisfactory measure of the family's ability to provide, since it does not include earnings and other forms of income from sources lying outside of the farm business. Family income would be more indicative of the ability to provide if this figure were available. In a recent study of 300 farm families of southeastern Ohio about one fourth of the cash available for family living purposes represented income from other than farm business sources, including work by different members of the family, except the operator, investments and gifts or inheritances.[4]

Neither farm income nor family income, for one year, is a complete measure of the ability to provide, however. Either may be far from the usual or average income, since it represents the returns for only one of the years during which the standard of living prevailing during the year under consideration has been in establishment. A part of the expenditures for goods during one year are often made before the income for that year is available. Funds accu-

[4] U. S. Dept. Agriculture, "Sources and Uses of Income Among 300 Farm Families," Preliminary Report, 1928.

mulated from previous years or anticipated from investments or the use of bank or store credit are not commonly
included in income. Considered from all angles, it is probable that certain other factors such as size of the farm
business, net worth of the farmer, or years since the farmer
began earning may be almost as indicative as is farm or
family income of the liquid assets available for family
living.

Size of farm. Size of the farm is indicative of the ability
of the farm family to provide to the extent that it is
reflected in the returns from farming. It is suggestive to
some degree of the net worth of the family, also considered
later as an index of the ability to provide.

Size of farm is most generally reckoned in terms of acres
operated per farm. The acre is not always a complete
measure of size of business, since it fails to account for
the intensity of farm operations. It is, however, the standard unit of land measurement, and acreage data are easily
obtained when other data which might be more indicative
of size of business are not available.

The acres operated per farm were obtained for almost
two thirds of the 2886 families of selected localities in
eleven States. To ascertain the relation of acres operated
per farm to the prevailing standard of living, the records for
which acres were reported were sorted into ten groups
starting with less than twenty-five acres and continuing by
fifty-acre groups up to 275 to 324 acres, and again by
100-acre groups to 525 acres or more.

The value of all goods used per family increased from
$1347 for families on farms of less than twenty-five acres
to $3086 for families on farms of 525 acres or more. The
percentage of the total value of goods going for food showed
a marked irregular decrease with increased size of farm

operated. The percentages devoted to advancement and to all other purposes showed fairly pronounced, irregular increases. The percentage for clothing showed a slight tendency to decrease, and the percentage for rent showed a slight tendency to increase with increased size of farm.

The larger farms apparently furnish more food, fuel and house rent value somewhat in proportion to the increased acreage and to the increased value of goods purchased per family.

The average number of persons per family remained almost constant as the average value of all goods rose with increased acreage per farm. From the standpoint of the individual, this favors a still higher standard of living among families on the larger farms.

Net worth of the farmer. Data from which the net worth of the farmer could be calculated were not obtained from the 2886 families. For the 861 white farm families of selected localities of Kentucky, Tennessee and Texas, 1919, net worth of the farmer appeared to have a more significant bearing than acres per farm on the prevailing standard of living.[5] This was expected, since net worth indicated the total value of all the unencumbered wealth of the family at the time of study, and acres per farm even when owned by the operator may have been held partially under mortgage. Net worth is largely the result of saving which usually has for its ultimate goal a higher standard of living properly balanced over life's span. Normally man's desires for goods are so multifarious that when he is supplied with accumulated purchasing power he is inclined to convert it into satisfactions contributing to his standard of living. It must be recognized, however, that man's wants

---

[5] U. S. Dept. Agriculture, "Relation Between the Ability to Pay and the Standard of Living," Bul. 1382, 1926.

for goods contributing directly to the family living are constantly being balanced against increased agencies of production—that is, more working capital, more land and the use of more labor. Sometimes the farmer's most intensive wants are along the line of greater production—larger business—at the expense of family living.

Years since the farmer began earning. Years since the farmer began earning—that is, the years he had spent at all occupations since having been employed without pay on his father's farm or elsewhere—appeared to be less closely related than net worth to the prevailing standard of living for the 861 families referred to above. When the records were sorted on the number of years the farmer had been earning, by five-year groups, beginning with five years or less and extending to fifty years or more, the average value of family living rose from $1059 for the lowest group to $1801 for the twenty-six to thirty year group and fell to $900 for the highest group. At the same time the size of family rose from 3.1 persons for the lowest group to 5.5 persons for the twenty-six to thirty year group and fell to 3.4 persons for the highest group. Thus the variation in the prevailing standard of living appeared to be accompanied by a corresponding variation in the size of the family.

The less significant relationship between years since the farmer began earning and the prevailing standard of living, than between net worth and the prevailing standard of living, is what one would expect, since the total amount of wealth available is of more significance than the time required for its accumulation. Ordinarily, one's earning life is characterized by a gradually rising accumulative ability until somewhere near the age of fifty. Allowances must be made for additional demands upon accumulative funds for the family living, due to more persons per family in many instances. But these demands may be met in some instances by the contributions made by the sons and daughters to the family living fund.

Number of years the farmer has been a farm owner. The number of years the farmer had been a farm owner at the time of study was tested for its relationship to the prevailing standard of living, for about 800 owner families of the 2886 families in eleven States. Records for these families were classified on the basis of years of ownership into ten groups, starting with less than 2.5 years and continuing by five-year periods to 42.5 years or over.

The average value of all goods used increased from $1298 for less than 2.5 years of ownership to $2061 for 27.5 to 32.4 years of ownership, after which it decreased to $1557 for 42.5 years or more of ownership. The percentage that the value of food is of the value of all goods increased and decreased inversely. The percentages that the values of clothing and advancement goods are of the value of all goods varied slightly in the same direction as the value of all goods. The percentages that the values of rent and of all other goods are of the value of all goods tended to vary without regard to years of ownership.

The average size of family varied in accordance with the average value of all goods used, the largest families (5.3 persons each) being supported during the 17.5 to 22.4 period of ownership.

These results are suggestive of a close correlation between the number of years the operator has been an owner, the age of the farm operator, the number of children per family and the standard of living. This is to be expected, since the earning power and the accumulative ability of the farmer is usually on the upward trend until somewhere

near the age of fifty. Similarly, the number of children and
the age of children per family are usually on the increase
until somewhere near the same age period of the operator,
at about which time the children begin to shift for themselves. Thus, the demands for goods of family living decline
with further increased ages and correspondingly longer
periods of ownership of the operator.

Income from other than farm business sources. Income
from other than farm business sources is often the means
of raising the standard of living through making available
desired and needed articles of clothing, furniture, musical
instruments, formal schooling or other goods of family
living. Sources of this additional income include especially
prepared home-canned or preserved products, articles of
fancy work, boarding and lodging of school-teachers or
others, teaching or other work performed by different members of the family, gifts and returns from investments.

Over two fifths of the 2886 families reported on the receipt of income from other than farm business sources.
These were classified according to the amount of this
income into eight groups. The average value of all goods
used rose somewhat irregularly from $1443 per family for
284 families having no other income to $3229 per family
for seventeen families having $2400 and more other income.
The percentage that food is of the value of all goods decreased slightly with increased additional income. The
percentage that the value of advancement goods is of the
value of all goods rose noticeably but very irregularly, and
the percentages that the values of other groups of goods
are of the value of all goods remained practically constant
with increased additional income. Allowance should be
made for a somewhat irregular increase in the size of
family, for additional persons per family sharing the use

of the larger values of goods means a less pronounced rise in the value of goods used per person than per family.

The findings cannot be accepted as absolute or final in regard to income from other than farm business sources. The additional incomes dealt with represent only a part, in many instances a minor part, of the total income available. The findings, however, are suggestive of further studies dealing with the entire available income of farm families.

Summary. From the foregoing considerations it appears that the use of time has less significant bearing than either the desires and demands coincident with the development of the family or than the ability to provide upon the prevailing standard of living. Desires and demands of the family seem to bear about the same relations to the standard of living as does ability to provide, if the factors selected and the measures used are equally indicative in both instances. This does not mean that the prevailing standard of living keeps pace with the multiplicity of new desires and demands developed through growth and through education—that is, through formal schooling, social participation and experience. Nor does it mean that greater ability to provide results automatically in higher standards of living. Undoubtedly the development of new desires and the growth of new demands and the ability to provide are dependent on each other. One is a "stimulus for and a condition of development of the other."

The prevailing standard of living, then, may be regarded as the resultant of the interaction between the life span or life cycle of the family, with its attendant growth and development of needs and desires, and the economic means of the present in relation to the economic efficiency of the

future. The satisfactions or values of life accruing from
the prevailing standard of living depend upon the efficient
use of time as well as the efficient use of goods by the
different persons composing the family. Both the prevailing standard of living and the satisfactions or values of
life for any group of families are as widely variable as are
the families composing the group. These variations or
differences which are not conveyed statistically are clearly
evident in the following characterizations taken from notes
kept by farm family living field agents and in the achievement records of two farm families as described by a former
county superintendent of schools.

"Two families visited to-day were especially interesting.
They were on about the same economic level and had the
same number of children. Both inherited their farms, married sisters and started out on adjoining farms. One home
was poorly kept, disorderly and uninviting. The other was
a splendid, well-kept, cozy place with a home atmosphere.
There was no difference in the size of the houses. The former home had twenty books and no musical instruments,
the children were dirty, cursed fluently and could talk only
of hunting. The oldest daughter was just back from the
city, where she had been a housekeeper. She had learned
quite a bit of cute slang. Her father was a chronic grouch,
seemingly disgusted with himself, and the mother appeared
to have given up all ambition if she had ever had any.
The latter home had a library of one hundred books and
a piano, and the children had a wholesome outlook on life.
They were in high school, interested in music and talked
of the books and magazines they had read. Their parents,
interested in good roads, schools and churches, were bearing
their share of the community's responsibilities."

"I walked a mile and a half down the hill to a little red house on one side of the road and two old patched-up barns on the other. One of the barns was over a ditch through which water flowed during a rain. Below this barn in the ditch by the road was a mud-hole fed by a spring from the hillside. In the mud-hole were eight ducks and three children, the oldest about seven years of age. The mud-hole was about thirty feet from the house and in full view from the front door. The porch was literally covered with mud and manure. The yard was strewn with everything. The children ran for the house when they sighted me. The youngest, failing to make the porch with the others, began to cry. This brought the mother to the door. She was a slim woman of about thirty summers. She seemed a bit frightened at first, but soon we were discussing the weather and the cozy home site in the side of the hill. She brought two chairs and asked me to sit. The small child, fresh from the mud-hole, crawled up into his mother's lap with all the mud and dirt that could cling to him. The schedule was finished at 11:30 and I was invited to stay for dinner.

"Presumably Mr. —— came in, a red-haired, broad-shouldered, husky farmer. We fed the horses and went in to dinner. The children had a bench at the end of the table. The father looked them over and decided that Theodore should go wash under his nose. Theodore after some argument obeyed in form only. There was no table-cloth on the table and the dishes were well worn and abused. But the table was well loaded with food; chicken in two dishes, ham, beef, potatoes, cabbage, lettuce and watermelon. There were two other guests, but the food was sufficient for half a dozen more. It was well cooked but poorly served.

"This family spent, in addition to table and household

operating expenses during the year, $50 for furnishings and equipment, $35 for a radio and $15 for reading materials, including a subscription to the 'Literary Digest.' They had fifty books in the home library. The husband and wife were both high-school graduates and the husband had taught five years in the rural schools. The teacher in the home school the past year 'didn't have any sense' and 'they ought to have better schools for taxes they paid.'"

"The next farmstead although located in an out-of-the-way spot occupied a beautiful site at the foot of the hill. A set of well-painted and well-kept buildings graced the setting which nature had provided. The lawn was planted as attractively as if a landscape architect had planned it. The house was not so large, but it was substantially built.

"I went to the front door and asked to stay for the night. The wife was not sure, but would ask her husband. I agreed to take chances with the husband and started for the barn. Soon he was adjusting himself to the new-comer, who discussed the merits of the milking-machine. Two little girls, eight and six, dressed in rompers, helped with cleaning the pails, which task along with the operation of the milk-ing-machine was in charge of an intelligent appearing brother about fourteen. Chores over, we went in to supper, a good meal; ham, eggs, potatoes, hot rolls, apple jelly, etc., served on a clean white table-cloth under a group of electric lights. When the meal was over, we visited until 11:30. All remained awake and we played games, told stories and talked about the vital problems they were grappling with, that of schools. They live so far from schools that the little girls can't go alone and the boy is going to high school next year. He is interested in bees and wants to come home at nights from high school to help with the chores. The girls could locate their home and others for five miles down the road on the map which I had with me. They told many interesting stories and recited short sayings. Both parents had only high-school education. But there is no question about their standard of living. It was reflected in unmistakable ways other than an attractive home, modern equipment, a good table and expenditures. It seemed to be a part of the folk, a well-rooted, never-failing, source of human culture."

Achievement Record. "Mr. A. and Mr. X. were both farmers living in the Willow Grove school community. Although not adjoining, the two farms were similar. Both contained 160 acres of tillable land of about the same topography and the same degree of fertility.

"At the time of my visit Mr. A. had been owner and operator of his farm for six years, during which time he had made minor improvements about the farmstead. The farm-house of some forty years had been repainted and substantial fences had been placed around the farm orchard and garden.

" 'We bought the place for a home,' said Mr. A., 'and we came over here from White Oak to be near a good school and a live church and to get into a better community. We had to get the children nearer to school. We have five and the third will start to school this fall. They must have the school, they need the church and they will enjoy the social life of the community.'

" 'This makes a satisfactory home for your family, then?' I inquired.

" 'Just now it does,' replied Mrs. A. 'but we'll need to improve it and fix it up as we go along. The children will need more room and better things in the house as they get older. We came here with the hope of being able to enjoy a comfortable farm home, school the children and share the social, religious and civic life of the community. In the six years we have the farm partially paid for. Presently, we will be able to give more attention to the children.'

" 'You'll soon need some more land,' I remarked, 'with the five children, four of them boys, coming on.'

" 'That will be for the children to help decide when they are older,' remarked Mrs. A. 'If in the future they prefer more land to farm instead of better home life and an education, then they may get it, but that is a good ways off. Now we have land enough to keep us all busy, and yet we find time for some leisure and recreation as we go along.'

"Calling on family X. several days after visiting family A., I learned that Mr. X. had owned and operated his farm of 160 acres for ten years, during which time he had tiled out each field, built new barns and rebuilt the farm-house. Both barns and house were modern for the period represented, about a generation ago. 'I came over here from Aspen to own a good farm, and folks will tell you I've got it,' said Mr. X. 'None better in the county, I guess.'

" 'Do you find good schools and things of that sort here?' I asked.

" 'The schools ought to be good, considerin' the taxes I pay. I don't plan to put 'em through school, anyway. The boys have more schoolin' now than I ever got, and if they want any more they'll get it of their own accord without my help. She [referring to his wife] plans to put the girl through school and send her on to college; but that's their affair.'

" 'But isn't it probable that in the future men will need more schooling to get on as well as you have?' I asked.

" 'Depends on the men and what they go into,' replied Mr. X. 'I'm fitting 'em out for farmers and it's no use to waste time and money on schoolin'.'

" 'And your church,' I reminded; 'you find a church of your liking here, I suppose?'

" 'Well, we still go over to Aspen when the weather and the roads are fit. When the weather's bad they [the children] go up here. I don't know much about their church up here, but at any rate it's only Sunday school.'

"Careful study from all angles for the decade following the time of these two visits revealed to me clearly the quality of life prevailing in each of the two homes. In home A. the farmer and his wife were happily engaged in sharing life, work, play, worship and ideals with their children. I knew Mr. A. to spend hours reasoning with his boys as to the best adjustment of cultivators, the handiest way of breaking colts or the most suitable plan of crop rotation. At the request of Mr. A. and Mrs. A., I spent many an evening at their home discussing different lines of work and relating my college experiences as best I could, in order that the children might develop a genuine desire for a college education.

" 'We want the children to know something of the outside world and of life,' was the common expression of either Mr. or Mrs. A. 'Then if they want to farm, they ought to make good farmers and better citizens of the communities in which they live.'

"In home X., Mr. and Mrs. X. seldom shared the work or play or discussed the ideals or the objectives of family life with their children. Here things went on with regularity; time to get up, time to chore and time to get to the field. Mr. X.'s farm hands, including the boys, were first in the community to get out in the mornings and the first to pull in evenings. But the longer evenings after supper were usually spent in 'prolonged choring,' looking after fences, cutting weeds from the pasture, working in the garden, greasing the wagons and storing the machinery. So far as I know, family X. never spent an evening playing games, singing or telling stories together. Quite true, the piano was played and books and papers were often read, but free and wholesome family fellowship was lacking.

"While Mr. and Mrs. A. enlarged, remodeled and refurnished their house to maintain a satisfactory home life, Mr. X. bought two additional farms, one of them in Canada, because he considered them good investments.

"Several years ago I took occasion to trace the children of these two families. Of the four sons of Family A., three had attended and graduated from the state agricultural college. The fourth was at that time attending a secular college and had made a splendid record in music. The daughter spent two years at this same college before marrying a farm boy in the home community. Of the three boys who attended the state agricultural college, two are farming (one on the home farm) in the home community and the other is a graduate student in agriculture. The two sons and the daughter living on farms are all leaders in the civic and social life of the community.

"Of the two sons of family X., neither finished high school. One became a garage mechanic, and the other after taking a business course became a clerk in a village bank. The daughter while attempting to work her way through college stopped to teach school and at the end of her first year's teaching became the wife of a village restaurant-keeper."

CHAPTER XII

ACCESSIBILITY OF GOODS, FACILITIES AND SERVICES TO FARM FAMILIES

DURING the past year the energies of the American Country Life Association have been directed toward the development of a national conference program on "urban-rural relations." The present "set-up" of the program proposes the presentation and discussion of five major questions: Are there fundamental differences between urbanism and ruralism? Should major social institutions center in town or open country? Is the farm family being destroyed by town influences? Are business interests of city and country inevitably opposed? and Must a community include both urban and rural? The score or more of sub-questions outlined as stimuli for interest in the program give no indication of attention to the major issue involved in the situation—namely, "How can 5,000,000 farm families attain a prevailing standard of living of which America need not be ashamed when adequate sources of the goods, facilities and services constituting this living are lacking?"

The economic goods of modern living are strikingly inaccessible to the farm family. Approximately 20,000,000 of over 28,000,000 farm people live more than five miles from cities or towns of more than 2500 population. And what can be said of the opportunities for obtaining modern goods, facilities and services in trading places or service centers of less than 2500 inhabitants, of which there are 39,000 all told?

For the most part these 39,000 small towns, villages and hamlets are providing in a way the goods, facilities and services demanded by the 20,000,000 families residing outside the five-mile radii of larger towns and cities.[1] Only a third of them are incorporated villages or towns, ranging in size from 100 to 2500 population. The remainder, 26,000, are smaller incorporated places ranging from a country store to a village of 300 people, "having two or three general stores, a church or two and a graded school."

One who is accustomed to the privilege of "shopping" with the other 8,000,000 farm people and all the urban people in centers of more than 2500 population needs only a limited experience in the smaller towns, hamlets and country stores to be convinced that a continuance of the practice is not for the best interests of his standard of living. He is soon impressed with the fact that "the best goods of all kinds, from clothing to pianos; the best doctors, hospitals, clinics; the best schools, churches and libraries; the best commercial amusements; the counselors at law, the experts in architecture, music, religion, education—all these tend to leave" the smaller places and flow to the larger centers where there are people enough to demand their wares and services.

The present layout of trading centers or service towns is incapable of meeting the modern needs and wants of the farmer. The volume of business for each is too small. The stocks of merchantable goods are too limited. The maintenance of adequate social institutions and organizations is too difficult, if at all possible.

[1] U. S. Dept. Agriculture, "An Income Spending Farm Program," Press Release, 1928.

There are authorities who hold that the situation in regard to the farmer's opportunities for purchasing goods and facilities is improving. Certain forces affecting rural communities are tending to destroy the long-established, conservative centers. Modern methods of travel and other means of communication are enabling the farmer to trade in the larger towns or the cities. City ideas of selling goods and services are permeating the open country. "Rural communities are becoming more urban; some are becoming satellites of cities," according to these authorities.

Also, "smaller communities are pooling their energies and resources to provide professional services, rural organizations are enlarging and rural churches are amalgamating," all of which are granted here. But attention needs to be called to a corresponding if not a more pronounced improvement in the purchasing opportunities for the people who patronize the urban centers. While satisfactory criteria for measuring the progress in each instance are not available, it is possible that the rate of improvement in the urban districts far outstrips that of the country districts, and that on the whole farm families continue to be the victims of an ineffective, non-modern and antiquated system of procuring goods, facilities and services in exchange for incomes.

The final result of the farmer's having to lag behind in the procurement of goods, facilities and services is inevitable. He will accept poorer qualities of many goods unless he chooses to go without altogether; either of which will lower his standard of living. Or perchance he will become "urbanized"—quit farming and go to the city in order to turn his income to the attainment of his desired standard of living.

This is what many farmers appear to be doing. The past

seven years have shown an average net loss of 400,000 farm people annually. A limited study of several thousand families of these 400,000 people showed that a third of them were in search of more income.[2] This was to be expected in an agricultural depression like that experienced during the seven-year period. It is much more significant that 14 per cent. of the families studied were in search of opportunities for spending their income, during a period of depression, effectively; that is, of exchanging it for goods, facilities and services of family living not accessible in the country.

There are no data on the extent to which the lack of available goods, facilities and services of quality lowers or depresses the standard of living generally among farmers. Limited information on some of the different aspects of the situation are of interest and this is presented to best advantage along with a brief consideration of the different principal groups of family living goods, facilities and services.

Food. "We have it whenever we can get it," is the usual response from farm women to the field agents' question, "How often do you buy fresh beef during the summer months?" Frequently this reply is elaborated upon with some such explanation as, "We drive over to 'Trading Post' to get meat for the threshers and the silo fillers, but the last we got over there was hardly usable."

The one consoling thought in respect to this matter is that the farm family purchases very little fresh meat, probably not more than fifty pounds of beef and several pounds of other meats, including veal, mutton and fish, per year, on an average. A considerable part of the beef is accounted

[2] U. S. Dept. Agriculture, "Analysis of Migration of Population to and from Farms," Preliminary Report, 1927.

for in the "quarters" purchased from neighboring farmers during the winter months.

It is fully as difficult for the farm family to obtain many of the fresh fruits and vegetables as it is to obtain good meats, especially when these are out of season in the immediate locality. This does not imply that the farm family needs to purchase out-of-season fruits and vegetables regularly, for proper foresight and attention will usually provide a satisfactory supply for ordinary usage. There are times, however, when certain kinds of fruits or vegetables are desired for "special events" or for an occasional change in the family diet.

Some one may question the worth-whileness of discussing the opportunity of the farm family to purchase foods, since approximately one half to two thirds of the average diet—in terms of value—is furnished by the farm. The remainder, amounting to $200 or more per family on an average, is sufficient to merit consideration, however. Among the more important items which it represents are sugar, flour and other cereals, coffee, citrus fruits, dried fruits, canned goods and other groceries.

For these staples and other groceries farm families tend to patronize the larger local trading centers so long as distance is not a limiting factor. With increased distance from larger trading centers patronage appears to go to the smaller towns, the hamlets or the country stores. A survey of 165 farm families of Pickaway county, Ohio, 1925, showed that 44 per cent. of the groceries used by these families were purchased in the largest trading center involved—Circleville, with about 7000 inhabitants.[3] The

[3] Ohio State University Bureau of Business Research, "The Social and Economic Relations of the Farmers with the Towns in Pickaway County, Ohio," Monograph 9, 1927.

other 56 per cent. were purchased in more than a dozen smaller trading centers, ranging in size from 1000 population down to the country store. The families buying in Circleville were seven miles out (distant from trading center), those buying at the next largest center were 4.5 miles out and those buying at the country stores were 1.3 miles out. Families living within a radius of five miles of Circleville reported the purchase of 86 per cent. of their groceries there, those living between the radii of five and ten miles 57 per cent. and those living beyond a radius of ten miles only 7 per cent. The study concludes that "beyond ten miles one could almost say Circleville held little interest as a grocery trading center."

In a study of the service relations of town and country in three counties of Wisconsin, 1923, approximately 800 farm families gave reasons for buying groceries at trading centers of different sizes. Generally the larger towns—those catering to the most people within the town and surrounding trade area—were favored with the reason "best goods." Country stores were favored with the reasons "nearest" and "most convenient." [4]

The summary of the replies from 325 farm families along certain rural postal routes, New York State, 1927, showed that 50 per cent. of these families purchase staples and other groceries, including flour, sugar, cured and fresh meats, breakfast cereals and citrus fruits, in villages under 2000 population. About 40 per cent. purchase these articles in towns of 2000 to 4999 and 10 per cent. purchase them in cities of 5000 or more population. Mail-order goods are not included in the summarization of the data.[5]

[4] University of Wisconsin Agricultural Experiment Station, "Service Relations of Town and Country," Research Bul. 58, 1923.
[5] Cornell University, "Farm Economics," March, 1928.

Further studies are needed as bases of adjustment and adaptation of the grocery supply to the needs and desires of the farm family. Until these studies are made, grocery "interests" attempting to serve the farmer will do well to keep in mind that the farm family will travel a reasonable distance to obtain "quality" goods at standard prices. At the same time the farmer will do well to press his demands for "quality" goods as one of the chief assurances of adequacy in the family diet. He will find the other chief assurance in increased attention to the provision and use of a wider variety of "quality" food products, garden produce especially, from the farm.

Clothing. Recently a farm family living field worker, a junior in college, went into the principal clothing store in a town of 5000 population, around which he was working, to buy a suit of clothes. After having been shown several samples which failed to please, he questioned the clerk, who happened to be the proprietor, as to when he expected his new goods to arrive. "Oh, they are here already," he was informed. "Now where are you from? I had you sized up as a farmer. These left-over suits are just as good; a little bit out of style, but that never matters for farmers."

While this practice is not held to be general, it may be prevalent enough to account in part for the tendency of farm families to purchase clothing in the larger centers. Better prices, better salesmanship and more effective advertising may be other factors.

More than half of the $33,000 worth of clothing purchased by 135 of the Pickaway county, Ohio, families referred to above was obtained in Circleville. More than 20 per cent., $7000 worth, was purchased in Columbus, twenty miles farther away, on an average, and almost 8 per cent. was purchased from mail-order houses. Families going to Columbus "went for better quality and greater variety from which to choose." Even Circleville, with at least fifteen stores handling clothing and dry-goods, was far from satisfying the farmer's purchasing needs, according to their statements, concludes the study.

Chief among the reasons given by those of 800 Wisconsin families that purchased clothing in the larger centers were "better variety and more selection" and "best goods." The principal reason given by those ordering from mail-order houses was "best price." Curiously enough, "best goods" led in the reasons given by the families purchasing clothing (work clothes primarily, no doubt) at the country stores. "Convenience" came next and "best price" last among the other specified reasons given by these families.

"The larger cities, from 10,000 to 600,000, receive the trade of the largest percentage of families for hats, coats, dresses and suits for all members of the family; underwear for the women, girls and younger children, shoes for the women, stockings for the girls and younger children [and] dress goods, . . ." according to the questionnaire study of 325 New York State families. "A very small percentage of the families bought these articles in villages under 2000 inhabitants." [6]

Village and open country stores will probably continue to be fairly satisfactory distributers of work clothes— shoes, overalls, jackets, shirts and the like—for the farm family for some time to come. Larger town and city stores must be resorted to, however, for the farmer's "better clothing," including overcoats, suits, hats, etc., for men and boys, and coats, ready-to-wear garments, hats and dress materials for women and girls.

[6] Cornell University, *op. cit.*, March, 1928.

Housing and household furnishings. A quarter of a century ago a certain agricultural village was noted for its "crew" of four first-class carpenters, who were recognized as builders of efficient farm-houses. Farmers within a radius of thirty miles from the village who desired to build sent for these workmen. Usually they were asked to plan the house, specify the needs, estimate the costs, order the materials and construct and "finish" the building. On the whole, their work was entirely satisfactory and the houses which they built met the needs of the farm family. At the present time, however, these men are not building farm-houses. Three have gone to the city, at better wages than the farmers could pay, one to supervise the building of apartments, another to do interior finishing, and the third to do expert drafting in a wood-work factory. The fourth has grown old in an unsuccessful attempt to fill the ranks of his crew with other workmen.

Lack of planners and scarcity of workmen who appreciate the farm family's needs in regard to housing and home equipment are contributing materially to the retarded progress in farm home improvement. Few landscape architects and builders capable of interpreting rural housing problems, capable of understanding and appreciating the satisfactions arising from a proper and artistic setting and planning of the farmstead as a whole and capable of planning houses of the best architectural designs with the most conveninent arrangement for living purposes are as yet catering to farm people. On the other hand, farm people are not requesting or demanding these goods or services.

The matter of furnishing the farm home presents a problem, ordinarily, owing to inconvenience of the family to a satisfactory furniture supply. Referring again to the Pickaway county, Ohio, study, almost half of the $4400 worth of furniture purchased by the fifty families purchasing was obtained in Circleville at an average of six miles distant. Over $500 worth was purchased in Columbus, at a distance of thirty-three miles, over $700 worth was purchased in other towns outside the county at a distance of twenty-nine miles, and over $1100 worth was obtained by mail order. Families living within a five-mile radius of Circleville bought 96 per cent. of their furniture there, those living between five-mile and ten-mile radii 55 per cent., and those living outside a ten-mile radius only 6 per cent. For the 325 New York State families furnishings were bought at an average distance of ten or eleven miles.

Transportation. The high percentage of farmers owning cars suggests that satisfactory automobile facilities and services are within the reach of the farm family. This may be the case so far as new cars are concerned if the farm family as a prospective buyer of a car is able to proceed sanely and satisfactorily amid a "bewilderment" of prices, makes or styles, engines, parts and accessories adapted to farm purposes. Probably few prospective buyers of cars are advised by local distributers of the average lifetime of a car or of the probable amounts of gasoline, oil, tires and accessories which it will use during its average lifetime.

If one may judge from the prevalence of filling stations and accessory shops along national, state and county highways the farm family should have ample opportunity to purchase the gasoline, oil and repairs needed for the car. It is probable also that quality of the workmanship which he obtains is equal to that given to passing tourists. The majority of farmers living off the main highways are much less favorably situated with regard to these facilities and services, however. Furthermore, the condition of unimproved roads cuts off the accessibility of these facilities and services and makes the use of the car impossible to many farm families during parts of the year: winter and spring months, especially.

Few farm families have access to insurance-rates and other services provided by the motor associations to urban families.

Condition of the roads over which it is used is one of the important factors determining the lifetime and the cost of up-keep of the car. The value of good roads to the car is likely to be underestimated, since roads are "tax-obtained" goods or facilities. There are farm families using cars who seem to think that satisfactory roads on which to use them can be provided and maintained at about the same costs as formerly when horse-drawn vehicles and even ox-carts were the prevailing methods of travel. The matter of roads demands as much consideration nowadays as the matter of a car.

Health maintenance. "Large and populous rural areas ready, willing and able to support a physician but unable to induce a physician to locate in them, and compelled to rely for medical attention on the uncertain services of practitioners perhaps twenty miles distant; this is the picture which has been drawn with increasing frequency in the past few years wherever physicians or public health workers gather. . . . Always and everywhere, the people of the towns have among them a substantially greater number of physicians than has an equal rural population." [7]

Approximately 63 per cent. of our physicians, located in cities and towns of 5000 or more inhabitants, are serving a little less than half of our total population. The remaining 37 per cent. of the physicians, in the towns, villages or ham-

---

[7] Mayers and Harrison, "The Distribution of Physicians in the United States," General Education Board, 1924.

lets of less than 5000 inhabitants, are serving in a way more than half of our total population.[8] To the farm family, their services are rendered less accessible and more costly owing to distances to be traveled, bad roads and poor communicative facilities.

Distance to be traveled adds materially to the cost of the physician's call in the open country. The study of rural health facilities of Ross county, Ohio, 1926, showed the most common fee for visits to the farm home to be $1.50 minimum plus a surcharge of $1 per mile among rural doctors and $2 minimum plus a surcharge of $1 per mile among urban doctors.[9] In the three areas included in a survey of sickness in Cortland county, New York, 1924, the maximum fees reported were $4.25, $5 and $6 per call for distances of nine miles, seven miles and ten miles traveled respectively. This study concludes that, considering the distance traveled, the physician's charges are reasonable, but it also holds that for those farms over five miles distant from a physician the cost is so great as to deter his employment except when absolutely necessary. Only one of the three areas included in the study had a resident physician, and the practice in one of the remaining areas was held insufficient to furnish an adequate living to a resident physician.

Hospital facilities and public health supervision are notoriously inaccessible to the farm family. In 1910 the general hospital, taken for granted for city people, was unknown as a rural institution. While since then hospitals have been established and maintained in some rural communities, on tax-provided funds in a few instances, farm families generally are outside the reach of hospital facilities.

[8] Hugh S. Cummings, "Country Gentleman," November 22, 1924.
[9] Ohio Agricultural Experiment Station, "The Rural Health Facilities of Ross County, Ohio," 1927.

At present not more than 20 per cent. of our rural population is provided with modern public health supervision. The farmer's health is less adequately safeguarded by the organization of medical care and by preventive measures than is the urban dweller's health, and the facilities and services that he gets are more costly in comparison.

The provision of adequate health facilities and services for the farm family must be attacked from the standpoint of the community. Practically any farming community can have a modern hospital if it really wants it. Every rural county can have public health supervision if it is willing to pay the cost, which ordinarily is reasonable. If other plans or methods of obtaining health maintenance do not appear feasible, unbiased consideration may well be given to taxation as a means of providing this essential element of farm family living.

Schools. For the most part school facilities for the farm family are tax-provided goods; and practically all aspects of the rural school problem center under one head, the provision of as good schools for farm children as for urban children. From the standpoint of its cost the rural school is "favored," for expenditures per year per pupil ($59) in centers of less than 2500 population is little more than half the expenditure per year per pupil for city schools ($108), according to estimates prepared by the United States Bureau of Education. Doubtless the expenditure per year per pupil would be still less for open country schools than for rural schools.

Comparative figures covering all of the annual costs of open country schools are not available, but it is of interest to know that the average teachers' salaries in one-teacher and two-teacher rural schools in 1924 were $761 and $743 respectively, in comparison with $996 in consolidated schools, $1124 in village schools and $1648 in city schools.[10]

The points of greatest interest lie in the character of the schooling obtained, however. The country school has approximately seven months of instruction, while the city school has nine months. The country school-teacher has one year of unsupervised experience and the city school-teacher has five years of closely supervised experience, on an average. The country school library has only a fiftieth as many books as the city school library.

Notwithstanding these and other drawbacks, the open country school has at least a few salient features, in particular locations especially. It is within easy reach of most farm boys and girls and it affords probably more opportunity for the development of primary group contacts. It would appear, however, that these features are not sufficient to warrant the retainment of all of our 150,000 or more one-room schools for many more years. The 4,750,000 farm boys and girls who are attending these schools are doubtless in need of better buildings, more adequate equipment, longer periods of instruction and more highly qualified teachers than are being provided in the majority of them.

There are, of course, other important institutions and agencies contributing to the education of farm boys and girls. The state agricultural colleges and state universities, maintained from tax-provided funds, are available to all who successfully avail themselves of the opportunities offered in the grade schools and the high schools.

Supplementary and continuing educational facilities in the form of extension service are accessible to those farm

[10] Information obtained by the writer from the Statistical Division of the U. S. Bureau of Education, 1928.

boys and girls as well as to adult farmers and home-makers who care to avail themselves of these opportunities. Rural library service is available to farm families of certain counties and certain communities.

The problem of providing proper educational facilities for the farm family is national in scope. The statement frequently made in many communities that the farmer cannot afford a high school must give way to the statement that the farmer cannot afford not to have a high school. Farmers, townsmen, community leaders and legislators—all must pool their efforts and their energies to equalize the educational opportunities for farm and city children.

Art. Several years ago a family living investigator conversing with a farmer mentioned the subject of pictures for the home. "Oh, yes," the farmer remarked, "you appreciate good pictures and I want to show you what I have." He led the way up a creaky stairs to a small sparsely furnished room, on the walls of which hung several highly prized paintings. "They're all my daughter's work. She was raised right here on this farm. They are all scenes from this window. See if you recognize any of them. Some of them are gone; but there's the best one yet just as it was when she painted it.

"I've been offered $1000 for that picture, but money can't buy it. It helps me to live; it rests me at night and it refreshes me in the morning. She [the daughter] got the idea of doing them from a visit to an art gallery. I took her to the city once when she was a wee girl. It was the best investment I ever made for my family."

Will farm people ever be provided with the opportunities which "will enable them to discover within themselves the emotional appreciations and the latent talents for painting, drama, poetry and music?" It is to hoped that they will.

There are those who hold that what they see as the farmer's lack of imagination and appreciation of the beautiful is due mainly to his burdensome struggle with the objects of nature. This is probable. On the other hand, it is equally probable that this apparent lack is due to the absence of "exposures" or contacts with the products of the creative arts, ordinarily farther from his reach than from the reach of the urban dweller.

All too slowly the creative arts are pushing out into country districts to vitalize and enervate the lives of farm people. The development of the little theater and the folk drama in North Dakota and North Carolina are commendable beginnings. University and state college dramatic clubs are contributing to the movement in certain other States.

But owing to the lack of satisfactory distributing centers, there is still a great unfilled demand for art in the open country districts. Farm families are waiting for the symbols of beauty and meaning which shape youth more than do lessons. These must come by way of plays, music, poetry, painting, craftwork, architecture and landscaping, all of which flow out most readily from the larger distributing centers.

Church facilities. For the most part the farm family relies on the rural church for its satisfactions or values in religion and morals. Almost limitless data are available which might be used to show that the rural church is meeting inadequately the religious and the social needs of the typical farm family.

A rather recent study based upon data obtained from 179 counties throughout the United States places the number of farm children living outside the reach of church or

Sunday school at 1,600,000.[11] In addition 2,750,000 farm children do not go to any Sunday school, either because the church to which their parents belong does not have any or because they do not care to connect themselves with any such organization. One in seven rural communities are without any church and two in five are without resident pastors. Many other communities appeared to have fared no better on account of being over-churched. Only one in six of the open country churches had a resident pastor.

Sixty-three members were enrolled in the rural church and forty-six were enrolled in the open country church. The average Sunday school membership was eighty-six for the rural church and sixty-four for the open country church.

Probably no single rural social institution is in a more deplorable state than the rural church. Fortunately, however, authorities who are concerned with the matter see signs of a reawakening of the farmer's church both from the standpoint of the local community and the overhead organizational tie-up. Appreciating the rôle of modern facilities for religion in family living, many farm families in separate groups in the open country or in rural communities, including villages and towns, have joined hands to reëstablish the church on a satisfactory functional basis. Plans of procedure, experiences encountered and results obtained are available to others who care to reëstablish their church activities to serve the local needs more effectively.

Local government facilities and services. Local government for the farmer has been characterized as the "weakest link in American democracy." [12] It is held by some authori-

---

[11] Morse and Brunner, "The Town and Country Churches in the United States," 1923.

[12] American Country Life Association, Report of Subcommittee on Local Government, Proceedings, 1919.

ties to be the most unbusinesslike, most wasteful, least efficient and least creditable of our rural institutions. Whether or not all these shortcomings can be heaped against it, undoubtedly our system of rural local government is about as primitive as the "ox and the wooden plow." Planned for the most part to take care of conditions prevailing almost a century ago, it has undergone little change to meet new situations. Rather it has tended to "grow along" without conscious direction as additional needs and additional functions have arisen.

In the main, county and township government is charged with the care of highways (except those under national and state control), the operation of schools, the recording of property titles, the maintenance of peace, the administration of justice and poor relief, the supervision of tax technique and election machinery. In some instances it has more recently acquired the functions of the establishment and maintenance of public libraries and hospitals, the furtherance of agricultural marketing agencies and the promotion of improved methods of farming. The care of highways and the operation of schools appear to be the paramount functions of government in most rural counties at the present time. This may account primarily for the prevailing opinion of many farmers that the character of the road bordering their farms or the quality of schools in their immediate "district" should be in exact keeping with the total amount of taxes paid.

More and more, the care of highways is bound to pass under state, and to a certain extent national, supervision. The former custom of the farmers of separate townships or of road districts working on the roads as they choose is no longer adequate or effective. The old plan of establishing and operating schools by district units has grown most ineffective and uneconomical in many rural counties. Larger school units than the "district" must be resorted to.

Also, the maintenance of peace and the administration of justice could now be handled to better advantage in larger units. Police officials answering to a central office representing a larger area than the township or even the county would make possible the employment of men equipped with special training. The recording of property titles, and in fact all matters of like proportions, could be carried on to-day in units or areas four times as large as originally with less difficulty than was encountered in the days of "pioneering." The time is ripe for an experiment in the readjustment of local government units better to suit the needs of the farmer; for, says the "Country Gentleman," "small counties are a relic of horse-and-buggy days, and fewer counties in agricultural districts would mean a reduction in taxes. With good roads, bus lines, automobiles, electric lines, and other means of transportation, a fifty-mile or even a 100-mile trip to the county seat would not be as great a hardship to-day as a ten-mile trip a few years ago. Why build so many court-houses and pay for their up-keep? What is the use of having three or four sheriffs when one could do the work? To-day there is a multiplicity of county officers being supported by tax-payers. With one county where we now have three or four, one set of officers with a little additional clerk hire could do the work of three or four sets, as it now stands."

Banking facilities. "I know of nothing that is quite so depressing on the farmer's standard of living as the failure of the bank in which at least a part of the family funds have been in keeping," stated a county home demonstration agent recently. "It seems to cut deep into the consumption of the goods, but deeper still into the spirit and morale of the family."

The disheartening effects of bank failures have been experienced by a number of farm families, since 1920 especially. The Agricultural Appropriation Bill for 1929 bears the record of 4071 bank failures during the preceding seven-year period. The primary cause of these failures will be attributed to the post-war agricultural depression. A careful study of the situation might show, however, that some of the failures were due, in part at least, to lack of adjustment to the larger trade and service center area. It is of interest that over four fifths of the failures represented private and state banks and less than one fifth represented national banks.

The study among 787 Wisconsin families referred to previously states that "The generalization regarding banking as one of the financial services of the farmer is to the effect that it follows general trade in both considerations of extent and reasons." "Trade center" was chief among the reasons given for banking in the different towns of two counties; and was a close second to "nearest," which led in the other county.

Further studies are needed to ascertain the extent and the effects of "over-banking" and "under-banking" in the rural areas. Too many small banks with limited patronage means high "overhead cost per unit of business, keen competition for deposits with high interest rates on such deposits, greater risks on loans concentrated in limited areas, and a lack of adequate reserves." [13] Also, too many small

[13] U. S. Dept. Agriculture, "Farm Credit, Farm Finance, and Farm Taxation," Year Book Separate 915, 1924.

banks or too few larger, more efficient banks may mean an undue strain on the farmer's standard of living.

Tax provided goods, facilities and services. Satisfactory progress will not be made in farm family living until tax-provided goods, facilities and services are given somewhat near the same consideration that is given to the other goods, facilities and services. Interest needs to be revived and energy needs to be redirected in the matter of tax technique for the provision of family living goods which can be obtained only by group action. The farmer who is inclined to say, as some farmers do say, "I'll tend to my affairs and the other fellow can run the government," must "right face" and join with his neighbor and his fellow-villager or townsman in a united effort to place within and to keep within his reach the essential elements of a truly American standard of living.

The farmer's trading post and service center. Under present-day conditions the city of 25,000 or more inhabitants appears to be able to provide all the principal kinds of goods essential to a high standard of family living—health facilities, schools, libraries, art, organized recreation, religion and government, in addition to food, clothing, housing, furnishings and transportation. Many towns with less inhabitants appear equally fortunate; in fact, some towns and villages of less than 2500 people seem to be well equipped with trading posts and service centers for all the goods and facilities needed by the villagers within their immediate limits, as well as the farmers within their trading areas. These towns appear, however, to have made the most of their opportunities in every respect, usually in coöperation with farm families of their surrounding trade area. Thus, there arise the questions of the numbers of families essential for efficient operation units in the matter of trading centers, health facilities, education, religion, recreation and government. Just how accessible must the families involved be to the particular kind of goods or services to be had? Attention has been called to the distances traveled by farm families of Pickaway county, Ohio, to purchase the different kinds of goods. The study of the 300 families of three other southeastern Ohio counties showed them to be traveling the following distances (in average number of miles) from the institutions and agencies named: Railroad station 5.1, general trading center 3.4, grocery supply 3.1, furniture store 13.1, clothing store 12.9, bank 11.3, doctor 6.8, high school 5.1, grade school 1.7 and church 1.9. Just why the farm family cannot travel as far for its religion as for its general store supplies, its doctors or its clothing has yet to be determined. What, after all, is the distance which farm families economically can go for the essential goods of family living? This must be ascertained, as must also the amount of competition which may be permitted to run *laissez-faire* fashion in the trade and service centers where farm families are obliged to obtain their major goods, facilities and services.

CHAPTER XIII

INVESTMENTS, SAVINGS, RECORDS OF EXPENDITURES AND BUDGETS FOR FARM FAMILIES

SEVERAL years ago a group of students from a state agricultural college, while driving one day to a neighboring college, amused themselves with deciding whether the farmer or the farmer's wife was "boss" on each of the farmsteads which they passed. Size and appearance of the house with its surroundings in comparison with size and appearance of the other farm buildings constituted the basis of their decision in each instance.

"Now look at the big barn and the new hog-house alongside of the tiny house; the husband is boss here," remarked one. "And look up the road at the nice big house and the little old barn; the wife gives orders there," said another. "Now look on this side at the imposing barn and the little house; oh! it's an old log-house; hubby has the say there," ejaculated a third. "Then, across the way is a pretty fair house and the ramshackle sheds; the wife is in charge again," commented a fourth. "And see what's coming—a charming house in a beautiful setting, and the fair-sized barns to match! I think there must be coöperation there," concluded the fifth.

In reality the five students, all farm reared, were making observations on the probable relative rates of growth or development of the farm business resources and the standard of living on the farms and in the homes which they passed. In each of the homes observed as well as in every farm home the balance of adjustment between these two aspects of farm life constitutes a knotty problem, with several important ramifications. There is the question of the goal or objective—the point at which the family wishes to arrive in regard to its family living; that is, the question of the desired standard of living. Then there is the matter of the amounts of funds to be reinvested in the farm to provide or maintain an efficient producing unit. Also, there is the question of the investment of funds in other securities for unanticipated needs, provided the farm business is already sufficiently large, when funds are available. Finally, there are the matter of records of the purposes for which the available funds are spent and the question of whether these records or other sets of figures may be made the basis for a more satisfactory use of funds in the future.

Investments. During the past seven-year period of postwar depression considerable attention has been given to the question of the investment of farm earnings in additional farm-land as one of the causes of the depression. A leading agricultural economist is now urging farmers to buy more family living and less land as a means of securing "a fair share in the national income." [1] "Farmers have been most unmerciful competitors of each other," according to this economist. "When they get a little increase in income it is too likely to go immediately into increased demand for land, labor and equipment for the purpose of expanding production, which tends to decrease prices. . . . In the long run any class of producers gets only what it consumes."

[1] H. C. Taylor, "Living Standards and Farm Income, Farm Income and Farm Life," p. 70, 1927.

Few data are available on the amounts of money invested annually in different securities or for different purposes by the farm family. Limited information for 357 Minnesota families, 1925, show an average investment of $579—one fifth of the total family "budget"—$260 of which went to pay interest on borrowed funds, mostly interest on mortgage debt.[2] Payments on the principal of the mortgage debt amounted to $172 per family. At this rate of repayment the families studied would pay off the mortgages in twenty-five years, which is less time than is required under the amortization plan of the Federal Farm Loan Bank, thirty-five to forty years. "Such thrift" is regarded as commendable from the standpoint of credit rating, but non-commendable if accomplished by holding down the prevailing standard of living.

Life-insurance premiums amounting to $38 per family constituted less than 7 per cent. of all investments. More first-class life-insurance would be a wise investment, undoubtedly, from the standpoints of diversity of investment, ease of handling in case of death, and the prevention of losses from such occurrences as forced sales and liquidation of estates, according to the study.

"All other" investments amounted to $109 per family, not including expenditures for live stock, farm machinery, new buildings, and clearing or tiling. It is held that these expenditures, amounting to about $350 per farm, should undoubtedly be added to the investments.

The study concludes that "farm investments are mostly tied up closely with the home farm and its related institutions, coöperatives and local banks," the only exception being life-insurance, which took 7 per cent. of the surplus

[2] University of Minnesota Agricultural Experiment Station, *op. cit.*, 1927.

funds. This lack of diversification of investment is looked upon as an important factor in most agricultural crises.

Knowledge of the bearing of mortgage indebtedness on the farm to the standard of living would be of interest. Limited results of two studies suggest little or no relationship between these two factors. For almost half of 402 Livingston county, New York, families with mortgaged capital there appeared to be little or no variation in the value of goods used during the year of study for family living purposes, or the percentage distribution of this value, as the percentage of indebtedness on capital increased from less than 10 per cent. to 50 per cent. or more.[3] About the same situation seemed to prevail among 874 owner families of selected localities in eleven States who reported on the question of mortgage indebtedness on the farm.[4] More than half of these families reported no mortgage indebtedness. For those reporting farm mortgages the average value of family living remained practically constant or varied with no regard to an increase in the per cent. of indebtedness. Also, the percentage distribution of the value of goods remained almost constant.

The validity of these figures is questioned by some authorities, who claim that mortgage indebtedness tends to cut into or to hold down the prevailing standard of living. These authorities may be right. On the other hand, it is probable that farm families are not widely different from urban families, some of which do not hesitate to place loans or trusts on their homes in order to buy automobiles, furniture or radios, or to pay for medical care and attention. The exact relationship between farm mort-

[3] Cornell University Agricultural Experiment Station, *op. cit.*, 1923.
[4] U. S. Dept. Agriculture, "The Farmer's Standard of Living," Bul. 1466, 1926.

gage indebtedness and family living is yet to be ascertained.

According to the United States Census of Agriculture, 1925, 36 per cent. of all farms operated by owners carried some mortgage debt. For the farms operated by full owners the mortgage debt amounted to 42 per cent. of the value of the farms (land and buildings value). For the mortgaged farms the average value of land and buildings was $9564 and the mortgage debt was $4004. While this amount of debt may seem large at first thought, farming does not appear to be overburdened with mortgages in comparison with holdings in other industries and institutions. Most industrial concerns and public utilities are mortgaged. Schools, highways and local government facilities are often bonded. City and suburban homes usually carry one or more trusts. A farm mortgage signifies disaster only when production and profits are not sufficient to meet the indebtedness as it becomes due.

Savings. "We added a little to our checking account, but it will soon be spent," "We made a payment on the mortgage; I reckon that is saved," and "We fixed up the house, if you call that saving," are typical replies made by farm women to queries of family living field workers on whether they were able during the preceding year to save anything. The amounts reported laid by during one year range from a few dollars in a Christmas savings club or postal savings account to as much as $6000 or more, obtained as gifts or inheritances, placed on interest in a few instances.

The amounts of savings reported have been compiled for two groups of families, 402 families of Livingston county, New York, 1921, and 360 families of Mason county, Kentucky, 1924.[5] These amounts averaged $38 for the

⁵ U. S. Dept. Agriculture, Bul. 1214, and Preliminary Report, 1924.

former and $91 for the latter families, not including premiums paid on life- or health-insurance. A part of the high average in the latter instance is due to the inclusion of a large amount of money from the sale of land, reported saved by each of two families.

The raising of such questions as, "What is meant by savings?" "Would savings include money to be used for a light plant?" and "Would the wheat which we are holding for a higher price be savings?" has almost thwarted the attempts of family living field workers to get estimates in regard to the matter. Amounts deposited in banks or with trust companies are not indicative of the exact situation usually, and yet it is doubtful if one should advise the farm family to regard all investments in real estate, payments on mortgages and improvements on farm buildings as savings. Banker's associations, trust companies and the like can perform an outstanding service by helping clarify or define the term savings for farm people.

The farm family should be no exception to all families in the effort and the ability to save something regularly from its wages or salary. There are rather regular needs to be met by farm families, including taxes, fuel and clothing, which can be met to best advantage if some attention has been paid to a savings account from time to time. There may be unanticipated needs, as sickness, accident or death, the costs of which should be provided for by means of a savings account, if not in the form of life,- health- or accident-insurance. Finally, there are usually certain anticipated goals or objectives which can be attained in many instances only by systematic saving during periods of several weeks, months or years. The provision for savings should be properly regarded as one of the principal elements of family living. No standard of living is complete without it. To save regularly means ability to meet emergencies, to invest wisely and finally to have some available income at the time of retirement from active or aggressive labor.

The amount to be saved is probably of less importance than the development of the habit of saving, which is best acquired in the light of a knowledge of the values of money. Doubtless the opportunity to teach the farm boy or girl the value of money and the "fine art of choice-making" is too seldom developed on the farm and in the farm home.

Some years ago a certain farm boy wanting a pony was given a pony with the understanding that he would feed it regularly and "be nice" to it. More than the pony this boy needed the training in earning, saving and spending which the purchase of the thing he most desired could have provided. The boy grew up to be kind to animals, but with no appreciation of how to provide for the needs of his family. There appears to be an almost untouched field for the development of saving, investing and spending habits of farm boys and girls. Fortunately, a start has been made by the Agricultural Extension Service and other similar agencies.

Saving, investing and owning are family matters. About ten years ago a field agent sent out from a certain state agricultural college to study the social aspects of farm tenancy made the acquaintance of a dozen or more farmers who were attempting to keep from their families the fact that they had invested money in a "promotion scheme" that had failed. The salesman had come along, the plan had looked good and the men had "invested." "It was bad enough to have the thing fall through and lose the $1000," said one of them, "but it would be worse for the family to find it out. I think I can make it back before they learn of it."

Too often farm family living has "gone on the rocks" because the principal members of the family were not consulted, were not informed or had no legal status in regard to matters of importance. "I don't know how to get on here," said a farm woman, after the death of her husband, recently. "He [the husband] did everything connected with the business. I couldn't prove that we own the farm, or the house or the automobile."

"I'm tired and sick of the thing," lamented another farm woman less than a decade ago after twelve years of attempting to run the 240-acre farm with hired help, following the death of her husband. "If only one of the three girls had been a boy I guess we could have made it. Or if I could sell the farm and move to town where the girls could get schooling and work that they like; but the law says I must hold on for four more long years."

The counsel of wives and the proper revision of existing state laws will contribute materially to the attainment of higher standards of family living in the open country. The time is ripe for the opening of this aspect of farm life to investigation and education in order that women who are copartners in the farming business may share on an equal basis the fruits of family toil.

Keeping records of family living expenditures. "We keep a record of all household expenditures, have for more than ten years and use the records kept year by year as a basis for our annual family living budget," stated a farmer last June at a farm bureau meeting where income and outgo were being discussed. "Tell us more about it; the kind of books you use, who does the work and how you make the books balance," came from another farmer.

Given the opportunity, the farmer called upon explained that an inexpensive day-book was used, that all the items of income and expenditure, with the amounts, were listed down the page daily by those who received the money and made the purchases. Amounts received from different sources were entered on a left hand page and amounts spent for different purposes were entered on a right hand page month by month. No attempt was made to classify the different items as they were listed except to place those most closely connected with family living near the front of the book and those most closely connected with the farm business near the back of the book. The different items were classified or grouped according to the principal kinds of family living goods and the main farm enterprises as desired, usually in early winter.

Produce furnished by the farm was listed on separate pages in order that it could be summed up as either farm income or family living outgo. In this way it did not become involved with the cash or trade transactions. The items were usually recorded in quantities as they were set aside for use, rather than in driblets as they were needed— daily or for separate meals.

"When you add things up for the year how long does it take?" queried a third farmer. "It sounds good, but my wife's never found time to do that sort of thing."

"Usually takes a week or two weeks of evenings," replied the one questioned. "We work along on it together. It makes a nice problem and sometimes a pretty good puzzle to see where we're coming out; that is, to see what part of the total went into foods, what part into clothing, what parts into furnishings and equipment and other things.

Each member of the family has always been eager to pick out and add up the cost of his own things to see where he stands. It might interest you to know that we have reduced the percentage that the cost of food is of all living costs year by year."

Some one insists that this was an exceptional farmer. He was. Also, this was an exceptional farm family. There are other exceptional farm families, however, where records are being kept of expenditures and goods for living purposes. As will be pointed out under budgets, farm families are beginning to appreciate the value of records or accounts in evolving plans for attaining the things which they most need or desire. Many farmers already are keeping records of farm expenses and farm receipts; analyzing the farm business from many aspects to determine if it is reasonably profitable and, if not, to discover ways and means of making it so. Family living, the objective or aim in view, is fully as important as the farm business, and in due time will be recorded and analyzed with as much or more care and patience than is now being given to the farm business. This worth-while activity awaits the development of a well-planned, simplified system of household or home accounting for the farm family.

Budgeting the family living. The past decade has been marked with the distribution of many publications on the different aspects of thrift, including "Modern Magic," "Budget Book with a Conscience," "Balance Wheel," "The Art of Spending," "How to S-T-R-E-T-C-H the Dollar" and "How to Get More for Your Money." Practically all of these are built around the same central theme, the budgeting of family living expenditures.

"To get what you want with any income you must plan its use, . . . make a budget," says one; ". . . plan and then spend according to plan, instead of spending for this and that as the impulse or need arises," says another, and ". . . planning a budget is the next best thing to a Fairy Godmother in helping you to meet your needs and realize your wishes," says a third.

After all, is it possible, is it practicable and is it profitable for the farm family to try to plan ahead in regard to family living expenditures? "We tried it last year and it didn't work," "We started but didn't get anywhere with it," and "We thought about it once or twice but never got at it yet," are among the responses of farm families who have given some thought to the matter. "We have tried it and found it works," "It's our way of getting ahead," and "It keeps us all working for a common purpose," are among the responses of those farm families that have given more thought to the matter.

The farmer who related his experience in keeping account of family living expenditures (above) explained also that the summaries obtained from the records kept facilitated in the making of a yearly budget by means of which the family got or came nearer to getting what it "wanted most each year." The averages of amounts and values or costs of the principal kinds of goods for the preceding five years were taken as a basis in making up the annual plan or budget of expenditures. Likewise the averages of income figures for the preceding five years were regarded as being typical of what might be expected under ordinary circumstances. Just as this family had not quit with keeping records when the accounts failed to balance to a penny, it did not abandon the budget idea when the plan made out failed to fit the situation exactly during any one year. "Even if it doesn't fit exactly, it gives us an indication of what we should or should not try to buy, shows us some of our mistakes, tells how far we have gone toward getting what we want and gives us a little better living each year," stated this farmer in a sort of summarization to his county agent at the close of the meeting referred to above.

Farm families are in dire need of specific information on the "why" and the "how" of planning ahead in regard to the needs and habits of well-balanced family living. Business, government, schools and churches, for the most part, are now run on the budget basis; that is, their needs are laid out at least a year ahead according to a carefully thought out plan. The adoption of the budget system by each of these institutions or agencies has resulted in wiser purchasing, more efficient using of goods and in many instances the realization of objectives which otherwise would not have been attained. Until this specific information is provided by research and extension workers in farm economics, home economics and rural sociology the following suggestions may prove helpful to the family which is ready to "experiment" in regard to its living.

Few farm families have figures for the past five years from which to obtain averages as bases from which to develop plans or budgets of spending. Many have some notion of what their living costs were during the past year, however, and others may choose some set of averages representing a particular group of families as tentative guides in the expenditure of money and the use of goods until actual figures from one, three or five years are available.

In choosing any set of figures as a guide for preparing a budget, allowances will need to be made for the number and ages of persons composing the family or household. Also, consideration will need to be given to the standard of living which the income will afford. In general, the higher standard of living possible on a higher income means a lower proportion of the value of all goods devoted to the more material needs, to food especially.

There are several possibilities for improvement in any sanely chosen set of averages of present habits of consumption of family living goods. One of these is the attempt by each farm family to save something, if only a little, annually for future needs not anticipated at present. Some farm families, and many urban families, try to save about 5 per cent. of their incomes. Savings are usually put into a savings account to be drawn on in case of absolute necessity or emergency. Christmas savings clubs, with the local bank or postal savings accounts, facilitate the matter of savings.

Another possibility of improvement in farm family living is the rational attempt to hold constant or reduce slightly the percentage that the value of food is of the total value of all goods. This reduction may mean also a reduction in the value of foods with some families. Care must be taken that the adequacy of the diet be held at the present level or raised if possible. No attempt at reducing the value of foods should mean that any family go hungry. Rather, all reductions in this direction should occur as a result of more intelligent planning of meals, greater care in the selection, purchase and preparation of foods and the providing of a greater variety of foods from the farm and the garden. In this way all members of the family may be as well or better nourished at less cost than previously. It is probable that many farm families fail to get the maximum quality and variety of vegetables and fruits which may be had from the farm, garden and orchard at relatively low costs in comparison with market prices of these products. If the attempt to feed the family at less expense is a success, a greater proportion of the total value of goods, more actual money

too, usually will be available for educational, recreational and social purposes—that is, for advancement.

Usually, the percentage that clothing costs are of the value of all family living will stand little, if any, reduction. Some families, however, may be able to gain economy in the purchase and through the care and repair of clothing. Where clothing which provides for the family the proper self-respect, as well as the necessary protection, can be had for less money than formerly, any money not needed for clothes may well go into savings or into a reserve fund for other purposes.

The budget may well include an allotment for use of the farm-house for family living purposes. Probably 10 per cent. of the value of the house, in so far as this can be determined, is the most satisfactory figure. Funds represented by this 10 per cent. will cover taxes (on the house only), insurance and ordinary repair and leave something in the way of accumulated funds which may be used later for rebuilding or enlarging the house or for installing modern improvements, including running water and central heating and central lighting systems. Or, if desired, the funds not needed for taxes, insurance and repair may be used for some other worthy purpose.

The percentage of the total value of goods to be devoted to the purchase of new furniture or other household equipment needs careful consideration. If no new furniture is needed during the year for which the expenditures are being apportioned, a small percentage of the total value of all goods may well go into a reserve fund to be used for new equipment in the future. It is well to consider furnishings in the apportionment of values of goods to be used, especially when the purchase of some new piece of furniture, or

a new picture, or something similar may mean a great deal to one or more members of the family.

The percentage of the total for operation goods probably will stand some reduction on the assumption that most families can effect a small saving through the practice of more efficient use of fuel and household supplies. With many families a study of the methods of doing housework might show ways of reducing money costs of operation. Probably ways of reducing the use of the automobile or cutting the costs of its operation can be determined. Depreciation on the car does not mean an actual expenditure where the car is paid for already, but a certain amount of money may well be put into a separate savings fund for the purchase of a new car when it is needed or for some other purpose.

Good health may be maintained with some families for less than the amount usually recommended for this purpose, but a certain sum should be held available if possible for this use when needed. If not used during the year for which plans are being made, the amount reserved may be added to the savings account as a protection against sickness expenses in the future. With all families attention should be given to the prevention of sickness or accident necessitating heavy expenditures for recovery.

The percentage of the total for advancement goods must be ample enough to meet the needs of any children in grade school, high school or college. This group of goods is worthy of all possible consideration and may well constitute a larger proportion of all goods as the needs become evident and as funds are available. Here as elsewhere, however, money need not be spent lavishly without due consideration merely because the purpose is regarded as educa-

tional or spiritual. Values to be obtained for money spent should have careful scrutiny.

Probably the percentage of the total for goods of a personal nature can be reduced slightly in some instances. A little saving through more attention to needs, purchases and use of goods of this type may mean greater satisfaction through the use of goods filling other needs.

An attempt to raise the amounts for life- and health-insurance might well be made by most families. Probably no farm family should be satisfied with carrying as little insurance as is suggested by the averages of premiums paid by the families of the prevailing standards of living shown by the sets of figures presented in several preceding chapters.

The percentage of the total for unclassified goods needs consideration in any plan of expenditures. If desired, money for goods of this type may comprise a part of a general reserve fund to be held for urgent unexpected needs during the year.

Other ways of improving the family living will be discovered by farm families which search earnestly for wiser expenditure of funds from year to year and for more efficient uses of the goods, facilities and services which are available.

The attempt to improve the family living on the same amount of money that has been available before will help the family to make the dollars go farther than formerly. This does not mean that more money could not be used advantageously in many cases. It does mean, however, an effort to raise the percentages of the total family living for clothing, for advancement goods and for life- and health-insurance, and to provide for a little savings and a reserve fund for improvement of the house or for unexpected future needs through more efficient uses of foods, operation goods and personal goods. It means undoubtedly giving more careful attention to quantities and qualities of goods, facilities and services to be obtained with the money available.

The attempt to raise the standard of living on the same income naturally will be followed by a careful study of the situation to discover possible ways of increasing the income. This will mean an analysis of the farm business procedure to see whether less money will adequately suffice in connection with farm expenses, thereby leaving more money for family living. The question of the amount of income for family living purposes hinges on a number of factors pertaining to both the home and the farm business. Farm ownership, freedom from indebtedness, and rational enlargement of the farm business for proper efficiency in production are aspects of the situation which cannot be ignored if a well-balanced, wholesome standard of living is to be enjoyed in the more mature years, as well as at present.

But whatever the money available, the art of getting better values for each dollar spent merits first consideration. The ability to get better values for money spent will be realized most readily through an attempt to attain a definite goal set by all members of the family. Cannot each farm family set up its own goal for a more rational standard of living? There would be zest in seeing how near the family might be able to go toward a definite goal set. Finally, if the more rational standard of living desired cannot be realized through a wiser expenditure of the funds which are available or from the attainment of more income from farming and from subsidiary sources, then the family may well consider some other type of work or some other location as a means of reaching its goal in family living, provided due consideration is given to the non-material satisfactions or values inherent in the occupation of farming.

CHAPTER XIV

THE SATISFACTIONS OF FARMING AND FARM LIFE

"IF you were starting over again now, would you choose to live in the country and would you pick farming as your particular line of work?" was answered in the affirmative by "more than 100 men and women," according to a recent issue of "Wallaces' Farmer." The people who answered the question, by letter, appear "to be farming because they believe the farm is still the best place to live." [1] Excerpts from several of the letters which were published indicate that there are yet farm people with "firm convictions about the desirability of country life and [farm] work."

"If I were starting over again, I would still choose to live in the country, for the very selfish reason that I think it's the pleasantest place to live," states one of the writers.

"The isolation that causes city-born folks to shudder, soothes and satisfies me. The solitude (after all, there's not so much) which fills some of our urban friends with uneasiness, brings to me a strange contentment. I cannot explain it. I simply know it is so.

"I am neither aloof nor unapproachable, but for all that I don't want too many people real close to me. I like a few at a time.

"I want my boys to have their creek and the wooded pasture through which it flows. They need that pasture

[1] "Wallaces' Farmer," December 9, 1927.

quite as much as the cattle that graze there. They need the creek as much as the beasts that drink therefrom."

"I am very sure," says another of the writers, "that if I should take time to sit down and really think clear down through the artificialities to the level of realities, I would again, with my husband, choose the farm as the place for our home and our work. . . .

"My girlhood home was in the city . . . and I am thoroughly aware of the advantages as well as the disadvantages which city life has to offer. I am sure it is more nearly possible for us to be successful fathers and mothers in the country than in the city, and the world is in far greater need of that type of success than it is of mere money-making success. Our four children have clean country air to breathe, an abundance of sunshine, space to play in and a bountiful supply of fresh foods produced through our own efforts. Nature's beauties on every hand to reveal God to them, a close-up to father's and mother's work and problems that make for comradeship and development, a convenient distance from cheap, trashy amusement that leaves room for the development of a taste for wholesome pleasures and a good consolidated school to attend . . . all these are distinct advantages. . . .

"As we work, there is a peace all about us that allows for deep thought and reflection. We are real comrades with our neighbors, for our work is a common interest."

"I know of no vocation entirely without trials," states a third writer. "Farming has its hardships, but it has great compensations, which are multiplying while science and education combine to relieve the one-time monotony and drudgery of farm life. . . .

"The farmer and his wife work and recreate together and their children learn to live and to work and to play with them. The country children are not sent home at night by a 'cop' or a curfew bell. And what greater compensation is there in this world than a contented family life?"

These statements call attention to some of the major satisfactions or values of farm life, the sources of which appear to be in danger of atrophying generally under a too lurid picturization of the economic ills of farming. Public sentiment to-day decrees that all farm families should be discontented if each cannot make money as rapidly as some city dwellers do. A general outpouring of gloom over the financial side of farming has doubtless influenced many farm families to give up farming and move to city, town or village during recent years. Data for the past seven years show an excess of nearly 3,000,000 people moving from farms to cities, towns or villages over and above those moving from cities, towns and villages to farms.

To some who are concerned about the future of farming the net movement of people from farms is alarming. It means that industry is outstripping agriculture and that the best farmers are going into trades and professions. To others it means simply an adjustment of the balance between agriculture and industry in accordance with the use of improved farm machinery, the practice of better farming methods and increased availability of agricultural produce from other countries. The quality of the people leaving the farm is seldom questioned by those who regard the net movement of farm population to cities, towns and villages as an adjustment of the balance between agriculture and industry.

To all who have any concern in the matter the decrease in farm population should mean serious consideration of the satisfactions or values accruing to the families involved in the process of moving from farms to cities, towns and villages and from cities, towns and villages to farms. A recent study of almost four thousand families moving in one or other of these directions showed that only 50 per cent. of those moving from farms to cities had tried other occupations than farming at the time of moving.[2] On the other hand, almost 90 per cent. of the families moving from cities to farms had had farm experience. Apparently higher percentages of the families seeking higher incomes, "bigger" opportunities, better living conditions, or more satisfactions of life off the farm were disillusioned with a trial in the city.

A third of the migrants from farms to cities were drawn by the lure of larger incomes. A fourth went on account of physical disability, old age primarily; a tenth went to school their children, and the rest went for various other reasons. Those going for larger incomes may have obtained them. It is probable, however, that many learned with regret that they had given too little serious thought to living costs, monotony of labor and the paucity of satisfactions of farm life within the city.

The farm family which moves to the city primarily in search of a larger income is likely to meet with disillusionment. The satisfactions of farm life are not all in the pay envelope.

The darker side of the farming picture is now subject to the danger of being painted too vividly in terms of labor income, farm income or per cent. of return on investment. These measures which were developed primarily as means of comparing the profitableness of farming in different

[2] U. S. Dept. Agriculture, "Analysis of Migration of Population to and from Farms," Preliminary Report, 1927.

localities, areas and regions were not meant to serve, and cannot be made to serve, as complete indexes of the satisfactions or values accruing from farming and farm life.

Most farm families find a wealth of satisfactions or values outside the realm of income, the rate of return on the investment or the "financial turnover" of the farm business. In fact, many if not most farm families obtain a large share of the values of life from sources not included in the goods, facilities and services of living. The sources of all the satisfactions or values of life for the farm family are the tangible goods furnished by the farm for family living purposes, the financial returns from farming (cash or credit) entitling the farm family to draw upon the community's supply of consumption goods not available from individual family effort, and the intangible factors inherent in no other occupation as in farming. A well-organized and operated farm is virtually a coöperative organization on a small scale; it involves the coöperation of all members of the family as does no other occupation or business. It creates a social and a business atmosphere which no other enterprise creates or permits. It carries a feeling of security of ownership which tends to develop a state of mind in harmony with an environment where individuals normally live at their best. These and other intangible factors "bulk large" in the satisfactions or values to be had from farming.

Although the satisfactions or values from the less tangible sources are for the most part immeasurable, indications of the degree of their prevalence appear in the available data on the opinions or attitudes of farm people toward farming and far life.

The opinions of several farm women toward farm life are expressed clearly in the letters quoted at the beginning of the chapter. Many letters of this type may be noted from time to time in the leading farm journals, the majority of them favoring farming and farm life, primarily because of the intangible satisfactions afforded therefrom. Pages of them could be presented if space were available. About 7000 letters written by as many farm women seven years ago bear hopeful testimony to the fact that the farm, in the open country, affords many major satisfactions in its advantages as a place to live and to rear children. In answer to the question whether, if they had daughters of marriageable ages, they in the light of their own experiences would want them to marry farmers, 94 per cent. of the 7000 women, in all sections of the United States, replied in the affirmative.[3] The reasons given for the "yes" answers included good living on moderate means, joy of working with nature's creative forces, natural balance of work and recreation for character building, family unity in work and pleasures, all-around opportunity to use highest mental faculties, true neighboring in the country, and the contribution of farming to the nation's progress.

Many who are concerned about the current financial dilemma of agriculture hold that the "votes" of the 7000 women may be non-typical of the "feeling" of the majority of farm women, and of farm people especially, since they represent only those women who were interested enough and hopeful enough to write about their situations. When proper allowance has been made for bias, however, the letters still show the "splendid courage, sanity, wholesomeness and clean-cut understanding" of farm women in a period of severe depression in agriculture. And to those who would question the authenticity of the letters, other data help to establish the fact that not all the satisfactions of

[3] "The Farmer's Wife," St. Paul, Minnesota, "What Farm Women Think About Farm Life," 1922.

farm life have been consumed by the "flame of farm financialism."

A recent study by the survey method among 150 farm families of two townships in South Dakota shows that 89 per cent. of the farm women, 88 per cent. of the farmers and 87 per cent. of the older farm boys and girls consulted answered "yes" to the question "Are you satisfied with farm life?" [4] Three out of four of the farmers, if starting over again, would farm, nine out of ten wanted their sons to farm and one out of six were making special effort to keep their children on the farm by trying to make farming more interesting, attractive and worth while.

A study by the questionnaire method among 6000 farm boys and girls of the ages of ten to twenty years shows the expression of an almost universal like for farm life. Ninety-five per cent. each of the boys and girls stated that they liked to live on the farm. More than half of the boys expressing a like for farm life gave farming as their choice of occupation as a means of making a living.[5] In regard to occupations other than farming, 10.9 per cent. of the farm boys preferred engineering, including telegraphy, etc., 6.1 per cent. preferred mechanics, including garage work, 7.4 per cent. preferred the professions, as lawyer, doctor or dentist, 5.6 per cent. preferred business, industry or commerce, 5.3 per cent. preferred teaching in school or college and 5.1 per cent. preferred other occupations. The majority of the girls liking farm life, 53.1 per cent., expressed a preference for teaching, 8.4 per cent. preferred nursing or social work, 17.1 per cent. preferred business, clerking or stenographic work, and 12.1 per cent. preferred other occupa-

[4] South Dakota Agricultural Experiment Station, "What Farmers Think of Farming," Bul. 223, 1927.

[5] U. S. Dept. Agriculture, "Attitudes and Problems of Farm Youth," Extension Service Circular 46, 1927.

tions, including engineering, mechanics and the professions. Only 4.2 per cent. of the girls preferred farming, but this relatively low percentage is doubtless due to confusion as to whether home-making should be regarded as an occupation and to hesitancy in stating a felt desire to be a home-maker, provided such desire were prevalent at the age period represented by the girl answering.

When the many reasons given by these boys and girls for liking farm life were grouped arbitrarily for convenience in tabulation into nature, including plants and animals, school and social advantages, health conditions and facilities, vocational and work aspects, recreational advantages or facilities, and all others, the vocational and work aspect appealed to farm boys liking farm life, with health conditions and facilities next in order. Health conditions and facilities included a variety of answers, ranging from "fresh air" to "plenty of milk to drink." School and social advantages seemed to make the least appeal. Health conditions and facilities appealed most to farm girls liking farm life, with nature, including plants and animals, and recreational advantages next.

The above and similar data do not refute the fact that farming has undesirable features. Farm life has certain disadvantages which need not be ignored nor minimized by those who think seriously of farming as an occupation and a way of life, nor by those concerned with the solution of the problems of agriculture.

But the disadvantages, the discomforts and the undesirable features of farming and country life have been overdrawn by recent writers in books of the "Main Street" type, including "Country People," "R. F. D. No. 3" and "Wild Geese." An urban dweller who had read one of these books recently remarked seriously to a farm life investigator, "I had no idea that country life was as drab and sordid and barren of satisfactions as that, and I'm glad to know somebody is studying it." Thoughtful and serious reading of books of this type can scarcely do other than raise in the mind of the reader the question, "Is there such a dearth of wholesome human values in farming and farm life?" If the reader could go from this type of book to another type represented by the "Blue Window" he would be reassured that contentment, joy, hope—wholesome satisfactions or values—are still to be found in farming. For example, ". . . they had all done woman's work, but when the war came on, with labor scarce, they toiled out of doors, sowing, planting, hoeing, weeding. None of them liked it except Hildegarde's mother. She had explained it to Hildegarde: 'When I plant a seed, I feel that it is an act of creation, as if I had painted a picture or written a poem—and I love the smell of the fresh earth with everything bursting into beauty.' " [6]

Further, ". . . it seemed to Crispin incredible that all that was left of that quick and burning spirit which had been Elizabeth Musgrove's [Hildegarde's mother] should be sleeping in that quiet place. . . . Whether he had found her digging in the garden or tending her stock, there had been an air of detachment from toil, as if the thing she did was not a task but an achievement." [7]

"One of the most cherished memories," says the author of "These Changing Times," "is that of father on a Sunday afternoon starting off for a walk across his farm.[8] I can see him yet as he went walking slowly down the lane with hands clasped behind his back. I can see him as he climbed

[6] Temple Bailey, "The Blue Window," p. 1, 1926.
[7] Temple Bailey, op. cit., p. 76.
[8] E. R. Eastman, "These Changing Times," p. 241, 1927.

the fence and sat for a time to look off across the meadows, the growing corn and potatoes, and the other crops that he was raising in partnership with God. Father was not an expressive man, but I know that as he looked at those things and realized his partnership with Nature he had a satisfaction, a sense of real happiness that no money could ever purchase."

"As a child I remember my father taking a great interest in fruit growing," says a trained social worker who was reared on a farm. "He read literature sent him, set and cared for his trees accordingly, grafted and budded successfully and had a fine orchard.

"For clear thinking, clean living and character building, there is no place like the farm. Let us go back fifteen years ago. There were the horses, the cattle and the sheep on the hillsides. There were fields of corn, and gardens and orchards and bees making honey. Not far from the farm was the village with its church and school and across the fields were the other farm homes with their roses and hollyhocks growing around them. There was peace and love and happiness; satisfactions not purchased with money, for there wasn't much money."

To the authors who care to portray them there are still sources of wholesome satisfactions or values on the farm— in the country. Not all farm families can be expected to "capitalize" equally on these satisfactions or values, it must be granted. Some have more means than others; some have larger capacities than others. Capacities to obtain values from farming and from living in the farming community, as well as capacities to acquire goods and to use goods and time efficiently, range from the minimum on the one hand, through 6,000,000 farm families, to the maximum on the other hand.

Essentially, in order to get the maximum of values from farming and from living in the farming community every family must have access to the goods, facilities and services which through efficient use will insure both the physical and the spiritual well-being of its members. There must be objectives or goals—desired standards of living—for different families, and these have been discussed in the preceding chapter. For any family the matter of the satisfactions or values to be had from the less tangible sources cannot be ignored in the "set-up" of a desired standard of living.

Farm families to whom farming and farm life appeal must insist upon striving to attain reasonably high standards of living. Farming should yield to every family that sees more of the desirable than the undesirable features of farm life "a reasonable measure of comforts and satisfactions both material and spiritual." May the time soon come when those families that like to farm will set their standards of living high enough to get the maximum of human values out of family and community life.

In regard to the families to whom the undesirable features and the discomforts loom larger than the satisfactions or values of farming and farm life, may the time soon come when our "programs for improving agriculture" will be of no more importance than our concern for the welfare of these families. Our first effort in this regard should be directed toward assisting these families to find more of the real satisfactions of farming and farm life. If this be unsuccessful, our next effort should be to encourage and to assist them to find at least an optimum amount of the satisfactions or values of life in some other occupation than farming and in some other location than the open country. It is not essential that these families be kept on the land if from farming they cannot obtain the satisfactions or values of life to be had from working and living elsewhere.

Emphatically, the question of the number of farmers to be kept on farms is secondary only to the values which these farmers and their families get from farming and from living in the farming community. Is the time not at hand for a coördinated program on the ways and means of assisting or enabling farmers to obtain the maximum of values from farm life? If farm families who appreciate fully the intangible satisfactions of farming have access to the satisfactions or values ordinarily accruing from a truly American standard of living, there need be little fear but that agriculture will continue to be our basic industry.

INDEX

Ability to provide, relation to standard of living, 228-234
Effected by:
Income from outside sources, 233; net worth of farmer, 230; number of years an owner, 232; size of farm, 229; years farmed, 231
Accounts, household. See records of expenditure.
Achievement record, of farm families, 238-241
Adult equivalent, 21, 22
Adult male equivalent, 22
Advancement, cultural, factors pertaining to, 216-221
"Advancement" goods, 27, 43; expenditures for, 181; importance of, 180; need for study of, 198
Age, relation to standard of living, children, 213; homemaker, 204-207; operator, 204, 207
American agricultural policy, 7
American Country Life Ass'n, 242
Ammain, 21, 24
Andrews, Benjamin R., 14
Art, distributing centers, 257
Atwater and Bryant, 94
Automobile, 157-160

Banking facilities, 260-262
"Blue Window, The," 290
Books, 188, 190
Budgets, 273-281
Burr, Walter, 173
Buying power, 38

Chapin, Robert Coit, 12, 41
Children per family, relation to standard of living, 207-216

Church, accessibility, 257; affiliations and attendance, 192; support, 191
Civilization, affected by communication, 37
Clarke, Edna L., 103, 118
Classification of family living goods, 26-30
Clothing, 5, 100-121; articles purchased, 107-114; costs, 102-107, 114; homemade, 116-120; importance of, 100; purpose of, 101; ready-made, 116-120; where purchased, 248
Comish, Newell H., 12
Communication, effect on standard of living, 37
Contacts, 37
Content of living, 16, 18
Cornell University Agricultural Experiment Station, 74
Cost consumption unit, 22, 24
Cost of living, definition, 17; as measure of standard of living, 17-19
"Country Gentleman," 260
Cultural advancement, factors pertaining to, 216-221
Custom and tradition, 36, 37

Davenport, H. J., 11
Death-rates, rural and urban, 173
Defect rates, 174
Desired standard of living, 16
Desires and demands, effect on standard of living, 234
Disadvantages of farm life, 289
Distribution of average value of goods, according to increase in value, 64; by localities, 61-64

295

POVERTY, U. S. A.

THE HISTORICAL RECORD

An Arno Press/New York Times Collection

Adams, Grace. **Workers on Relief.** 1939.

The Almshouse Experience: Collected Reports. 1821-1827.

Armstrong, Louise V. **We Too Are The People.** 1938.

Bloodworth, Jessie A. and Elizabeth J. Greenwood.
The Personal Side. 1939.

Brunner, Edmund de S. and Irving Lorge.
**Rural Trends in Depression Years: A Survey of
Village-Centered Agricultural Communities, 1930-1936.**
1937.

Calkins, Raymond.
**Substitutes for the Saloon: An Investigation Originally
made for The Committee of Fifty.** 1919.

Cavan, Ruth Shonle and Katherine Howland Ranck.
**The Family and the Depression: A Study of
One Hundred Chicago Families.** 1938.

Chapin, Robert Coit.
**The Standard of Living Among Workingmen's Families
in New York City.** 1909.

**The Charitable Impulse in Eighteenth Century America:
Collected Papers.** 1711-1797.

Children's Aid Society.
Children's Aid Society Annual Reports, 1-10.
February 1854-February 1863.

Conference on the Care of Dependent Children.
**Proceedings of the Conference on the Care
of Dependent Children.** 1909.

Conyngton, Mary.
How to Help: A Manual of Practical Charity. 1909.

Devine, Edward T. **Misery and its Causes.** 1909.

Devine, Edward T. **Principles of Relief.** 1904.

Dix, Dorothea L.
On Behalf of the Insane Poor: Selected Reports. 1843-1852.

Douglas, Paul H.
**Social Security in the United States: An Analysis and
Appraisal of the Federal Social Security Act.** 1936.

Farm Tenancy: Black and White. Two Reports. 1935, 1937.

Feder, Leah Hannah.
**Unemployment Relief in Periods of Depression:
A Study of Measures Adopted in Certain American
Cities, 1857 through 1922.** 1936.

Folks, Homer.
**The Care of Destitute, Neglected, and
Delinquent Children.** 1900.

Guardians of the Poor.
**A Compilation of the Poor Laws of the State of
Pennsylvania from the Year 1700 to 1788, Inclusive.** 1788.

Hart, Hastings, H.
Preventive Treatment of Neglected Children.
(Correction and Prevention, Vol. 4) 1910.

Herring, Harriet L.
**Welfare Work in Mill Villages: The Story of Extra-Mill
Activities in North Carolina.** 1929.

The Jacksonians on the Poor: Collected Pamphlets.
1822-1844.

Karpf, Maurice J.
Jewish Community Organization in the United States.
1938.

Kellor, Frances A.
Out of Work: A Study of Unemployment. 1915.

Kirkpatrick, Ellis Lore.
The Farmer's Standard of Living. 1929.

Komarovsky, Mirra.
The Unemployed Man and His Family: The Effect of Unemployment Upon the Status of the Man in Fifty-Nine Families. 1940.

Leupp, Francis E. **The Indian and His Problem.** 1910.

Lowell, Josephine Shaw.
Public Relief and Private Charity. 1884.

More, Louise Bolard.
Wage Earners' Budgets: A Study of Standards and Cost of Living in New York City. 1907.

New York Association for Improving the Condition of the Poor.
AICP First Annual Reports Investigating Poverty. 1845-1853.

O'Grady, John.
Catholic Charities in the United States: History and Problems. 1930.

Raper, Arthur F.
Preface to Peasantry: A Tale of Two Black Belt Counties. 1936.

Raper, Arthur F. **Tenants of The Almighty.** 1943.

Richmond, Mary E.
What is Social Case Work? An Introductory Description. 1922.

Riis, Jacob A. **The Children of the Poor.** 1892.

Rural Poor in the Great Depression: Three Studies. 1938.

Sedgwick, Theodore.
Public and Private Economy: Part I. 1836.

Smith, Reginald Heber. **Justice and the Poor.** 1919.

Sutherland, Edwin H. and Harvey J. Locke.
Twenty Thousand Homeless Men: A Study of Unemployed Men in the Chicago Shelters. 1936.

Tuckerman, Joseph.
On the Elevation of the Poor: A Selection From His Reports as Minister at Large in Boston. 1874.

Warner, Amos G. **American Charities.** 1894.

Watson, Frank Dekker.
The Charity Organization Movement in the United States: A Study in American Philanthropy. 1922.

Woods, Robert A., et al. **The Poor in Great Cities.** 1895.